GW00368131

LEAVING CERTIFICATE

LATER MODERN HISTORY OF EUROPE AND THE WIDER WORLD TOPIC 6

The United States and the World 1945–1989

MÁIRE DE BUITLÉIR

STEPHEN TONGE

Edco

THE EDUCATIONAL COMPANY OF IRELAND

First published 2015

The Educational Company of Ireland
Ballymount Road
Walkinstown
Dublin 12
www.edco.ie

A member of the Smurfit Kappa Group plc
© Máire de Buitléir, Stephen Tonge 2015

ISBN: 978-1-84536-497-7

Editor and indexer: Jane Rogers
Interior and cover design: Design Image
Layout: Carole Lynch
Illustrations: Brian Fitzgerald
Cover photography: Shutterstock (lower right) and TopFoto (top left, top right
and lower left)
Interior photography: Alamy, Corbis, Getty Images, Shutterstock, TopFoto

The paper used in this book comes from Managed Forests in Northern Europe For every tree felled, at least one new tree is planted

Acknowledgements: 'You Mean I'm Supposed to Stand on That?', a 1950 Herblock Cartoon, © The Herb
Block Foundation; 'The World According to Reagan' © David Horsey, 1982. Reprinted by permission of *The
Seattle Post-Intelligencer*; excerpt from Martin Luther King's 'I Have a Dream' speech, 28 August 1963 © 1963
Dr Martin Luther King, Jr. © renewed 1991 Coretta Scott King. Reprinted by arrangement with The Heirs to
the Estate of Martin Luther King Jr., c/o Writers House as agent for the proprietor New York, NY; excerpt from
Montgomery (Alabama) City Code, 1938, Chapter 6, Sections 10 and 11, Alabama Department of Archives and
History, Montgomery, Alabama; excerpt from *Voices of Freedom* by Henry Hampton and Steve Fayer, published
by Vintage. Reprinted by permission of The Random House Group; excerpt from a memo to Eisenhower on
the Korean War from the Dwight D. Eisenhower Presidential Library; excerpt from *The Pentagon Papers*, Gravel
Edition, Vol. 3; excerpt from President L.B. Johnson's broadcast to the nation, 31 March 1968; excerpt from
'The Reason Why' from 'Part II: Stars, Stripes, and Stigmas' from *Naming Names* by Victor S. Navasky. Copyright
© 1980, 1991 by Victor S. Navasky. Reprinted by permission of Hill & Wang, a division of Farrar, Straus and
Giroux, LLC; excerpt from J.F. Kennedy speech to Greater Houston Ministerial Association, 12 September 1960;
edited excerpt from *American Experience, Race for the Superbomb* (http://www.pbs.org/wgbh/amex/bomb/
peopleevents/pandeAMEX51.html) © 1996 –2015 WGBH Educational Foundation; excerpt from 'Men Walk On
Moon' by John Noble Wilford, *New York Times*, 21 July 1969

While every care has been taken to trace and acknowledge copyright, the publishers tender their apologies
for any accidental infringement where copyright has proved untraceable. They would be pleased to come to
a suitable arrangement with the rightful owner in each case.

Web references in this book are intended as a guide for teachers. At the time of going to press, all
web addresses were active and contained information relevant to the topics in this book. However, The
Educational Company of Ireland and the authors do not accept responsibility for the views or information
contained on these websites.

CONTENTS

USEFUL WEBSITES

Below is a list of websites that both students and teachers may find useful as aids to the different topics covered in the book. Many contain videos, interactive timelines or primary sources. More useful websites are listed at the end of Chapter 1, page 16.

General Sources
www.digitalhistory.uh.edu
www.gilderlehrman.org/history-by-era/1945-present
www.presidentialtimeline.org/#/home
www.digitalvaults.org
www.let.rug.nl/usa/outlines/history-2005/decades-of-change/

US Economy 1945–1989
www.countrystudies.us/united-states/history-114.htm
www.ushistory.org/us/58b.asp

Racial Conflict and Montgomery Bus Boycott
www.history.com/topics/black-history/civil-rights-movement
www.biography.com/search/9365086
www.pbs.org/wgbh/amex/eyesontheprize/
www.nps.gov/nr/travel/civilrights/
www.civilrights.jfklibrary.org
www.montgomeryboycott.com/
www.archives.gov/education/lessons/rosa-parks/
www.pbs.org/wgbh/amex/eyesontheprize/story/02_bus.html

Foreign Policy 1945–1972
www.history.state.gov/milestones/1945-1952/berlin-airlift
www.pbs.org/wgbh/amex/airlift/
www.history.com/topics/korean-war
www.koreanwar60.com
www.history.com/topics/cold-war/red-scare
www.ushistory.org/us/53a.asp
www.foundationnationalarchives.org/cmc/
www.history.com/topics/cold-war/cuban-missile-crisis

LB Johnson and Vietnam
www.lbjlibrary.org/exhibits/the-vietnam-conflict
www.presidentialtimeline.org/#/exhibit/36/01
www.pbs.org/wgbh/amex/vietnam/
www.history.com/topics/vietnam-war
www.vvmf.org/Wall-of-Faces/

Foreign Policy 1973–1989
www.history.state.gov/milestones/1969-1976/detente
www.coldwar.org/articles/80s/SDI-StarWars.asp

Moon Landing / Information Technology
www.airandspace.si.edu/exhibitions/apollo-to-the-moon/online/
www.wechoosethemoon.org
www.thespacerace.com
www.livescience.com/20718-computer-history.html

US Society and Religion
www.pbs.org/opb/thesixties/
www.ushistory.org/us/53f.asp
www.docsteach.org
www.ushistory.org/us/57a.asp

FOREWORD

This revised textbook is designed to prepare students for the Leaving Certificate in an engaging manner. Written with the students in mind, the language used is accessible. Key questions make chapters more manageable and allow students to focus on the main themes. Special emphasis is given to three case studies and their historical context.

Full-colour illustrations and photographs are used throughout. There are helpful timelines and glossaries. There are also useful websites, biographies of the key personalities and a section explaining key concepts.

End-of-chapter questions for both Higher and Ordinary Level students reinforce learning. These exam-focused questions are a mix of document questions, paragraph-style answers and essays.

The textbook follows closely the prescribed syllabus in examining the history of the USA. It covers the country's political and foreign policy, dominated by the background of the Cold War with the USSR. Developments in the society and economy of the USA are covered, along with cultural, scientific and religious changes.

The textbook also examines the Cuban Missile Crisis that nearly led to nuclear destruction, the struggle of African Americans for equality and the achievement of the long-held dream of man walking on the moon. It looks at how US society changed from the conformity of the 1950s to the rebellion of the 1960s and the disillusionment of the 1970s.

The topic of the USA and the Wider World 1945–1989 allows students to explore the history of the most powerful country of the 20th century. This history is rich and exciting and familiar to many of us from films and television. The USA is also the world's largest economy with a very strong cultural impact around the globe. Developments in the USA, and its actions, affect us all.

The Government of the United States

KEY QUESTIONS

The US Constitution, drawn up in 1787, defines the political structure of the USA

THE US CONSTITUTION

The US Constitution states how the United States is governed. Americans are very proud of their Constitution as it set up one of the first democratic governments in the world.

It was drawn up in 1787 and, with amendments (changes), still sets out the political system of the USA. In this chapter we will examine how the US system of government works.

WHAT IS THE FEDERAL SYSTEM OF GOVERNMENT?

The US Constitution made the country a **republic** with a president as head of state. It set up a **federal system** where power was shared between the national and state governments. The people who wrote the Constitution were determined to preserve the rights of each state and prevent the federal government becoming too powerful. Each state has its own capital where there is a legislature (parliament) elected by the people from that state. The most important official in each state is the **governor**, who is elected by popular vote. This federal system has been copied throughout the world, for example in Germany after World War II.

Today this means that there is a federal government in **Washington, DC** with responsibility for matters that cross state borders and for relations with foreign countries. These include trade, war, treaties, the army and the navy. Currency and coinage and the postal service are also controlled by the federal government. The states have control of areas such as business, transport, policing and education. Each state also decides whether or not to have the death penalty.

There are a lot of areas where the federal government and the states share responsibility, for example taxation, health care, social welfare and the protection of natural resources. The **Federal Bureau of Investigation** (FBI) was established to deal with crime that involved more than one state, e.g. organised crime.

> **Washington, DC:** The nation's capital was named after the first president of the United States, George Washington. The DC stands for 'District of Columbia'. The city was deliberately located on land between the states of Virginia and Maryland but was not part of either state. Why do you think the capital is not located in a state?

HOW DOES THE FEDERAL GOVERNMENT IN WASHINGTON OPERATE?

Separation of Powers

Study the diagram below. It shows how the federal government is separated by the Constitution into three branches. Americans call this the **separation of powers**.

One of the main concerns of the drafters of the Constitution in 1787 was to prevent the president or Congress from becoming too powerful.

Let us look at each of the branches of government:

Role of the Executive

As head of state the president's role is to run the country. He (or she) is assisted by the heads of different government departments, who are called Secretaries. The main functions of the president are:

- ◎ enforcing the laws of the nation
- ◎ acting as Commander-in-Chief of the army
- ◎ conducting foreign affairs and negotiating treaties
- ◎ appointing government officials.

The president is usually a highly respected figure whose views are very important. Presidents have a major role in influencing popular opinion. They are also the recognised leader of the political party they represent. The president usually has a major input in setting the law-making agenda during the presidency but, as we shall see, only a member of Congress can actually introduce a bill into one of the Houses of Congress. Therefore the attitude of Congress is crucial if a president is to see proposals become law.

The **vice-president** is usually elected as part of the presidential ticket along with the president. He (or

THE FEDERAL SYSTEM OF GOVERNMENT		
The Legislature Congress Makes the country's laws Made up of two houses: The House of Representatives The Senate	**The Executive** **(Head of State)** The President Runs the country Is assisted by a number of ministers called **Secretaries**.	**The Judiciary** The Supreme Court Makes sure that all laws that are passed are constitutional.

The separation of powers in the US federal government

The White House, where the president lives and works

she) is the president of the **Senate** and succeeds the president if the president fails to serve a full term. This has happened three times since 1945:

- In 1945, when President Roosevelt died, Harry S. Truman became president.

- In 1963 Lyndon Johnson took over as president when John F. Kennedy was assassinated.

- In 1974 Richard Nixon was forced to resign and Gerald Ford succeeded him.

Some vice-presidents have successfully stood as candidates for the presidency. In 1968 Richard Nixon, who had served as vice-president between 1952 and 1960, was elected; and George Bush succeeded Ronald Reagan as president in 1988.

While in theory a powerful figure, in most cases the vice-president does not have a major role in the executive. Instead, to help the president run the country there are a number of departments called collectively the **administration**. The most important are **State** (foreign affairs), **Defense**, **Treasury**, **Education** and **Justice**. The president

appoints the heads of these departments. They are called **Secretaries** and are similar to our ministers in Ireland.

Presidential Bureaucracy

The **bureaucracy** or civil service is responsible for the day-to-day running of the country. The size of the bureaucracy grew dramatically in the twentieth century. There are hundreds of government agencies that implement policies, protect the citizens or provide social services. These include the **Environmental Protection Agency**, the **FBI** and the **Postal Service**. The number of people directly employed by the government grew from 2.5 million in 1960 to over three million by 2012. This figure does not include the two million or so soldiers in the different branches of the US Army. Furthermore, millions of Americans work in companies that depend on the federal government for work, e.g. the arms industry.

The federal budget, which sets out how much the government spends on running the country each year, has also grown dramatically. In 1988 it amounted to over $1.7 trillion (that's 1,700,000,000,000 dollars!). Fifty per cent of the budget that year was spent on **social security and health care** and 27 per cent was spent on **defence**. The federal budget is submitted by the president for approval of Congress every year.

The large number of government agencies and employees and the sheer size of the federal budget have led many Americans to criticise the **presidential bureaucracy** – or 'Big Government'. Many Americans see personal liberty as very important and are deeply suspicious of the greater role the government plays in their lives.

The Republican Party in particular is opposed to increased government spending unless it is on defence.

Role of Congress

Capitol Hill, where the House of Congress meets

As we have seen, while presidents have a major role in deciding what laws they want, they cannot actually introduce or pass a law. That is the job of the legislature, or parliament, which the Americans call **Congress**. When the Constitution was being drafted in the eighteenth century there was a serious disagreement between the states as to what type of parliament the federal government would have. Smaller states feared that they would be dominated by the larger ones and have little say in the federal government. So a compromise was agreed that set up two Houses of Congress:

- The lower house is the **House of Representatives**. It has 435 members and the number of representatives from each state is decided according to its population. Today there are fifty-three members from California but only one from Alaska. Members are chosen every two years. Bills relating to taxes can only be introduced here.

- The upper house is the **Senate**, which was set up to protect the rights of states. Each state has two senators, whatever its population (so California and Alaska both have two senators). There are one hundred senators in total, who are elected every six years. The Senate has a major role in foreign affairs: while the president has the power to negotiate a foreign treaty, it must be ratified by the Senate by a two-thirds majority. Famously, **President Wilson** did not get the Treaty of Versailles approved by the Senate.

How are Laws Passed?

The law-making process in the USA, set out below, clearly shows the separation of powers.

1 A **bill** is introduced and passed by both Houses of Congress.

2 It is signed into **law** by the president.

3 It is checked by the **Supreme Court** to make sure that it is constitutional (see page 6).

Only a member of Congress can introduce a bill. Bills come from different sources. Many come from the president and his (or her) administration and are introduced by a member of the president's party. Others are proposed by a member of Congress or a group of members. A large number are introduced on behalf of paid **lobbyists** acting for interest groups. These groups represent big business, unions, farmers, foreign governments, etc. Many Americans are worried about the influence that some interest groups (e.g. big business) have on the democratic process.

A bill must be introduced when Congress is meeting or in **session**. Both Houses of Congress have committees that will examine the proposed legislation. If the bill is approved by a committee, both Houses of Congress vote on it.

If it passes, the bill is then sent to the president, who signs it into law. If they do not like a law or part of it, they can stop or **veto** it. Often the threat of a veto is enough to get the changes to a bill that the president wants. If the president does veto a bill, Congress can overturn it with a two-thirds majority vote.

Why is the Relationship between the President and Congress Important?

For laws to be passed the relationship between the president and Congress is crucial. If the president's party has a majority in Congress this usually (but not always!) makes it easier for the president to get laws passed.

However, presidents often face a Congress dominated by their political opponents. For example, the House of Representatives is elected every two years and these elections are often won by the party opposing a sitting president. So compromise is the order of the day and this is crucial to the president's success in working with Congress. Presidents often have to work with senators and representatives they do not agree with politically. If presidents refused to pass all bills they disagreed with and Congress did likewise, government would come to a halt. As a result, presidents are often forced to accept changes that they do not like to get the bills they want passed.

Difficulties also occur when a president becomes unpopular. Members of Congress are very conscious of popular opinion, and because members of the House of Representatives and one-third of senators are elected every two years this can make it very difficult for unpopular presidents to get laws they want passed by Congress.

Successive presidents have met a lot of resistance to their policies from Congress:

- Southern senators opposed or watered down both Truman's and Eisenhower's **civil rights** legislation.

- Kennedy's proposals for education and health reforms were resisted.

- Gerald Ford was at odds with Congress over the best policy to adopt to deal with the economic difficulties of the 1970s.

- The Strategic Arms Limitation Treaty (SALT II), agreed with the USSR by Jimmy Carter, was delayed by Congress until it was abandoned by his successor Ronald Reagan.

The Electoral College

Although the president is elected in a popular election, the actual method of being chosen is complicated:

- In each state the voters vote for their candidate for president. The winner then takes the delegates from that state to an **Electoral College**.
- The number of delegates is usually the same as the number of senators and representatives from the state. For example, California has fifty-five delegates, which is equal to the number of senators and representatives from that state; Alaska has three.
- All delegates from a state must vote for the candidate who got the majority of votes in their state – no matter how small the majority.
- The candidate who receives the most delegates in the Electoral College becomes the president.
- It is possible for a president to win the vote in the Electoral College and not get a majority of the popular vote – George W. Bush won the 2000 election but received fewer individual votes than his rival Al Gore. A number of other elections have been very close, especially John F. Kennedy's victory in 1960.
- While most states are traditionally either Democrat or Republican, presidential candidates tend to concentrate on states where support for the parties is neck and neck. These are so-called swing states; examples include Florida and Ohio.

Role of the Supreme Court

This is the top court in the land. Its role is to interpret the Constitution and make sure that all laws that are passed – at both federal and state level – are in keeping with the Constitution. Its rulings are final and can only be changed by a later Supreme Court ruling or by an amendment to the Constitution. If the Supreme Court finds that any federal or state law is in breach of the Constitution, that law must be changed.

There are nine judges and they are appointed for life. The most important judge is the **Chief Justice**. The members can only be removed from the court if they are **impeached** (tried) and convicted by the Senate. Although its members are nominated by the president and approved by the Senate, it is very independent-minded and very powerful.

The Supreme Court has played a very important role in interpreting the Constitution in line with the changing values of US society. In the 1960s and 1970s the court brought in a number of rulings that reflected the greater emphasis on personal freedom in America. The most controversial was the court's decision in 1973 in the **Roe versus Wade judgment** to legalise abortion. It played a very important role in dismantling the laws that existed in many states which discriminated against African Americans (see Chapter 4).

QUESTIONS

1   Explain the term 'federal system'.

2   What are the president's main powers under the Constitution?

3   What is the 'presidential bureaucracy'?

4   What is the role of the vice-president?

5   Briefly describe the role of (a) the Senate and (b) the House of Representatives.

6   Explain the process by which a bill becomes a law.

7   What tensions can exist between Congress and the president?

8   Why is the Supreme Court so important in the federal system of government?

HOW DOES THE SYSTEM OF CHECKS AND BALANCES WORK?

As we have read, the US Constitution made sure that no branch of government could become too powerful. The decision-making power of each branch is limited and each can stop any misuse of power by the other branches. This is referred to as a system of **checks and balances**.

Here are some examples:

- The president can veto any law passed by Congress, but Congress can overturn the veto.

- The Supreme Court can declare any law passed by Congress or action taken by the president as unconstitutional.

- Congress can **impeach** (**try**) a president or a Supreme Court judge accused of misuse of power. Bill Clinton was impeached in 1999 but found not guilty. In 1974 Richard Nixon resigned before he was impeached.

Changing the Constitution

The Constitution can only be changed by an **amendment**, and it is not easy to get an amendment passed. First of all a proposed amendment must be passed by a two-thirds majority in both Houses of Congress and then it must be approved by three-quarters of all states.

There have been twenty-seven amendments since the Constitution was passed in 1789. Many have reflected the changes in attitudes and values of US society over the years.

Some of the most important in the twentieth century were:

- The 18th made it illegal to sell alcohol (known as Prohibition) and the 21st repealed this ban!

- The 19th gave women the right to vote (1920).

- Under the 22nd a president can only serve two terms.

- The 24th made poll taxes illegal. As we shall see in Chapter 4, some southern states had introduced this tax to make it difficult for African Americans to vote.

- The 26th lowered the voting age to 18.

The Main Political Parties in the USA

There are two main political parties in the USA: the **Republicans** and the **Democrats**. Traditionally the Republicans were viewed as more conservative and pro-big business while the Democrats were more reforming on social issues. Issues that have divided the parties include **abortion**, **taxation** and **federal spending**. For example, on federal spending Democrats usually favour more resources going to health and education. Republicans, while accepting the role of government spending in helping the poor, want to see it limited and greater stress put on individual responsibility.

Given the size of the country, there were often **divisions on geographic lines** as well. Until the 1960s Democrats from southern states opposed civil rights for African Americans, while Democrats from the rest of the country were more sympathetic. One of the results of the civil rights campaign was a big switch among southern whites from Democrat to Republican.

Voters can often choose different parties at local and national level. A voter can choose a Democrat as senator and a Republican for president. For example, many traditional Democrats supported **Ronald Reagan**.

Tension between the States and the Federal Government

As we have seen, the Constitution divided the responsibility for running the country between the different states and the federal government in Washington. As a rule this federal system works quite well, but a number of issues – usually involving race – have caused tensions between the federal government and different states.

- Most famously, the **Civil War** (1861–65) was caused by the determination of southern states to maintain their right to have slavery. When Abraham Lincoln, who opposed slavery, was elected president, eleven slave-owning states left the United States. They set up their own country, which they called the Confederacy. A bloody civil war followed that resulted in the deaths of over 620,000 Americans – more than the American dead in the two World Wars combined. The northern states (the Union) won, slavery was abolished and the southern states were reincorporated into the USA.

- After World War II **Civil Rights** for African Americans caused tension as the southern states opposed federal measures. As we have seen, the Supreme Court played a very important role. It declared state laws unconstitutional if they discriminated against African Americans.

- Nonetheless the southern states were very slow to apply the Supreme Court rulings. **President Eisenhower** sent troops to **Little Rock** in **Arkansas** to enforce a Supreme Court ruling that ended **segregated** (separate) schooling.

- In 1965 the federal government was forced to pass a law ensuring that African Americans could vote in a number of southern states. This right had been guaranteed by the Constitution since 1870 but had been obstructed throughout the south through various measures such as taxes, literacy tests, etc. The Voting Rights Act banned these practices.

QUESTIONS

1 What is meant by the system of checks and balances in the US system of government?

2 Give three examples of important amendments to the US Constitution.

3 What issues divide the Democratic and Republican parties?

4 Give three areas where states have control over their own affairs.

5 What power does the Supreme Court have over the different states?

6 Examine two historical instances of tension between the federal government and the different states.

HOW DID THE PRESIDENCY DEVELOP FROM ROOSEVELT TO REAGAN?

The president is the most powerful figure in the US political system. He (or she) is elected every four years and can only serve for two terms. This rule was brought in in 1945 after the death of President Roosevelt, who had been elected four times: in 1932, 1936, 1940 and 1944.

The president is the head of state, in charge of the government or the **executive**, and is the Commander-in-Chief of the US armed forces.

US Presidents 1932–1989

Franklin Delano Roosevelt (1882–1945)
Franklin D. Roosevelt (FDR) was the 32nd president of the USA. He came from a wealthy New York background and following the example of his distant cousin, President Theodore Roosevelt, entered politics as a Democrat. He was elected to the New York Senate in 1910 and was the Democratic nominee for vice-president in 1920.

In 1921 he was stricken with polio, which left him disabled from the waist down; but he was careful to hide the illness from the public. In 1928 Roosevelt became Governor of New York.

He was elected President in November 1932. In response to the Great Depression he introduced his **New Deal** programme to help revive the economy. By 1935 the nation had achieved some measure of recovery, but businesspeople and bankers were turning more and more against Roosevelt's New Deal. Roosevelt responded with a new programme of reform: social security; heavier taxes on the wealthy; new controls over banks; and an enormous work relief programme for the unemployed.

In 1936 he was re-elected by a large margin. He was elected again in 1940 and 1944 – the only president to serve more than two terms.

In foreign relations, his policy in the 1930s reflected the dominant isolationist mood in the USA at the time. He brought in neutrality legislation to keep the USA out of a war in Europe, but following the success of the Germans in the early stages of World War II he sent military aid to Great Britain under the **Lend-Lease** programme.

The USA entered the war in December 1941 following the Japanese attack on Pearl Harbor. Roosevelt directed organisation of the nation's labour and resources for global war. Feeling that the future peace of the world would depend on relations between the United States and Russia, he worked to see the establishment of the United Nations (UN), hoping that this organisation would preserve world peace after the war. His leadership during the war helped to establish the USA as a leader in world affairs.

As the war drew to a close, Roosevelt's health deteriorated, and on 12 April 1945 he died of a stroke. His policies during the Great Depression and his wartime leadership led him to be regarded by Americans as one of the greatest presidents in the history of the USA.

Harry S. Truman (1884–1972) – Key Personality

The 33rd president of the United States, Harry Truman was famous for his plain speaking and his motto, 'the buck stops here'. He is best remembered as the man who ended World War II by using the atom bomb on Japan and committing the USA to containing the spread of communism.

Truman was born in Lamar, Missouri and served in France during World War I. Active in the Democratic Party, he was elected as a senator for Missouri in 1934. He was a supporter of President Roosevelt's 'New Deal' policies.

In 1944 he was chosen as vice-president, and he became president following Roosevelt's death on 12 April 1945. After Germany's surrender, he met with **Stalin** at **Potsdam**, where disputes broke out between the Americans and the Soviets about the future of Europe, sowing the seeds of the Cold War. Controversially, he authorised the dropping of atomic bombs on Hiroshima and Nagasaki, which led to the surrender of the Japanese and the end of World War II. The morality of the president's decision has been debated to this day. 'Let there be no mistake about it,' Truman said later, 'I regarded the bomb as a military weapon and never had any doubt that it should be used.'

Domestically Truman proposed a 21-point programme, the **Fair Deal**, which included civil rights laws to improve the position of African Americans, better social welfare and public housing to help the poor. However, Congress obstructed many of his proposals; and battles with Congress were to be a feature of his presidency. For example, his civil rights legislation was blocked by southern senators, many of whom were from his own party. One major success was implementing the **GI Bill**, which enabled former soldiers to buy homes at low interest rates and allowed them access to university education by helping to fund the cost.

Internationally Truman believed that it was the role of the USA to stop the spread of communism. The **Truman Doctrine** committed the USA to supporting all countries fighting communism. This policy, also known as **containment**, became US strategy throughout the **Cold War**. In 1947 the USA announced that it would provide massive aid to help the economies of war-torn Europe to recover. This was known as the **Marshall Plan** after Truman's Secretary of State, **George Marshall**. In 1948, when Berlin was blockaded by the Soviets, he authorised an airlift to supply the city until the Soviets backed down in May 1949.

Re-elected as president in 1948, Truman continued to press for civil rights domestically and to contain communism abroad. The **Red Scare** began during his second term and this saw the rise to prominence of Senator **Joseph McCarthy**.

However, it was international relations that would again dominate his second term. In 1949 he negotiated the formation of the **North Atlantic Treaty Organization** (**NATO**) to defend Western Europe against communism. He committed US troops to South Korea when it was invaded by communist North Korea. He later fired the commander of US troops in Korea, **General Douglas MacArthur**, for publicly questioning his orders.

Relevant chapters:

You will find events and topics relevant to Truman in Chapters 2, 4, 6 and 9.

In 1952 Truman's poll ratings slumped to record lows. The war in Korea was unpopular and there were a number of corruption allegations against officials in his government. He announced that he would not seek a third term as president. He retired to Independence, Missouri, and died in 1972. Today he is regarded by many Americans as one of the greatest US presidents.

Dwight D. Eisenhower (1890–1969)

Dwight Eisenhower, the 34th president, served two terms from 1953 until 1961. A World War II hero, Eisenhower was a popular president throughout his two terms. He was so completely honest that even his political opponents never questioned his honour. His health was poor in his second term and this weakened his effectiveness.

In the area of foreign relations he obtained a truce in Korea and worked during his two terms to ease tensions between the USA and the USSR. At the same time, his administration worked hard to stop the spread of communism in Asia, Africa and South America. He cut defence spending and in his farewell address in 1961 warned against the unchecked growth of a **military–industrial complex** (see page 161).

Relevant chapters:

You will find events and topics relevant to Eisenhower in Chapters 2, 4 and 6.

At home his economic policies were successful. Eisenhower promoted a stable economy and fought to balance the budget – making sure the government spent no more than it raised in taxes. His two terms produced eight years of growth and prosperity. In 1956 he launched the **Interstate Highway System**, the single largest public works scheme in US history, which provided much employment. He signed the bill setting up the **National Aeronautics and Space Administration (NASA)** in 1958.

He was very cautious on reform in the area of civil rights: as a southerner he disliked having to deal with race issues. Nonetheless he implemented some limited civil rights reforms and desegregated the army. In 1954 the US Supreme Court declared that the segregation of white and black children in public schools was unconstitutional. Eisenhower hoped for peaceful integration of the races in schools throughout the south, but when the Governor of Arkansas refused to follow the Supreme Court ruling he was forced to take action. In 1957 he ordered US military units to the capital of Arkansas, **Little Rock**, to enforce the law. Today most Americans would view his presidency as a success.

Relevant chapters:

You will find events and topics relevant to Kennedy in Chapters 2, 4, 6 and 12.

John F. Kennedy (1917–1963)

In 1960 John F. Kennedy narrowly defeated Richard Nixon to become the 35th president. Kennedy was the first Catholic president, and at the age of 43, he was also the youngest person ever elected to the office of president. He came from a very wealthy background, was a World War II hero and had been elected as a senator for Massachusetts in 1952. There were great hopes for his presidency, but these hopes were largely unfulfilled as his term in office was cut short by his assassination in 1963. The events surrounding his death are a matter of dispute to this day.

As president, Kennedy supported tax cuts, civil rights legislation and the exploration of outer space. In 1961 he promised that the USA would land a man on the moon by the end of the decade. The shortness of his presidency meant that many of his policies had not passed Congress.

On the international stage Kennedy successfully handled major crises with the Soviet Union over Berlin (1961) and Cuba (1962). His leadership during the Cuban Missile Crisis is seen by many historians as his finest hour. The crisis led to improved relations with the USSR, and he signed a **Test Ban Treaty** with the USSR in 1963. Nonetheless he was committed to supporting South Vietnam and stopping the spread of communism. As a result he increased US military involvement in the country.

Lyndon B. Johnson (1908–1969) – Key Personality

Lyndon B. Johnson became president following the death of John F. Kennedy in 1963. He pursued a reform agenda at home, tackling poverty through his Great Society project and racial discrimination through the Civil Rights Act and the Voting Rights Act. However, his presidency is best remembered for the disastrous involvement of the USA in Vietnam that ultimately saw him resign rather than seek re-election.

L.B. Johnson was born into a farming family in Texas in 1908. In 1934 he married Claudia Alta Taylor and they had two daughters. In 1937 he was elected as a Democratic member of the House of Representatives. He was a firm supporter of the reforming New Deal policies of President Franklin Roosevelt.

In 1948 he was elected as a senator for Texas and in 1953 he became the youngest leader of the Democrats in Senate history.

In 1960 he lost the party's nomination for president to John F. Kennedy. Despite this, Kennedy asked Johnson to join him as his running mate in the forthcoming election. He needed the Texan senator to help him win votes in the south. As vice-president, Johnson served Kennedy loyally, but he had no meaningful involvement in policy. On 22 November 1963, after the assassination of President Kennedy, Johnson took the oath of office as the 36th president.

As president, Johnson brought in a new civil rights bill that banned discrimination on the grounds of race, and a popular tax cut. In the 1964 election he campaigned on a programme of domestic reform called the '**Great Society**'. This vision proved popular and he was re-elected with the largest margin in US history.

Domestically his presidency was a success. A wide-scale fight against poverty, aid for education and medical help for the elderly (**Medicare**) and the poor (**Medicaid)** were the highlights of his policies. These policies saw the number of Americans living in poverty fall from 25 per cent to 12 per cent.

He also introduced the **Voting Rights Act** in 1965, which removed obstacles to African Americans voting in elections. His support of civil rights helped to transform the south and ended segregation there. He was also an active supporter of the space programme as the USA made spectacular progress in the **space race** with the USSR.

His domestic achievements were overshadowed by the war in Vietnam. Influenced by the **domino theory** (a fear that the loss of South Vietnam would lead to the loss of many other Asian countries to communism), he greatly increased US involvement. By 1968 there were over 500,000 US troops in Vietnam.

Protests against the war erupted throughout the country, and racial tensions were also growing at the same time. Race riots broke out in the overcrowded slums of Chicago, Detroit, Los Angeles and New York.

Relevant chapters:

You will find events and topics relevant to Johnson in Chapters 2, 3, 4, 7 and 9.

On 31 March 1968, facing mounting domestic criticism over the war in Vietnam, Johnson announced, to widespread surprise, that he would not stand for re-election. He helped to start peace negotiations with North Vietnam before he retired as president. He died of a heart attack in 1973 at his Texas ranch, five days before a peace treaty was concluded with North Vietnam.

Richard Nixon (1913–1994)

Richard Nixon came from a poor background and had a long political career before becoming the 37th president. Elected as a Republican senator for California in 1950, he served as vice-president to President Eisenhower from 1952 until 1960. He lost the 1960 election to John F. Kennedy. After a failed campaign to become governor of California, he stood successfully against Democrat vice-president Hubert Humphrey in 1968, and his first term saw the dramatic moon landing in 1969. A liberal Republican, he continued many of his Democratic predecessor's programmes, for example supporting the **Equal Rights Amendment** of 1972. Responding to public concern about the environment, he created the **Environmental Protection Agency**.

Nixon took a number of steps to try to improve the nation's economy. These included a temporary freeze on wages and prices and a devaluation of the dollar. US support for Israel during the **Yom Kippur War** of 1973 resulted in an **oil embargo** by Arab nations. This led to an energy crisis in the USA and worsening economic conditions, with rising inflation and unemployment.

Nixon ended American military involvement in **Vietnam**, but it was a long, drawn-out process and US troops did not pull out until 1973. He achieved major foreign policy breakthroughs in 1972 when he visited both **Moscow** and **Beijing**. This laid the basis for **détente** with the USSR and full US recognition of communist China.

In 1972 Nixon was swept to an overwhelming victory in the presidential election. However, during the campaign there had been a break-in at the Democratic Party headquarters in the Watergate building in Washington. In the ensuing **Watergate scandal**, the president was implicated in the break-in and he was forced to resign rather than face impeachment in 1974. He was the only president ever to be forced from office for misconduct.

Relevant chapters:

You will find events and topics relevant to Nixon in Chapters 2, 4, 6 and 8.

The cynical actions of his administration contributed to a growing distrust of politicians and government among Americans. A national opinion survey in 1975 revealed that 69 per cent of Americans felt that 'over the last ten years the country's leaders had consistently lied to the people.'

Gerald Ford (1913–2006)

The 38th President of the United States, Gerald Ford, succeeded to both the vice-presidency and the presidency without having contested an election. He was elected as a member of the House of Representatives from Michigan, and was appointed vice-president in 1973 following the resignation of Spiro Agnew.

Nixon's departure the following year saw Ford rise to the highest office in the land.

Domestically he faced serious economic difficulties. The US economy was in **recession**, with rising unemployment, inflation and high interest rates. He failed to tackle these problems effectively – for example, his **Whip Inflation Now (WIN)** policy failed – and he was not helped by a hostile Congress. His pardon of Richard Nixon was unpopular and cost him political support. Economic problems and the pardon contributed to his defeat by Jimmy Carter in the 1976 election.

> **Relevant chapters:**
>
> You will find events and topics relevant to Ford in Chapters 2 and 8.

In the area of foreign relations the fall of **South Vietnam**, **Cambodia** and **Laos** to the communists was a blow to the administration. He continued Nixon's policy of **détente** with the USSR. This resulted in the joint **Apollo–Soyuz** space mission of 1975 and the signing of the **Helsinki Accords** that aimed to improve relations between East and West. He helped to preserve peace in the Middle East between **Israel** and **Egypt** after the war between the two countries in 1973.

Jimmy Carter (1924–)

Jimmy Carter became the 39th president of the United States in 1976. He had entered politics in 1962 and as Governor of Georgia he had ended segregation in the state. Surprisingly selected as the Democratic candidate for president in 1976, he successfully campaigned on a platform of political honesty. Carter was well intentioned but very unlucky as president. By the end of his term he was widely viewed as being weak and was seen as a failure.

Domestically Carter tried to combat inflation and unemployment. By the end of his administration there was an increase of nearly eight million jobs, but inflation and interest rates were still high. These economic problems were made worse by the **Second Oil Crisis** of 1979 that saw oil prices increase dramatically. He improved social services by creating the Department of Education and strengthening the social security system.

In foreign affairs he helped to negotiate the **Camp David Agreement** of 1978 that brought peace between Egypt and Israel. He established full diplomatic relations with the **People's Republic of China** and completed negotiation of the **SALT II** treaty with the Soviet Union. He made human rights a centrepiece of his foreign policy and suspended economic and military aid to Chile, El Salvador and Nicaragua in protest against those regimes' human rights abuses.

Relevant chapters:
You will find events and topics relevant to Carter in Chapters 2 and 8.

There were serious setbacks, though. The Soviet invasion of **Afghanistan** in 1979 saw the suspension of plans for ratification of the SALT II pact limiting nuclear weapons. The **Iran Hostage Crisis** dominated the news during the last fourteen months of his administration. This crisis, together with continuing inflation at home, contributed to Carter's defeat by **Ronald Reagan** in 1980. He was the first president since 1932 to fail to be re-elected.

Ronald Reagan (1911–2004)

Ronald Reagan, who became the 40th president of the United States in 1980, was at the age of 69 the oldest man elected to the post.

Reagan was a former Hollywood actor turned politician. He served as the governor of **California** between 1967 and 1975. In the 1980 election he won a landslide victory over Jimmy Carter. Nicknamed 'the **Gipper**' and 'the **Great Communicator**', he was famous for his charm and sense of humour. In 1981 he survived an assassination attempt and was re-elected easily in 1984.

Domestically Reagan's controversial economic policies, known as **Reaganomics**, saw large tax cuts and increased military spending. He took a tough line against trade unions. To control inflation he kept interest rates high as they made borrowing less attractive. The economy improved although the country's **budget deficit** – the amount it borrowed to pay for spending – grew to record levels. During his second term, Reagan passed a major tax reform bill, inflation was reduced, and unemployment fell to 5 per cent.

Internationally he was an **anti-communist crusader**. His aim was to rebuild the American strength and self-confidence that had been damaged by the **Vietnam War**. Reagan referred to the USSR as an '**evil empire**'. His **Star Wars** proposal and military build-up contributed to one of the 'hottest' periods of the Cold War (1981–84), when there was a widespread fear of a nuclear war between the superpowers.

His administration intervened in South and Central America to oppose the spread of communism, reversing the human rights-centred policy of his predecessor Jimmy Carter. In the process the administration backed some unsavoury regimes (e.g. El Salvador) that were guilty of terrible violations of human rights.

However, Reagan was horrified at the prospect of ever using nuclear weapons and was prepared to negotiate with the USSR. In 1985 the election of the new Soviet leader **Mikhail Gorbachev** saw a change in direction in the USSR. Reagan surprised many by entering into serious arms reduction talks with the new Soviet leader, thus making an important contribution to ending the Cold War.

His second term was tainted by the **Iran–Contra** affair. It was uncovered that officials in his administration had secretly used the Israelis to sell American weapons to Iran. At first the USA had hoped these sales would help gain the release of US hostages in Lebanon, but later the USA used the profits from the sales to aid the Contra rebels who were fighting the left-wing government of Nicaragua. These actions were illegal; selling arms to Iran and funding the Contras had both been banned by Congress. Nonetheless Reagan's popularity recovered and in 1989 he left office with the highest approval rating of any president since Franklin D. Roosevelt.

> **Relevant chapters:**
> You will find events and topics relevant to Reagan in Chapters 2 and 8.

Where Can You Research the Lives of the Presidents?

Every president has a presidential library established in their honour and you can visit the libraries' websites. Here you will find a wealth of information about the events during the terms of each president.

- Franklin D. Roosevelt Presidential Library and Museum: www.fdrlibrary.marist.edu

- Harry S. Truman Library and Museum: www.trumanlibrary.org

- Eisenhower Presidential Library: www.eisenhower.archives.gov

- John F Kennedy Presidential Library and Museum: www.jfklibrary.org

- LBJ Presidential Library: www.lbjlibrary.org

- Nixon Presidential Library and Museum: http://nixon.archives.gov/index.php

- Gerald Ford Presidential Library and Museum: www.ford.utexas.edu

- Jimmy Carter Library and Museum: www.jimmycarterlibrary.gov

- Ronald Reagan Presidential Library and Museum: www.reagan.utexas.edu

1 THE US SYSTEM OF GOVERNMENT

State whether each of the following statements is true or false. If false, write a sentence explaining your answer.

a) The term 'separation of powers' refers to the fact that there are three branches of the US government.
b) The president has complete control over treaties that are signed with other countries.
c) The Supreme Court's main role is to make sure that all laws that are passed are constitutional.
d) Each state has the same number of members of the House of Representatives.
e) A senator is elected every six years.
f) Paid lobbyists get members of Congress to introduce bills.
g) A bill needs to be passed by only one of the Houses of Congress before the president has to sign it.
h) The power of veto means that a president can stop a bill.
i) California can send an ambassador to China and print her own money.
j) A state government can ignore a Supreme Court ruling about one of its laws.

2 ORDINARY LEVEL QUESTIONS

a) Outline the role played by the president and Congress in the US political system.
b) What were the tensions between the federal government and the states?
c) What did Harry Truman achieve as president of the United States? (Leaving Cert 2011)

3 HIGHER LEVEL ESSAYS

a) How does the separation of powers operate in the government of the USA?
b) What are the main tensions that have been present at state and federal level in the US system of government?
c) How did the US Presidency develop from Roosevelt to Reagan? (Leaving Cert 2011)

② The US Economy after World War II

Economic Terms Explained

In this chapter we will refer to a lot of economic terms and ideas. Here are explanations of some of the economic terms that you will read about:

inflation A situation in which prices are rising. Usually measured as an annual percentage (e.g. 5 per cent). High inflation means that ordinary people can buy fewer goods and services with their income.

real purchasing power Inflation affects what people can buy for their wages. This means that even if wages are rising they may not be keeping up with inflation. Real purchasing power looks at what a person can actually buy with their wages, not the money value of the wages they receive.

real income Takes into account the effect of inflation. For example, if inflation is higher than the yearly rise in your wages you can actually buy fewer goods with your money.

interest rates The cost of borrowing money. A rise in interest rates will help to tackle

inflation; a reduction can help to create employment.

federal revenue Money collected by the US federal government that is then spent on defence, education, social security, health care, etc.

deficit spending Government spending is greater than revenue (tax). The difference is made up by borrowing (deficit). If this continues for a few years it leads to a federal deficit.

government bonds When a government wants to raise money it can sell bonds. These are loans that are repaid, with interest, a few years later. US government bonds were traditionally the most sought after internationally and therefore the US government had little difficulty borrowing money.

mergers When two companies agree to join together to form one company. Mergers are different from takeovers, where a larger company takes over a smaller one.

boom A period of rising growth and employment when the economy is doing very well.

recession/depression A period of low or falling growth leading to rising unemployment.

exports Goods or services a country sells abroad.

imports Foreign goods or services bought in the home country.

trade balance The difference between exports and imports. If imports are greater than exports, a country has a trade deficit. If exports are greater than imports, the country has a trade surplus.

devaluation Reducing the value of your currency compared to other currencies. This makes your exports cheaper but can cause inflation as goods bought from other countries become more expensive.

multinational corporation A company that operates in more than one country. Many US companies had (or have) production facilities throughout the world, e.g. Coca-Cola.

WHY DID THE USA EXPERIENCE AN ECONOMIC BOOM AFTER WORLD WAR II?

The USA emerged from World War II as the most powerful economy in the world. Its economic boom continued well into the 1960s. In 1950, with only 7 per cent of the world's population, the USA was producing half of all the manufactured goods in the world. Between 1945 and 1960 the economy almost doubled, exports rose dramatically and unemployment and inflation rates were low. The booming economy allowed Americans to enjoy the highest standard of living in the world.

Many factors contributed to the development of this economic boom.

1. World War II

The war boosted American production. Largely untouched by the fighting and out of the range of enemy bombers, American industry was able to produce vast amounts of military equipment and supplies for the Allies. For example, Ford alone produced more military equipment than the whole of Italy! Increased production meant more jobs. The unemployment rate dropped from nearly 15 per cent in 1940 to less than 2 per cent in 1944. Over six million women joined the workforce, replacing the millions of men serving in the armed forces. Wages were high and overtime work was plentiful as industry tried to keep up with war demands. The government began collecting income tax from paychecks for the first time in 1943. With high employment this provided a rich source of federal revenue. For example, nearly half the cost of the war was paid for with taxes.

Millions of women joined the workforce during the American industrial boom caused by World War II

However, with resources directed towards the war effort, few consumer goods were made for people to buy. This forced many Americans to save their money. By 1945 ordinary Americans had $134 billion in bank accounts and/or invested in government bonds, which were sold by the government to finance the war. After the war consumer goods became available again and this led to a huge increase in spending on cars, homes and a range of household consumer goods with wartime savings.

The boom continued in the years after 1945 as the wartime economy converted to peacetime production. The USA became the leading exporter of a range of goods and services. While many new industries emerged, older ones began modernising and expanding. One particular growth sector was franchises such as McDonald's (1955). These enabled business people to set up a company using an established and successful business formula.

There was a trend towards mergers, leading to the concentration of businesses and industry into giant corporations (companies). By the mid-1960s 150 large corporations controlled half of America's manufacturing industry, and in 1962 General Motors was the largest company in the world. During the 1960s US corporations began operating in many locations abroad, becoming **multinational corporations**. The process of worldwide integration of markets became known as **globalisation**. Between 1945 and the late 1960s the global economy was dominated by American multinational corporations such as General Electric and Exxon (Esso).

2. Public Investment

After the war the US government followed the economic policies of the British economist **John Maynard Keynes**. He believed that government spending (public investment) would help tackle an economic recession. His idea, known as 'priming the pump', involved government pumping money into the economy in order to increase demand for goods and services. This increased demand would lead to a rise in employment, more tax revenue and greater consumer spending power. Many people expected an economic recession after the war when industrial production based on military demands ended and millions of soldiers returned looking for work, so the government continued to invest money in the economy.

In 1944 the Servicemen's Readjustment Act (known as the GI Bill) was passed by Congress. It provided government funding for returning war veterans, offering low-interest loans to set up businesses or buy family houses, and financial help for university education. Between 1945 and 1955 $20 billion was made available to over 7.8 million veterans. The GI Bill greatly helped the economy, contributing to a boom in the building industry, education and other services, and promoting consumer spending.

In 1948 President Truman announced his Fair Deal reforms, a programme that increased public spending. Though much of this package was rejected by Congress, he did manage to raise the minimum wage and extend social security to help those who were unemployed. The number of people working for the government (the federal bureaucracy) also increased.

Thousands of kilometres of highways were built in the 1950s and 1960s, connecting American cities and states

Public spending continued to rise in the 1950s and 1960s. In 1956 the Eisenhower administration introduced the **Interstate Highway Act**, under which $33.5 billion was spent building 65,970km of roads around the country. In 1964 President Johnson's Great Society programme spent $800 million on social welfare reforms. His reforms in both health care and social security had a dramatic effect on reducing poverty in the United States. Unfortunately, some resources allocated for the programme were diverted to funding the Vietnam War.

During the Cold War there was huge US government investment abroad. The **Marshall Plan** (1947) provided $13.5 billion of US government aid to post-war Europe. This came in cash, equipment, food and technical assistance. Participating countries agreed to buy US goods and to allow US companies to invest in their economies. As a result American public and private investment in Western Europe increased dramatically.

The US government spent billions of dollars on defence during the Cold War. Military bases were set up in thirty countries. The US fought wars in Korea (1950–53) and Vietnam (1965–73). The **arms race** (see Chapter 11) and the **space race** (Chapter 12) resulted in heavy government investment in defence-related industries such as weapons research and development. All of these created further demand in the economy, providing more jobs.

The growing government investment in defence led to industrial expansion in the south and west of the country. Texas, California and the states between them became known as the 'gun belt'.

3. Energy

The USA had access to an abundant supply of cheap energy, particularly oil. As the economy continued to grow, the demand for oil was greater than the USA was able to supply from domestic production. US oil consumption rose from 6.5 million barrels of oil a day in 1950 to nearly 14 million barrels of oil a day in 1970. As a result the USA began to import oil, particularly from the Middle East. Five US oil companies, together with one British and one Anglo-Dutch oil company – known collectively as the Seven Sisters – controlled 85 per cent of oil reserves in the world prior to the oil crisis of 1973.

Between 1950 and 1970 the average price for a barrel of oil was $2. The low cost of fuel kept production and transport costs low, helping businesses to grow.

After the war the atomic industry expanded, not only for military purposes but also to generate electricity. The first nuclear power stations opened in 1957 and by 1970 over 100 nuclear stations were generating almost 8 per cent of the country's electricity supply.

4. Technology

Advances in sciences and technology during the war led to the development of new industries after 1945. The electronics industry expanded, making the USA a world leader in the production of televisions, computers, transistor radios, and a range of household consumer products. Power-driven machinery and increasingly more complex equipment replaced hand tools in industry, farming and the home. The technological revolution after 1945 led to a dramatic rise in production and economic growth.

5. The Baby Boom and the Growth of Suburbs

In 1946 nearly four million babies were born in the USA. This was the first year of the so-called '**baby boom**' (or increased birth rate) that lasted for nearly twenty years. It resulted in a demand for a growing range of goods and services. By 1958 children under 15 made up nearly one-third of the population, and provided a growing market for clothes, food and toys. This consumer society kept the post-war economy booming.

The baby boom created a demand for housing, schools and leisure facilities. Developers built huge suburban housing developments, complete with schools, shopping centres, churches, banks and recreational amenities, all over the USA. During the 1950s many more suburbs appeared around the country, including large suburban developments known as 'Levittowns' (after the company – Levitt & Sons – that built the first one – see page 30). By the end of the decade 25 per cent of Americans had moved to the suburbs.

The move to the suburbs prompted a demand for more cars. In 1945 there were 26 million cars on the American roads; by the mid-1950s there were over 130 million.

The movement to the suburbs was also accompanied by a movement of the population to cities in the west and south-west of the country, an area that became known as the '**Sun Belt**'. Crucial to this population movement was the invention of air conditioning. Cities located there, such as Houston, Miami and Phoenix, grew rapidly. The biggest, Los Angeles, overtook Chicago to become the second largest city in the USA. By 1970 California had overtaken New York as the country's most populous state.

HOW DID THE US ECONOMY PERFORM BETWEEN 1968 AND 1989?

The Great Society and the Vietnam War

When J.F. Kennedy was elected president in 1960 he announced his ambitious 'New Frontier' programme, which combined domestic and foreign policy objectives. At home his priorities were tax reform, social welfare reform and civil rights. He also increased federal spending on defence. To fund this ambitious programme, federal deficits (a situation where the government spends more than its income) were introduced.

Following Kennedy's assassination in November 1963, Lyndon B. Johnson became president. He cut income taxes, announced his **Great Society** programme and declared a 'war on poverty', making $800 million available to improve health and education for the poor, and to tackle the problem of urban poverty.

During his presidency the USA became more involved in the long and costly war in Vietnam (see Chapter 7). The war placed huge strains on the federal budget. By 1968 it was costing the USA $100 billion a year. To avoid raising unpopular taxes to pay for the war, Johnson increased government borrowing. The national debt soared and federal deficit spending grew out of control.

Domestic Recession

As a result, by the late 1960s the economy was beginning to slow down. Inflation and unemployment were increasing. Continued deficit spending, together with a decline in production and in export sales, led to a negative trade balance as the country was importing more than it was exporting. To combat inflation the government raised interest rates.

This economic downturn was to worsen considerably in 1973. Following a war between Israel and Egypt, the USA offered Israel a $2.2 billion arms deal. The Organization of Petroleum Exporting Countries (OPEC), which was dominated by Arab countries, increased the price of oil fourfold and imposed cutbacks in supplies to countries that supported Israel. The USA imported 30 per cent of OPEC's oil exports and as a result was badly affected. OPEC's embargo impacted heavily on industry and on consumers. Unemployment rose and high inflation resulted in a drop in real income for workers.

Continuing deficit spending increased inflation as the government was printing money to pay for the services it provided. The complex economy of the 1970s and 1980s required a skilled workforce, but millions of Americans lacked these high-tech skills and were therefore unemployable. The unprecedented combination of high inflation, low growth and high unemployment became known

Homelessness became a huge issue in the 1970s. These people are waiting to get into a Seattle shelter

as **stagflation**. Stagflation presented the US government with a unique economic dilemma because high unemployment and inflation do not usually exist together. The normal policy to curb inflation is to raise interest rates or cut government spending. However, these policies will have the effect of creating unemployment. This is why US presidents found it very difficult to deal with the country's economic problems in the 1970s.

In 1974, when Nixon was forced to resign following the Watergate scandal, Gerald Ford became president. The economy continued in recession and trade deficits worsened.

The USA had a trade deficit in eight of the ten years of the 1970s. These trade deficits led to a devaluation of the dollar to try to encourage exports. After a second oil crisis in 1979, Ford's successor, Jimmy Carter, increased interest rates. He hoped this would discourage borrowing and reduce inflation, but it had little impact.

The Economic Policies of Ronald Reagan

In 1980, when Ronald Reagan became president, the USA was in deep recession. Unemployment was running at 10 per cent and almost a third of US industrial plants remained idle. Economic rivals Germany and Japan were taking a greater share of world trade. Matters were not helped by record interest rates of 20 per cent. Reagan's economic policies – **Reaganomics** – involved cutting federal welfare spending and reducing personal and corporate taxes. He believed that cutting taxes would provide an incentive to business and for people to work harder.

Inflation fell and the US economy turned around, contributing to Reagan's re-election in 1984. In his second term he signed the biggest tax reform measure in 75 years, which cut taxes further, mainly for the rich.

In 1989 Reagan left office with the economy in its longest post-World War II expansion. Tax cuts had led to increased consumer spending; the economy was growing faster than at any time since the mid-1960s; personal income rose 20 per cent per person after 1980; annual inflation fell from 13 per cent

American prosperity in the Reagan era – executives at Sun Microsystems

in 1981 to less than 4 per cent; and unemployment was down to around 5 per cent as the economy created 13 million new jobs.

However, a lot of the growth had been as a result of deficit spending. For example, the Reagan administration greatly increased military spending. In 1982 a new defence plan costing $1.2 trillion was adopted. Government borrowing now soared, causing bigger federal deficits than had ever been seen before. It increased from $930 billion in 1980 to $2.6 trillion in 1988. This was three times more than the debt accumulated by the previous 39 presidents!

The number of millionaires increased by 100,000 every year and there was a great spending spree. A stock market crash in 1987 (the largest in history) had little impact. However, Reagan's policies did little to help the poorest Americans, who saw their income fall. The gap between rich and poor increased as many of the new jobs that had been created were in low-wage service industries.

What Impact Did Competition from Abroad Have on the US Economy?

By the mid-1970s, as we have seen, the problem of trade deficits emerged. Americans were spending more on imports than they were gaining from selling exports.

The most serious competitors were West Germany and Japan, the defeated powers in 1945. Much of their economic recovery was due to US aid, but by the 1980s they had become more efficient and more productive than the USA. Traditionally strong American industries such as steel, textiles, consumer and electrical goods began to decline. These industries, which had been big exporters since 1945, saw many of their products replaced by foreign imports.

The US car industry, dominated by **Chrysler**, **General Motors** and **Ford**, which had been the leader in the world for so long, lost out to competition in foreign markets. The domestic market was also shrinking due to competition from companies such as Mercedes-Benz and Toyota. In 1955 imported cars accounted for only 1 per cent of sales in the USA; by 1987 this figure had risen to 31 per cent. By the end of the 1980s America was producing fewer cars than Germany and Japan.

Foreign investment in the US economy increased, and Americans became alarmed as foreigners bought up US stocks and property. In 1988 Japanese investment in California, New York, Texas and Washington ran into billions of dollars. When a Japanese company bought the Rockefeller Center in New York many Americans feared that their heritage was being sold out to foreigners.

Under Reagan the USA remained committed to **free trade**. This open market policy worked well when the US economy was booming, as it allowed favourable trading conditions for US exporters, but in times of recession the reverse was true. America became flooded with cheap imports and was unable to find markets abroad for its exports.

The quality of American manufacturing was clearly slipping. Some critics blamed the education system for not producing skilled business and scientific experts; others blamed the workforce for demanding high wages, or corporations for wanting quick profit at the cost of long-term investment.

The result of the growing competition from abroad was a decline in domestic production, a large trade deficit and a rise in unemployment in traditional industries.

END-OF-CHAPTER REVIEW

1 ORDINARY LEVEL QUESTIONS
Write a paragraph on the following:
a) The multinational corporation, 1945–68. (Leaving Cert 2012)
b) The sources of the US economic boom after World War II.
c) The impact of competition from Japan and Europe.
d) The economic policies of Ronald Reagan.

2 HIGHER LEVEL ESSAYS
a) Why did the United States experience an economic boom, 1945–68, and what was its impact on society? (Leaving Cert 2010)
b) To what extent did the US economy experience both success and decline during the period 1945–89? (Leaving Cert 2012)
c) What was the impact on the US economy of one or more of the following: the multinational corporation; the military–industrial complex; international competition from Japan and Europe? (Leaving Cert 2013)
d) What were the significant developments in the US economy, 1945–89? (Leaving Cert 2014)

KEY QUESTIONS

As we saw in Chapter 2, post-war American society was marked by dramatic growth and change. There was unprecedented growth in the economy, in population and in prosperity, and great changes in traditional social values. The world of leisure, work, the role of women and the family were transformed. The phrase 'the American way of life' came to symbolise a society based on abundance, with a large section of society enjoying a very good standard of living. This kind of society, where a great many ordinary people enjoyed such affluence, was unheard of in the USA, or elsewhere in the world, before 1945.

The causes of the post-war economic prosperity and the recessions of the 1970s and 1980s were examined in Chapter 2. This chapter looks at the social trends that emerged between 1945 and 1989 and the impact they had on the American way of life.

WHAT WERE THE DEMOGRAPHIC CHANGES IN THE USA?

The Baby Boom

The post-war generation had lived through economic depression and war. By the end of the war people were eager to put the bad times behind them. One clear indication of the sense of confidence in the future was the increase in the national **birth rate**. During the war there had been a trend towards earlier marriages and rising birth rates. Birth rates continued to rise until well into the 1950s. In 1946 alone, a record 3.8 million babies were born in the USA. From 1948 to 1953, more babies were born than in the previous thirty years. This dramatic rise in the birth rate became known as the **baby boom**. The post-war baby boom would have a profound effect on the American way of life for decades into the future:

- It helped stimulate demand for a range of consumer goods and services. By 1958, children under 15 made up nearly one-third of the population and provided a market for clothes, food and toys. In that year toy sales reached $1.25 billion.

- It created a demand for houses, suburban development, schools, and recreation and sports facilities. One leading supplier of school furniture saw its business triple between 1945 and 1958.

- By 1965, these baby boomers had reached their teens or early 20s, when they contributed to a new **youth culture** that would shock the older generations and change American society.

- The baby boom provided new opportunities for American businesses. However, it also presented new challenges for teachers, parents and society in general.

Immigration

During the baby boom years, immigration into the USA contributed to the dramatic rise in population.

There were four main sources of immigration during this period:

1 World War II: Refugees, mainly from Western Europe, came to the USA after the war.

2 The Korean War (1950–53): Between 1953 and 1968, 17,000 Koreans, mostly wives (war brides) and children of American servicemen, settled in the USA.

3 The Cold War: Immigrants from Eastern Europe came to the USA. Under the **Displaced Persons Act** (1948), many of these émigrés took up academic and research jobs.

4 Over 275,000 Mexicans became US citizens during the 1950s. Most of them settled in California, Arizona and Texas, where they worked as farm labourers.

As the national birth rate began to stabilise after the mid-1960s, immigrants began to make up a growing percentage of the population. During the late 1960s and early 1970s, around 400,000 legal immigrants arrived each year. By the 1980s, their numbers had grown to an average of 730,000

A 'baby boom' family in the 1950s

annually. In 1960, there were 9.7 million foreign-born Americans. Twenty years later, 14 million people living in the USA were foreign born.

Death Rate

Improvements in health care, medical advancements and a better diet led to increased life expectancy in the USA after 1945. In 1954, a combination of a high birth rate, a low death rate and the influx of 144,000 immigrants led to the largest one-year population growth recorded by the Census Bureau in US history. Americans were living longer. In 1975 the average life expectancy for American males was 72 years, and for females it was 81 years.

Migration

Americans began to spread into new areas of the country after 1945. The region known as the Sun Belt (Florida, Texas, Arizona and California) saw a rapid rise in population. Between 1945 and 1949, California alone gained two million extra inhabitants. By 1970, it was the most populous state in the USA, with a population of 20 million. This huge demographic shift would have far-reaching social, political, economic and cultural effects.

In the 1970s, one out of every five Americans was moving to a new place of residence in the country every year. Three distinct trends in migration emerged:

1   Movement away from farms and rural areas to cities

2   Movement of the middle classes out of city centres to suburbs

3   Movement of African Americans out of the south to the north and west of the country.

In 1940 the population of the USA was 130 million. By the mid-1950s it had increased to 165 million, in 1960 to 179 million and by 1989 it had reached 249 million.

HOW AFFLUENT WAS THE USA?

World War II brought full employment to the USA. Wages were high, with average yearly earnings increasing from $754 in 1940 to $1,289 in 1944. But during the war there was a shortage of consumer goods, as priority was given to the production of goods needed for the war effort. By the time the war was over, Americans had saved over $134 billion in cash, bank accounts and government bonds. Having gone without material comforts during the war, Americans now wanted to spend their savings.

Incomes continued to rise after the war. Between 1950 and 1968, average family income grew from $3,319 per year to more than $8,000. Real purchasing power increased by 66 per cent in the first twenty years after the war. The majority of

Millions of immigrants took the citizenship pledge to become American citizens during the 1960s, 1970s and 1980s

Americans now had a standard of living that would have been unheard of before the war.

Economists in the 1950s attributed this new prosperity to what they called 'an economy of abundance' – an economic system that could produce more goods and services than Americans were capable of consuming. This economic wealth created great affluence in post-war America.

From 1960 onwards white-collar workers outnumbered blue-collar workers

The New Rich

The number of very rich Americans grew dramatically in the post-war years. The established wealthy class, the 'old rich', retained and expanded their wealth. However, after the war another wealthy class emerged. By the 1960s there were approximately 100,000 millionaires in the USA; these 'new rich' had made their money in oil, insurance and property.

When the economy recovered again after the recessions of the 1970s, it was the very rich who benefited most. In 1980, there were 574,000 millionaires in the USA; by 1988 there were 1.3 million, over fifty of whom were billionaires. The post-1970s generation of 'new rich' had made their fortunes in the information and communication industries. Bill Gates of Microsoft, and Ted Turner of Turner Network Television (TNT) and Cable News Network (CNN) became the symbols of this new generation of very wealthy Americans.

The Middle Class

After World War II the American middle class grew in size and prosperity. In 1945 'blue-collar' workers (wage earners in industrial jobs) were the largest group of workers in America. In the post-war years, however, more and more Americans stopped wearing overalls to work and started wearing suits. By 1960, the number of 'white-collar' workers (earning salaries in professional and managerial jobs) outnumbered blue-collar workers for the first time in American history. In the 1970s, for every blue-collar worker there were two white-collar workers in the workforce.

The majority of middle-class Americans now worked in service industries such as advertising, technical and clerical jobs, publishing, teaching, nursing, medicine, law and accounting. This new middle class earned good incomes and developed affluent lifestyles.

The age of affluence came to an end during the 1970s (see pages 23–24). This decade proved to be the most difficult for the American economy since the Depression of the 1930s. Incomes failed to keep up with the rising cost of living. Unemployment rates increased dramatically and general living standards fell. Despite this downturn, however, the majority of middle-class Americans continued to enjoy comfortable living standards relative to the rest of the world.

QUESTIONS

1 Why had Americans managed to save so much money during World War II?

2 Explain 'economy of abundance'.

3 What is meant by the term 'baby boom' in post-war American history?

4 List some of the effects of the baby boom.

WHAT WAS THE CONSUMER SOCIETY?

Consumption and spending became the driving force of the post-war American way of life. Affluence led to a growing demand for consumer goods. While the old and new rich lived in great luxury, it was the middle class that increasingly defined the consumer society in post-war America.

Range of Goods

As the economy quickly converted to peacetime production, a whole range of consumer goods and services became available. Manufacturers produced an abundance of appliances and gadgets to make everyday home life easier and more comfortable – washing machines, fridges, air conditioners, vacuum cleaners, TVs, furniture, cars, etc. Sales of all these consumer goods rose steadily in the post-war years.

Suburbia

The post-war marriage and baby boom created a demand for housing. Economic prosperity and generous government subsidies (the GI Bill – see page 20) made home ownership possible for the new middle class. For the first time in American history the majority of families lived in houses they owned.

The demand for new housing led to a construction boom. Developers built huge suburban housing complexes, many of them complete with schools, shopping centres, churches, banks and recreational amenities. One enterprising builder, Abraham Levitt, came up with the idea of mass production of suburban houses. In 1947, the company began building the first Levittown on Long Island, New York State. Every house had the same floor plan and was equipped with a refrigerator, electric cooker and washing machine, and a TV set built into the living room wall. When this suburb was completed in 1951, it had 17,447 homes, as well as schools, shops and parks. Throughout the 1950s 'Levittowns' were built all over the country.

The affluent middle class wanted space to bring up their families. Suburbia offered protection from urban unrest and congestion, as well as

Suburban living offered children more space to play than they would have in high-rise apartments

an escape from class and racial conflict (see Chapter 4). It reinforced traditional family values and represented the 'American dream' of the good life. Houses were designed for married couples with an average-sized family. Women stayed at home to look after the children and run the home. Men commuted to work.

By the end of the 1950s, one-quarter of the population in the USA had moved to the suburbs, and by 1970 the majority of Americans were living in suburbia.

The Car Culture

The mass movement of people to the suburbs prompted a demand for cars. Very few cities had good public transport systems, making car ownership necessary for work, shopping and recreation.

In 1945 there were 26 million cars on American roads. Most of them were old and in need of repair. Car manufacturers produced 2.1 million new cars in 1946. Ten years later, new car sales reached 8 million. In 1955, there were 52 million cars registered in the USA, in 1960 over 70 million, and by the mid-1970s over 130 million.

The dramatic increase in car sales led to significant changes in the American way of life. The countryside was transformed to facilitate car users. The Federal-Aid Highway Act 1956 provided for the building of 68,395 kilometres of highways

(motorways). Billions of dollars were spent on constructing roads and parking facilities. By 1976, 6.4 million kilometres of paved roads and streets had been built.

The '**drive-in**' idea had been developed in California during the 1920s, but after 1945 it expanded rapidly around the country. In the 1950s, banks, cinemas, theatres and restaurants all catered for car drivers by offering 'drive-in' services. Motels, designed for the car-travelling public, sprang up along the new highways.

Cars became important for image and status. In suburbia, the station wagon was popular and became the badge of affluence for middle-class families. The ultimate status symbol in America in the 1950s was the Cadillac, which was considered the embodiment of the American dream. Car manufacturers produced bigger cars that had no great transportation advantages, but were in demand by customers who saw in them powerful expressions of image and self-esteem.

Petrol (gas) was cheap and plentiful in the post-war years. As Americans increased their consumption, they became increasingly dependent on imported oil. Between 1971 and 1973 oil imports quadrupled. Disaster struck in 1973 when OPEC increased the price of oil from $3 to $5 a barrel. During the winter of 1973–74, Americans faced long queues at petrol stations and prices rose dramatically. Car manufacturing levels fell by nearly 22 per cent and continued to decline for the rest of the decade. Consumers began to demand smaller, more fuel-efficient cars. In the 1970s and 1980s, the car became less a status symbol and more a practical form of transport.

'Buy Now, Pay Later'

Anxious to promote spending after the war, retailers and manufacturers offered consumers attractive conditions with low interest rates and small down-payments on a range of goods and services. The giant car manufacturers General Motors coined the phrase 'Buy now, pay later' to entice people to buy their products even if they could not afford them. Soon millions of Americans were using instalment plans to acquire household appliances and furnishings.

The rapid expansion of car ownership led to competition between petrol companies. To attract motorists to their brands, they offered loyalty cards that could be used for credit in thousands of outlets around the country. In 1950, Diner's Club took up the idea when it distributed credit cards to wealthy New Yorkers who wanted to eat in expensive restaurants and not have to deal in cash. During the 1950s, American Express, Sears Roebuck and several other banks and department stores issued credit cards to customers. As a result of instalment buying and credit card use, private debt shot up from $104.8 billion to $263 billion during the 1950s.

By the end of the 1970s, there were over 600 million credit cards in use by 150 million Americans. Excluding mortgages, the average American was spending 18 per cent of net income to pay for consumer loans (credit).

> In Arthur Miller's play *Death of a Salesman* (1949), the character Willy Loman complained, 'Once in my life I would like to own something outright before it is broken. I'm always in a race with the junk yard! I just finished paying for the car and it's on its last legs. The refrigerator consumes belts like a goddam maniac. They time those things. They time them so when you finally paid for them, they're used up.'

Advertising

Advertising promoted consumer spending and borrowing. As more and more products were made, manufacturers stimulated demand by vigorous advertising. They employed psychologists and sociologists to study public buying habits and develop profitable marketing strategies.

By 1960, 90 per cent of American homes had television. Advertisers were quick to exploit this new medium. Before the end of the decade, two out of every ten minutes of broadcasting time went on commercials (advertisements).

Criticisms of the Consumer Society

Some critics of the consumer society pointed to the decline in the quality of life in America. They complained about suburban sprawl invading the countryside, about traffic and overcrowded highways, about relentless shopping and advertising, and about the loss of traditional values such as thrift and saving money. To many, the new way of life after 1945 was vulgar and crass. Novels

Images of domestic wealth and ease like this one from 1955 were widely used to 'sell' the ideal of modern suburban living

such as *The Man in the Gray Flannel Suit* and *The Crack in the Picture Window* highlighted what the writers saw as the empty consumption-driven world of middle-class Americans who lived in suburbia.

In San Francisco a new generation of poets and writers, known as the **beats** or **beatniks,** emerged. Between 1957 and 1960, this group came to represent the voice of opposition to consumer culture. The best-known beatniks were the poet **Allen Ginsberg** and the writer **Jack Kerouac.** The movement began to fade after 1960 but had a powerful influence on youth culture in the 1960s and 1970s (see page 142).

Vance Packard wrote three best-selling books highlighting the power advertising had in the consumer society: *The Hidden Persuaders* (1957), *The Status Seekers* (1959) and *The Waste Makers* (1960). Packard claimed consumers were being fooled into buying products by advertisements that appealed to their subconscious fears or desires.

In *The Lonely Crowd* (1950), sociologist **David Riesman** described the growth of conformist values among the middle classes. He found that Americans were becoming 'other-directed', influenced by peer groups and living as society expected them to live. Riesman's study drew attention to the lack of individualism in mass consumer-driven society.

William H. Whyte, in *The Organization Man* (1956) (see page 187), described the change in attitudes to work and career. He claimed that the values of individualism and personal ambition were being replaced by loyalty to the company and the demands of business. He also criticised suburban life, which forced people to conform and live according to social expectations.

John Kenneth Galbraith, the Harvard professor of economics, wrote *The Affluent Society* in 1958. He showed that while Americans spent billions of dollars on cars, TVs and household appliances, spending on services such as education, health and social services was inadequate. He saw a massive contrast between private affluence and public poverty. A booming economy, according to Galbraith, had not improved the quality of life in America. He called for increased spending on public education and higher taxes to pay for better social services.

By the mid-1960s, some people were beginning to complain that many consumer products were useless, dangerous, falsely advertised, over-priced or defective. A lawyer called **Ralph Nader** became the leader of a new movement aimed at protecting consumers. In 1965, he published *Unsafe at Any Speed*, exposing the lack of safety features in American cars. He started consumer organisations in an attempt to bring public pressure on business and government.

Leisure

The post-war economic boom brought new economic and social freedoms. Millions of Americans had more time off work and more disposable income to spend. They were now getting more pay for less work. In 1900, the average working week was 55 hours. By 1950, this had been reduced to 40 hours and workers were given annual paid holidays.

The demand for entertainment and recreational activities increased, and the leisure industry expanded dramatically. By the end of the 1960s, Americans were spending nearly $40 billion a year on a wide range of leisure activities.

Television

In 1946 there were fewer than 7,000 TV sets in the USA. The basic set cost between $375 and $500, which was beyond the budget of most ordinary Americans. There were only a few channels on offer, and viewing time was limited to a few hours in the evening.

By 1950, the price of TV sets had dropped considerably. In 1955, there were 32 million sets in use and nearly 75 per cent of all homes had TV. By 1960, that figure was 90 per cent.

The television boom had a great impact on American social life. Attendance at cinemas, sports events, restaurants and night clubs declined as TV became widespread in homes.

Colour TV sets first became available in the USA in 1954. Initially, colour sets cost four or five times as much as black and white sets. Not surprisingly, few coloured sets were sold in the 1950s. Black and white TVs out-sold colour sets until 1968, when their price dropped dramatically. By 1970, 24 million homes had colour TV sets.

Twenty per cent of broadcasting time was taken up with commercials (ads). TV advertising influenced consumer spending and proved to be a powerful force in promoting the consumer society.

Soap operas, which first featured on US radio in the 1920s, became popular during the 1950s. The term 'soap opera' originated in their association with companies like Procter & Gamble and other manufacturers of soap, laundry and cleaning products, who sponsored the programmes. At first they were broadcast during the day and were aimed at housewives, but from 1956 soap operas were shown as prime time evening viewing. Soaps continued to attract large audiences throughout the 1960s, 1970s and 1980s.

By the 1960s, polls were reporting that television viewing was the favourite leisure-time activity of almost 50 per cent of the American population. TV sets were on for three hours or more a day in the average American home.

Sport

Public interest in sport – both watching and participating – increased dramatically in the post-war years. Increased car and TV ownership contributed greatly to the new popularity of sport as a leisure activity.

In the 1940s and early 1950s, attendance at sporting events grew because:

- People could drive to a baseball or American football game.

- The baby boom and the growth of suburbia led to a demand for family-centred sports activities.

Millions of viewers could watch a range of sporting events regularly on TV. By the 1960s, sport was earning more revenue from TV rights than it was taking in from ticket sales. In 1967, more than 65 million TV viewers watched the first televised Super Bowl (the Green Bay Packers defeated the Kansas City Chiefs).

Before the advent of TV, sports such as tennis and golf were largely the preserve of the rich. TV exposure increased their popularity with all classes. President Eisenhower was a keen golf fan and his interest helped to make golf one of the most popular sports among ordinary Americans in the 1950s.

A 1950s family gathered in front of the television watching a favourite show

Baseball, the national game of the USA, remained the most popular spectator sport in the 1950s and 1960s. The game was organised at a professional level, with players earning good salaries. As with all professional sports, television turned baseball into a multi-million-dollar business.

Nationwide competitions were also organised in American football, basketball, hockey, soccer and tennis. The number of professional teams in these sports grew rapidly during the 1950s. In the 1960s, college football (American) became very popular, attracting even larger numbers of fans than baseball before the end of the decade.

By the 1970s active participation in sport had grown dramatically. It is estimated that 88 million adults were involved in some kind of sporting activity.

Sport reflected the **racial tensions** of post-war America. It was affected by the growing demands by African Americans for civil rights during the 1960s: African-American athletes were prominent in amateur sports such as the Olympics, but boxing was the only professional sport in which they competed. In 1947, the race barrier was broken in baseball when the talented African-American player Jackie Robinson was hired by the Brooklyn Dodgers. It was not until 1977 that an African-American manager was appointed to any major league baseball team.

Other professional sports remained predominantly white until the 1960s. Since most private tennis and golf clubs excluded African Americans, there were few opportunities to compete in these sports. In 1990, when the Professional Golfers Association (PGA) championship was played in the Birmingham country club in Alabama, African-American players were still excluded from membership of this club. In most sports, racial discrimination was only gradually removed.

The Popular Arts

Post-war prosperity led to an expansion of interest in the arts. In 1964, Americans spent around $1 billion on books, $600 million on musical instruments, $200 million on paintings and art supplies, and $400 million on theatre and musical performances. Entertainment became the dominant feature in the popular arts of drama, music, film and literature. Musicals attracted large audiences in the 1950s, and the 1957 hit stage

Eisenhower (right) and Nixon playing golf at a course in Denver, 1953. Sport had strong political backing

musical *West Side Story* became a Hollywood movie in 1961. During the 1960s and 1970s, the cost of live production and the growth of TV resulted in a decline in attendance at musicals and live stage performances.

The expansion in TV ownership led to a drop in cinema attendance during the 1950s and 1960s. By the mid-1960s, Hollywood was beginning to recover, and in the 1970s attendances at the cinema increased again. The 1977 disco movie *Saturday Night Fever* made over $108 million by the end of 1978.

The widespread production of books in paperback (rather than the more expensive hardback) meant that by 1960, paperbacks were outselling hardback books. Both fiction and non-fiction were more widely read than ever before. Books were easily available and sold in department stores, train and bus stations, airports and many other outlets. The number of publishing houses increased dramatically.

Holidays and Travel

The expansion of holiday travel businesses after 1945 clearly indicated the growth in leisure time enjoyed by the general public. With more holidays and rising living standards, Americans could afford a wide choice of holiday pursuits both at home and abroad.

New roads, the growth of car ownership and the development of new recreational attractions across the country led to a dramatic boom in the holiday industry. During the summer months, families took to the roads to spend holidays at camp sites or visit theme parks. The first Disneyland opened in 1955 in Anaheim, California, and millions travelled long distances to visit it.

Mass holiday travel contributed to changes in the nation's eating habits. Roadside and drive-in takeaway restaurants became popular. In 1954, the entrepreneur Ray Kroc developed a business catering for people who wanted fast, cheap food. The business expanded and became the McDonald's fast food chain. By 1960, there were 228 McDonald's franchises, worth $37 million in annual sales.

Foreign travel, once the preserve of the rich, became available to millions of Americans in the 1950s. By 1966, they were spending $3.7 billion on foreign travel. Air travel expanded with the arrival of jet aircraft in 1958. By the 1970s, jumbo jets had the capacity to carry 360 passengers.

QUESTIONS

1 Explain some of the reasons for the growth of the 'consumer society' in the USA after 1945.

2 How did the growth of suburbia contribute to the boom in consumer spending?

3 Name some of the critics of the consumer society and list their arguments.

4 List some of the effects TV had on American society in the 1950s and 1960s.

5 Outline how sport was affected by racism in the USA.

HOW DID THE ROLE OF WORK CHANGE IN US SOCIETY?

Americans have traditionally believed that what a person **achieves** is more important than where they come from. This was a central theme in the great **American Dream**, the belief that in America anyone could become rich and successful, regardless of their social or economic background. The key to material success was **hard work**. Millions of Americans in the nineteenth century and well into the twentieth believed in this dream. The 'rags to riches' story came true for many. For millions of others, it became a driving aspiration and sustained a dedicated work ethic.

Agriculture

The number of people employed in agriculture had been declining since the early twentieth century. Small family farms struggled to compete as prices for agricultural produce continued to drop after 1945. Farm workers left the land in droves to find better-paying jobs in factories around the country. By 1956, only 22.3 million, one-ninth of the population, were employed in agriculture.

During the years of economic boom, agriculture remained excluded from the general prosperity enjoyed by other workers in the USA. During the 1960s, large farming corporations took over small farms, amalgamating them into huge multi-billion-dollar businesses. Farm sizes continued to grow, but the numbers employed in farming declined. The profile of farming gradually changed: it had become an **agribusiness**, rather than the simple pastoral occupation it had been until then.

Manufacturing

In the 1950s, 83 per cent of American workers were employed in the non-agricultural sector. Most of them were in unskilled or semi-skilled jobs – blue-collar workers. The largest section of the workforce was involved in manufacturing, working in factories where goods were mass produced. Two men significantly influenced the development of the system of mass production in twentieth-century America, creating models that would be replicated worldwide.

- **Henry Ford**
  In the early twentieth century, car manufacturer Henry Ford invented what became known as **assembly line production**. This system involved dividing production into separate tasks. Ford's method speeded up production, and became common practice in manufacturing until the arrival of computers.

- **F.W. Taylor**
  In the 1890s Taylor, an industrial engineer, developed the system of **scientific management**. He believed that if workers, like the machines they operated, were carefully managed and timed, they would work more effectively, and output would increase. Taylor's ideas influenced the organisation of work and its management.

In 1945, the leading American manufacturing industries were steel, textiles and the automobile industry. By the end of the 1980s, the numbers employed in each of these industries had declined dramatically due to competition from foreign

Ford automobile assembly line, 1958

manufacturers and increased **automation** (use of machines to assemble products). Between 1945 and 1990, the American workforce changed from being mainly employed in manufacturing products to earning a living by providing services to customers.

Service Sector

The service sector employs workers in offices as clerical and administrative workers – white-collar workers. This sector grew rapidly in the post-war years. Jobs in the service area required professional and technical skills – teaching, science, communications, law, medicine and engineering. The expansion of third-level education after 1945 contributed to the growth of white-collar employment. Jobs in government services also increased significantly in the post-war years. By the 1970s, one out of every five workers in the USA was employed by the government.

Unemployment

During the 1950s and 1960s, when the economy prospered, jobs were plentiful and unemployment rates were low. At the end of the 1960s, fewer than 4 per cent of the working population were out of work. However, as a result of two oil crises in the 1970s and the cost of the war in Vietnam, the economy went into recession. In 1975, unemployment stood at almost 8 per cent and by 1982 had risen to nearly 11 per cent. African Americans, women, teenagers and unskilled workers were the worst affected. Twenty per cent of African Americans and 24 per cent of all teenagers were unemployed that year. The most extreme figure was for young African Americans aged between 16 and 24, 32.1 per cent of whom were out of work. By the late 1980s, unemployment rates had dropped to 6 per cent, but critics argued that too many jobs were unskilled and paid minimum-wage rates.

Labour Unions

The labour movement in the USA was always weaker than it was in Western Europe. In America, trade union membership had always been strongest among male workers in heavy industries such as coal, steel and car manufacturing.

During World War II, union membership grew from 28 per cent of the non-agricultural workforce in 1941 to 36 per cent in 1945 (13 million workers). In 1955, the two biggest unions, the **American Federation of Labor** (AFL) and the **Congress of Industrial Organizations** (CIO), combined to form one union representing 15 million workers.

However, trade union membership began to decline from the mid-1950s. Between 1955 and 1968, it went from 33 per cent of the non-agricultural workforce to 28 per cent. This trend continued throughout the 1970s and 1980s. By 1987, it was down to 17 per cent. A number of factors contributed to this decline:

- Government introduced legislation to restrict trade union activity (the **Taft-Hartley Act**, 1947). More anti-union legislation followed in the post-war years.

- During the years of post-war prosperity, American workers wanted consumer goods and job security, and they did not want conflict with employers. Most paid their union dues, but had little time for socialist politics and union leaders.

- The 'Red Scare' (see page 140) contributed to turning public opinion against trade unions.

- After the war, many industries moved from the midwest and north-east to the south, where there was hostility to trade unions.

- The decline of heavy industries and manufacturing resulted in lower union membership. White-collar workers were less inclined to join unions, and they represented a growing proportion of the American workforce, many of whom worked in small private businesses.

- The emergence of women in the labour market affected union membership. Most women worked in the service area, and many did part-time work, which was difficult to unionise.

- Many unions had links with the criminal world. A series of corruption scandals in the late 1950s weakened the trade union movement. The writer Norman Mailer (see page 191) wrote that some unions were closer 'to the Mafia than to Marx'.

Changes in the Work Ethic

In the post-war years, both the nature and the structure of work changed. Labour-saving technology led to a decline in the percentage of the workforce employed in difficult and low-paid work in mining and agriculture. Women joined the workforce in record numbers. Large corporations dominated industry. By 1960, half of American manufacturing was controlled by 150 corporations.

Some critics complained that work had become routine and meaningless for millions of workers. In the 1950s, **Paul Goodman** claimed that America had become a 'rat race', where individual talent had become stifled in the workplace. Workers were becoming increasingly dissatisfied and forced to conform to the needs of society. **William H. Whyte**'s *The Organization Man* (see page 187) considered middle management workers in large corporations, but his analysis applied to most large institutions.

The continued growth of large corporations and the service economy led to a new work ethic. This demanded loyalty to the corporation and the expectations of society, and placed less importance on the role of the individual.

HOW DID WOMEN'S LIVES CHANGE?

In 1956, *Life* magazine published a feature entitled 'The American Woman'. It portrayed the typical American woman as a suburban housewife and mother. Throughout the decade, marriage and motherhood were considered the 'proper' role for women. Women married young (the average age was 20), and stayed at home to rear their families. Marriage rates were high. In 1957, 97 per cent of women of marriageable age were in fact married. Divorce rates were low, only 1.4 per cent by the end of the 1950s, and birth rates were high. The figures for 1957 show a record birth rate of 25.2 per thousand women. The media, advertising and the consumer society reinforced the image of domestic bliss, and all that this implied for women.

Over the following decades, a number of social and economic developments brought about changes in the role of women in the USA.

In 1940, fewer than 25 per cent of American women worked outside the home. During the war the number of women in employment rose dramatically. The majority of them were married. When the war ended, married women left their jobs to make way for returning male soldiers.

Women in the Workforce

During the 1950s, the number of women employed outside the home began to increase again. By 1960, 40 per cent of all women aged over 16 were employed. Between 1950 and 1970 the percentage of working women rose from

By 1990 nearly 53 million American women were employed in the workforce.

28 per cent to 37 per cent. In 1990, 43 per cent of American workers were women (nearly 53 million women).

Growing numbers of married women were joining the workforce. In 1960, only 19 per cent of married women with children under the age of six worked outside the home: by 1980 this number had increased to 45 per cent. Another trend began to emerge in the late 1960s: the number of women over 35 who, having stayed at home while their children were young, now began to return to work. Most women worked in the service industries, many in part-time jobs (often without employment rights or security).

At first most married women went out to work to supplement family incomes. Some took up jobs to fund a mortgage or buy consumer appliances for the home. But the increasing divorce rates since the 1960s meant a rise in the number of households headed by women, and it became necessary to find employment to pay bills and maintain a standard of living.

Women and Education

During the 1950s, the number of women attending university declined; and there was a high drop-out rate among those who did attend. In 1960, fewer women graduated from university than in 1930. There was no pressure on women to have careers. Instead, they were expected to find a husband. For most middle-class women in the 1950s, the best place to find a suitable husband was at college.

Over the next decade, more women went into third-level education, as having a career became more important to them. Many qualified women wanted access to professional jobs.

Despite their growing numbers and better qualifications, women faced many forms of discrimination in the workplace. Women's salaries were lower than men's; in 1971, the average annual salary for a man was $9,630, while for a woman it was $5,700. In the late 1960s, only 7 per cent of medical doctors were women, and fewer than 4 per cent of lawyers. Even in jobs traditionally considered female areas of employment, such as teaching and social work, women were being replaced by men. The number of women in senior management positions in business remained low.

Women's Rights Movement

During the 1960s, changing social and economic trends led some women to question their traditional role. The emergence of the civil rights movement was another important development for women. Martin Luther King's campaign to end discrimination against African Americans (see page 55) inspired many women.

The publication in 1963 of **Betty Friedan**'s book *The Feminine Mystique* (see page 188) was a landmark in the development of a new feminist movement. The book exposed the reality behind the myth of the happy American housewife. It attacked the 'cult of domesticity' and the consumerism that went with it. Women, according to

Friedan, had been brainwashed into believing that their proper role was in the home as wife and mother.

Friedan highlighted the widespread dissatisfaction felt by millions of American housewives with this role. Despite all the labour-saving devices in the home, women at home complained of tiredness. Doctors called this 'housewife fatigue', and many prescribed tranquillisers as the solution. The problem, Friedan insisted, was not caused by domestic duties, but by boredom. She advised women to develop themselves through education and a career outside the home. Urging women to 'get a life plan', she concluded, 'Who knows what women can be when they are finally free to become themselves.'

The Feminine Mystique appealed to middle-class American women, and influenced their demand for equal rights. In 1964, the government intro-duced the **Civil Rights Act**, which outlawed job discrimination on grounds not only of race, but also of gender (male or female). It set up the **Equal Employment Opportunity Commission** to ensure that the law was upheld. Women were able to send complaints about discrimination at work to this body.

However, other forms of discrimination against women continued. In some states women could not serve on juries, make contracts or hold property. Co-founded by Betty Friedan in 1966, the **National Organization for Women** (**NOW**) campaigned for full civil, political and social rights for women and for an **Equal Rights Amendment** (ERA) to the Constitution. NOW later expanded its demands to include paid maternity leave, childcare facilities and legal abortion. It planned to work through the courts and legislation to bring about change. NOW was the moderate voice of the new feminist movement; its members were mainly middle-class, college-educated, professional women.

On 26 August 1970, NOW organised the **Women's Strike for Equality**. In New York and many other cities, thousands of women marched and held rallies. In 1977, the first **National Women's Conference**, financed by the federal government, was held in Houston, Texas.

The campaign for women's rights was helped by Congress and the Supreme Court. In 1972, Congress passed the **Educational Amendments Act**, ensuring equality for women in education. This Act brought in **affirmative action** (see page 58), a policy giving preferential treatment to women and minorities. Later, the policy was extended, making it a legal requirement for employers to give more jobs to women. Also in 1972, ERA was approved by Congress, but failed

The National Organization for Women (NOW) picket the White House, 1969

to get passed by enough states to make it law in the USA. In 1973, the Supreme Court upheld the right to abortion in the **Roe v Wade** ruling.

By the end of the 1960s, the women's movement became more militant. Younger, more radical women wanted greater change. They attacked Western society as 'male-dominated', and believed that the only way to end discrimination against women was to destroy '**patriarchy**', which would involve a complete restructuring of institutions such as family and marriage. They began demanding an end to sexism in advertising. In September 1968, they picketed the Miss America Pageant in Atlantic City, claiming that the event degraded women.

During the 1970s, clear divisions developed in the women's movement. The moderate middle-class mainstream were criticised by a vocal and militant minority for ignoring the plight of poor and racial minority women.

The growth of militancy led to a backlash from more traditional elements. Some women did not agree with the feminists, and objected to their attack on the traditional role of women as wives and mothers. In 1977, while 2,000 women were attending the National Women's Conference in Houston, 11,000 other women calling themselves the Pro-Family Coalition also met in Houston. Their programme was anti-ERA, anti-abortion and anti-homosexuality. They claimed to be the real representatives of American women.

HOW DID THE FAMILY CHANGE?

As we have seen, during the late 1940s and into the 1950s, marriage rates were high. Couples married young, had their children early and most people stayed with their spouse for life. The typical American family comprised a working father, a stay-at-home mother and their dependent children (the **nuclear family**). However, by the late 1970s, only one in five families followed this pattern. A number of factors brought about this huge transformation:

- Marriage patterns changed from the mid-1960s on. In 1960, there were 148 marriages for every

1,000 women aged between 15 and 45. By 1980, there were only 108. Many young people opted to live with their partner rather than commit to permanent relationships. Divorce rates increased: in 1960, the rate was 2.2 per cent per thousand people, while by 1970 it was 3.5 per cent, and in 1980 it reached 5.2 per cent.

- As the baby boom began to tail off from the late 1960s onwards, families became smaller. In 1960, there were almost 24 births per thousand population; this was down to 18.4 by 1970. In 1976 the figure had dropped to 14.8.

- The growth of suburban living and relocations for work had a negative effect on families. They became isolated from their relatives, losing the supportive back-up of grandparents and other relatives.

- The growing number of married women joining the workforce also put strains on family life. Fathers now had to take a more active role in rearing children and running the home. In the 1970s, affluent young adults were less inclined to have families.

- The number of children born to unmarried women increased. Many of these single mothers were teenagers. By the late 1980s, 30 per cent of all births were to single women. From the 1960s, single-parent, female-headed families increased. While many of these were the result of soaring divorce rates, there was a big increase in the number of women having children outside marriage.

- The emergence of the women's movement brought changes in the family. The new mood of liberation led many women to reject traditional roles and the idea of the nuclear family. For some women, liberation meant choosing not to have children. The availability of contraception and abortion allowed them this choice.

By the 1980s, sociologists and other commentators were writing about the breakdown of family structures. Some believed that the decline in the importance of the family was producing a range of social problems, including crime, drug abuse and poverty. The problems were particularly evident among African Americans (see Chapter 4). However, it was clear that across all classes and racial groups, the typical American family had changed dramatically. Politicians and religious leaders talked about restoring 'family values', but by the end of the 1980s it was clear that the institution of the family had been transformed by changing social and economic forces.

QUESTIONS

1 Outline Henry Ford's and F.W. Taylor's contributions to American manufacturing.

2 Explain why employment in manufacturing declined in post-war America.

3 In which area of the economy was there a marked growth in employment?

4 Why did the number of working women in the USA increase from the 1950s on?

5 What kinds of discrimination did women face in employment?

6 Why was the publication of *The Feminine Mystique* important for the feminist movement?

7 Outline the main changes that took place in the traditional American family, 1945–89.

TROUBLED AFFLUENCE: DID ALL AMERICANS BENEFIT?

Not all Americans benefited from the economic boom and post-war affluence. In 1959, according to the US Census Bureau, 22 per cent of American people were living in poverty. Most of them were African Americans, other minorities, and the elderly. Many of them lived in rural areas, but the vast majority lived in inner cities.

In 1962, **Michael Harrington**'s book *The Other Half* received national attention when he claimed that nearly 25 per cent of the population (almost 40 million people) were living below the poverty line in 1960. The problem, according to Harrington, was that the poor were invisible. They lived in urban slums or in depressed rural areas, where they were cut off from educational and medical facilities and from job opportunities. He also showed that the poor were trapped in a vicious cycle of poverty where children of the poor had no hope of improving their situation and their children too would fall into the same culture of poverty.

In 1963, President J.F. Kennedy said, 'Poverty in the midst of plenty is a paradox that must not go unchallenged.' In 1964, L.B. Johnson announced, 'This administration, today, here and now, declares unconditional war on poverty in America.'

Urban Poverty

In the post-war years the population structure of US cities changed:

1 Large numbers of African Americans migrated from the rural south into northern cities.

2 White people moved to the suburbs ('white flight'), leaving inner cities to become ethnic and racial ghettoes.

3 Growing numbers of Hispanic emigrants settled in US cities.

4 Many poor whites from depressed rural areas moved to the cities.

These changes led to greater urban poverty, caused by many factors, including:

- **Unemployment** – Earlier immigrants came to cities like New York, Boston or Chicago from Europe. Most of them were unskilled, but found work and eventually became prosperous. However, the American economy had changed since the arrival of these immigrants. In the post-war years, there were not as many jobs for the unskilled. The decline in manufacturing meant that there were few jobs in industry. African-American and Hispanic women usually managed to get jobs as waitresses and domestic servants, but unskilled men found it difficult to get work. They were left with the lowest-paying jobs, often only working part-time hours. In the new technological age many of them became unemployable. Unemployment rates in the urban ghettoes were twice the national average.

- **Housing** – The urban poor moved into housing vacated by the white middle classes when they left for the suburbs. The **Housing Act** (1949) provided for public housing in cities, but this housing tended to be high-rise, ugly apartment developments called **projects**. In 1960, African Americans made up 23 per cent of the population of Chicago and occupied only 4 per cent of the physical space of the city. This situation was mirrored in most of the big urban centres in the country.

- **Welfare and taxation** – As the affluent suburbs grew, businesses followed them out of the cities. The loss of tax revenues to the cities was significant. Added to this problem was the fact that the majority of inner-city inhabitants depended on welfare payments. As a result, many cities did not have money to spend on schools, hospitals or public services, such as bin collections. As a result, inner cities stagnated.

By the early 1960s, urban poverty had become a national issue, and it was against this background that President Johnson began his war on poverty, as part of his **Great Society** programme. In dealing with poverty he had two main aims:

1 Give the poor a chance to help themselves

2 Provide them with direct financial government assistance.

In 1964, he brought in the **Economic Opportunity Act**, providing $1 billion to fight poverty. This set up the **Office of Economic Opportunity (OEO)**, which had the task of organising a number of programmes, including:

- A Jobs Corps to give training in skills for the job market to young people in inner cities.

- Head Start, to provide pre-school education for poor inner-city children. It also provided school meals and medical examinations for these children.

- Neighbourhood Youth Corps to provide work and training for poor students and inner-city school drop-outs.

- A programme to provide training for unskilled, unemployed poor people.

- Loans to small businesses in poor areas.

In 1965, Johnson provided direct aid to the poor by allocating billions of dollars to a **Food Stamp Program**, rent subsidies and housing, health care (Medicare and Medicaid), and educational grants. City governors were given $375 million to improve transport facilities in poor neighbourhoods.

The war on poverty succeeded in reducing the number of people living in poverty by 10 million between 1964 and 1967. However, critics complained that the government was merely throwing money at the problem, and many middle-class taxpayers resented the huge increase in welfare spending (during the 1960s the number of people receiving welfare doubled, reaching 25 million by 1975). Others claimed that many millions of dollars were being spent on administration of the various programmes, benefiting middle-class bureaucrats and businesses rather than the poor. Many poor people resented the 'do-gooder' white middle classes who seemed to be trying to impose their ways on the ghettoes.

Urban Riots

Poverty and racial tensions in inner cities were already reaching crisis point by 1963. In that year **rent strikes** broke out in Harlem in New York. In the following year, disturbances occurred in many other northern slums. In 1965, a major riot took place in Watts, Los Angeles (see page 58). Watts was a typical African-American ghetto – run down, overcrowded (80,000 crammed into a small area) and with high unemployment (30 per cent). Most buildings, shops and businesses were owned by white absentee landlords. The riot began on 11 August, after a white policeman drew his gun on a young African-American driver he suspected of being drunk. Over the next five days, tens of thousands of people from the ghetto took to the streets, looting and burning white-owned property. The National Guard was sent in to restore order.

A woman with her children in a New York City tenement, 1960

When the riots ended, 34 people were dead and over 1,000 injured.

Urban riots continued in inner-city ghettoes across the country for the following three summers. In 1967, rioters in Detroit and Newark, New Jersey chanted 'Get Whitey' and 'Burn, baby, burn', but the causes of the riots had as much to do with poverty as with racial conflict. Decaying urban ghettoes were centres of poverty, broken families, crime, drug abuse and hopelessness. By 1969, the Kennedy–Johnson policies to renew inner cities seemed to have failed. By then, too, the war in Vietnam was draining both federal finance and commitment away from the problem of urban poverty.

Economic recession in the 1970s led to further impoverishment in the ghettoes. The South Bronx in New York, home to thousands of unemployed people, was littered with burnt-out cars and blackened derelict shops and houses. In 1975, New York, with a population of eight million, had one million people living on welfare, costing the city over $2 billion a year. To balance the budget the city needed to borrow, and as debts soared, New York City faced bankruptcy by the mid-1970s.

Nixon left Johnson's reforms in place. He tried to introduce a **Family Assistance Plan (FAP)** to help poor families by providing federally guaranteed incomes. Michael Harrington (see page 43) called the plan 'the most radical idea since the New Deal', but it was defeated in Congress. Under Nixon, federal spending on education and health care for the poor increased.

The Reagan administration cut federal spending for the poor, believing that private charities should take care of the less fortunate. He introduced **Workfare**, a policy which required that people on welfare had to accept a job to qualify for welfare benefits. Though unemployment dropped, many jobs that had been created were low-paid. The problem of homelessness also increased in cities. In New York alone, 23,000 people were living on the streets. By 1989 most of the problems Johnson had tried to address two decades earlier were still in evidence in urban areas.

Crime

Urban poverty resulted in dramatic increases in crime levels. The urban riots of the 1960s focused attention on law and order. Crime was mainly an urban problem, with 30 per cent of all crimes taking place in the six largest cities in the USA. Most criminals were young, poor, male African Americans. Many of them were repeat offenders. The USA had the highest crime rate and the highest number of prison inmates (426 per 100,000 of the population) in the world. Tough measures were taken by governments. Arrests were made, and prisons were filled.

However, a number of factors prevented progress in dealing with crime:

- In the 1970s and 1980s the Nixon and Reagan administrations invested much effort and funding into reducing crime levels. However, they also shifted responsibility to state and local authorities. Many city authorities were not able to provide adequate policing because they could not afford to pay salaries and maintain a large police force.

Ten years after the 1967 riots, which left 27 people dead, buildings are boarded up and children play in a rubble-strewn vacant lot in Newark

- US gun laws were lenient (citizens have a constitutional right to bear arms), and guns widely available. The number of murders and crimes involving firearms increased during the 1970s and 1980s.

- The emergence of a drug culture in the 1960s and 1970s led to a marked increase in organised crime.

Drugs

Drug use became common during the 1960s, when many middle-class young white people began experimenting with marijuana. This continued through the following decades. In 1973, Nixon set up the **Drug Enforcement Administration (DEA)** to stop the importation of drugs into the country.

Cocaine had been considered a recreational drug used by the rich, but by the end of the 1970s it had spread to the general public. Costing $100 per gram, it was widely seen as a party drug, but it had the potential to cause serious brain damage or death from overdosing. By 1986, it was estimated that 5.8 million Americans were using cocaine at

least once a month, and over 600,000 were addicts. The public became alarmed by reports of deaths from cocaine use (for example, the well-known comic actor **John Belushi** died from an overdose), and the rising crime rates resulting from the use of crack cocaine in the ghettoes.

Drug trafficking involving international criminal gangs became a big business in the 1980s. Drugs were imported from poorer countries like Columbia, Afghanistan and Turkey by **drug barons** (wealthy criminals). It was a lucrative business involving a network of individuals, from poor farmers tempted to grow a crop that yielded high prices to organised 'runners' who risked arrest at ports and airports.

In 1982, First Lady Nancy Reagan made drug education her special national project. Under the slogan '**Just Say No**', she launched a campaign to inform schools, churches and civic groups about the dangers of cocaine and other drugs. This did help the educated middle classes, but had little or no effect on drug abusers in the ghettoes.

By 1989 more cocaine than ever before was flooding the American market and addiction remained a major national problem.

QUESTIONS

1 List the causes of urban poverty in the USA.

2 How did President Johnson plan to fight poverty? Did his policies work? Explain your answer.

3 Why did riots occur in urban ghettoes during the 1960s?

4 Why, do you think, was Watts a typical urban ghetto?

5 Why did crime rates increase in the USA after the 1960s?

6 Explain how the drug problem contributed to rising crime rates.

1 ORDINARY LEVEL QUESTIONS

Write a paragraph on the following:

a) The consumer society in the USA, 1945–89.

b) In what ways did the life and work of Betty Friedan reflect the changing role of women and the family in modern America? (Leaving Cert 2013)

c) Urban poverty, drugs and crime. (Leaving Cert 2014)

2 HIGHER LEVEL ESSAYS

a) During the period 1945–89, what were the major changes which took place in the role of women and the family?

b) What contribution did Betty Friedan and/or Norman Mailer make to society in the United States? (Leaving Cert 2007)

c) During the period 1948–89, what was the impact of one or more of the following on American society: racial conflict; urban poverty; organised crime? (Leaving Cert 2006)

④ Racial Conflict

WHAT WAS THE STATUS OF THE AFRICAN-AMERICAN POPULATION ?

Slavery was introduced to the American colonies in the late seventeenth century. Black slaves were brought from Africa to work on the cotton and tobacco plantations and as domestic servants.

After the Civil War (1861–65), Abraham Lincoln issued the **Emancipation Proclamation**, and the 13th Amendment to the US Constitution outlawed slavery in the USA. The **14th Amendment** (1866) broadened the definition of American citizenship to include African Americans.

Despite these legal changes, African Americans did not have equality with whites. In the northern states the majority of African Americans were unskilled labourers. They could vote, but were discriminated against in jobs and housing. In the south they were even worse off – very harsh laws,

called the Black Codes, were passed there to control former slaves.

Segregation

By the end of the nineteenth century, most southern states had passed segregation laws (known as **Jim Crow** laws – see the box below), enforcing separation of blacks and whites in public transport, restaurants, schools, and a whole range of other public facilities. In 1896, in the *Plessy v. Ferguson* case, the Supreme Court ruled that segregation was legal as long as the facilities provided for each race were equal (see page 52).

All citizens in the south had to pay a poll tax (a local council tax) before they were allowed to vote. Most African Americans could not afford the tax and therefore could not vote. Many southern states also had a literacy test which voters had to pass before being allowed to vote. African Americans were given more difficult tests than

The Jim Crow laws allowed segregation to continue in the southern states. This sign was in place until 1958 in Alabama

Jim Crow Laws

This term describes the laws and customs that enforced segregation between African Americans and whites in the southern states of the USA. Jim Crow was a stereotypical African-American character in the minstrel shows of the mid-nineteenth century. The most common types of Jim Crow law prohibited black people from sharing public facilities with whites and forbade intermarriage between the races. However, different states and different cities had their own local segregation laws. Various court decisions and government legislation from 1954 onwards dismantled Jim Crow laws, but the customs lingered on long after the laws had changed.

Here are some examples of Jim Crow laws passed by different states:

- 'No colored barber shall serve as a barber to white women or girls.' (*Atlanta, Georgia*)
- 'The marriage of a person of Caucasian blood with a Negro, Mongolian, Malay, or Hindu shall be null and void.' (*Arizona*)
- 'Any person ... presenting for public acceptance or general information, arguments or suggestions in favor of social equality or of intermarriage between whites and negroes, shall be guilty of a misdemeanor and subject to a fine not exceeding five hundred dollars or imprisonment not exceeding six months or both fine and imprisonment in the discretion of the court.' (*Mississippi*)
- 'Separate free schools shall be established for the education of children of African descent; and it shall be unlawful for any colored child to attend any white school, or any white child to attend a colored school.' (*Missouri*)
- 'All railroads carrying passengers in the state (other than street railroads) shall provide equal but separate accommodations for the white and colored races, by providing two or more passenger cars for each passenger train, or by dividing the cars by a partition, so as to secure separate accommodations.' (*Tennessee*)
- 'Nurses: No person or corporation shall require any white female nurse to nurse in wards or rooms in hospitals, either public or private, in which negro men are placed.' (*Alabama*)
- 'Buses: All passenger stations in this state operated by any motor transportation company shall have separate waiting rooms or space and separate ticket windows for the white and colored races.' (*Alabama*)
- 'Lunch Counters: No persons, firms, or corporations, who or which furnish meals to passengers at station restaurants or station eating houses, in times limited by common carriers of said passengers, shall furnish said meals to white and colored passengers in the same room, or at the same table, or at the same counter.' (*South Carolina*)

KKK members, wearing white hooded robes, and the symbolic burning cross, which were used to intimidate African Americans in the south

whites, which meant they were more likely to fail and were then unable to vote.

Intimidation

The white supremacist group the **Ku Klux Klan** (**KKK**) terrorised African-American communities and intimidated any white people who tried to help their black neighbours. The most common form of abuse carried out by the KKK was lynching (killing someone without a trial, usually by hanging). During the 1880s more than one hundred lynchings a year were reported, most of them in the south.

The Ku Klux Klan

The KKK was founded in 1866, in the aftermath of the American Civil War. It is thought that the name may have come from the Greek word *kuklos*, meaning circle, while the *klan* may refer to 'clan' or family. The KKK opposed the abolition of slavery and carried out acts of violence and intimidation against African Americans. It went into decline in the late nineteenth century, but resurfaced again in 1915. During the 1920s, the KKK was very active in organising anti-equality marches and in recruiting new members. By 1925, it is estimated, it had achieved a membership of five million. As well as being anti-African American, it was hostile to Jews, Catholics, socialists, communists and foreigners in general. It advocated a policy of 'native white Protestant supremacy', believing that American values were under threat from foreign influences.

After World War II the Klan was disbanded, but it never died out. With the emergence of the civil rights movement in the 1950s, it reappeared in the south, and it was active in Montgomery during the bus boycott (see Chapter 5).

WHAT WAS THE IMPACT OF WORLD WAR II?

The war focused attention on racial discrimination. Nearly one million African Americans served in the army, where they were put into segregated units under the command of white officers. They were not allowed serve in the Marine or Air Corps. In army training camps in the south, northern African-American recruits came face to face with the discriminatory Jim Crow system. Fights and riots frequently broke out. African Americans also faced prejudice when they looked for work in the defence industry.

During the war the need for military efficiency led to changes for African Americans. They were admitted into the marines and the navy for the first time. Following protests against job discrimination in the defence industry, the government set up the **Fair Employment Practice Committee**. As more people were needed in the armed forces, employers in northern states started to hire southern African Americans to work in factories. The promise of good jobs and high wages drew millions of southern African Americans to cities like New York, Chicago, Los Angeles and Detroit.

World War II brought some economic gains for African Americans, but also highlighted their status as second-class citizens. In the post-war decades they began to challenge this. During the 1950s and 1960s African Americans began to use three different tactics to win racial equality:

1 Political and economic pressure

2 Legal pressure

3 Violence.

The war also caused many white people to address the question of racism. America had gone to war against imperialist Japan and its allies, Nazi Germany and fascist Italy. By 1945, many white Americans felt that dealing with racial problems at home should become a national priority.

HOW DID POST-WAR SOCIAL AND ECONOMIC CHANGES AFFECT RACE RELATIONS?

After the war, the movement of African Americans from the rural south to urban centres increased. Some moved to cities in the south to look for work

in industry. Many migrated to the big industrial cities in the north and west. The transformation from a mainly rural to an urban environment had profound effects on African Americans, north and south. The sheer concentration of numbers in cities made it easier for African Americans to organise and address discrimination by setting up pressure groups, some advocating peaceful means and others promoting angry direct action.

The changing social and economic trends in post-war America greatly affected African Americans. These included:

1 *The economic boom:* African Americans got jobs and better wages.

2 *Growth of suburbs:* After the white middle classes moved to the suburbs, large African-American populations lived in inner cities. Ghettoes emerged, where overcrowding and poor housing conditions were the norm, and African Americans became more aware of racial injustices.

3 *Better educational opportunities:* Some African Americans were able to improve their skills and job prospects. More African-American students attended university, and an educated African-American leadership emerged in the USA that made a significant contribution to the civil rights movement.

Children's programmes, such as **Sesame Street***, from the late 1960s onwards did much to counter racial discrimination in the USA*

4 *Affluence:* Better living standards for African Americans also led to rising expectations and a demand for equal treatment with whites.

5 *The development of television and the mass media* exposed racial discrimination, and focused African-American attention on racial issues. TV was to play a major role in winning the support of northern whites to the cause of African-American civil rights.

The Cold War

The race issue was affected by the Cold War. The USA claimed to be the leader of the 'free world', and accused communist governments of denying human rights in Eastern Europe and Asia. African Americans saw the hypocrisy of fighting for human rights around the world while at the same time allowing racial inequality to exist at home, and their leaders were quick to point this out. Many whites were also aware that segregation damaged America's image abroad.

During the McCarthy witch hunt for communists at home (see pages 84–86), many whites became alarmed by McCarthy's attacks on civil liberties. The 'Red Scare' helped to highlight the issue of civil rights, including racial inequality, among certain sections of the white population.

WHAT WAS DESEGREGATION?

Armed Forces

In 1946, President Truman set up a **Committee on Civil Rights**. In its report a year later, this committee advised the government to set up a permanent Commission on Civil Rights, bring in laws to ban lynching, stop discrimination in voting practices, and stop segregation in the armed forces (desegregation). Truman was prevented by Congress from introducing all these reforms, but he did use his presidential power to end segregation in the armed forces. He won the 1948 presidential election partly with the support of urban African-American voters in the north and west, but southern opposition in Congress continued to block his proposals to bring in civil rights legislation.

Truman's successor, Eisenhower, completed the process of desegregating the armed forces. He did not need the African-American vote, and was less enthusiastic about pushing for civil rights than Truman had been. However, it was during his presidency that dramatic legal changes happened for African Americans in the south.

Eisenhower appointed **Earl Warren** as Chief Justice of the Supreme Court. Warren was a liberal who believed in extending the Court's powers to protect the individual's rights over the state's rights. He later headed the Warren Commission, which investigated the assassination of J.F. Kennedy.

Education

The African-American civil rights group the **National Association for the Advancement of Colored People** (**NAACP**) (see box on the next page) had for decades been campaigning for an end to segregation in education. They concentrated their efforts on bringing cases to court to try to win admission for African-American students to colleges and universities. In 1954, they began challenging segregation in public schools and brought the case of Linda Brown to the Supreme Court.

Segregation laws meant that **Linda Brown**, a young African-American girl in Topeka, Kansas, was not allowed to attend a local white school. Instead she had to travel further away to an all-black school. In 1896, the Supreme Court had ruled that segregation was legal provided the facilities were equal (*Plessy v. Ferguson*). In 1954, a team of NAACP lawyers led by **Thurgood Marshall** argued that separate schools caused psychological damage to African-American children and thereby denied them their rights under the 14th Amendment. The NAACP won the case (*Brown v. Board of Education of Topeka*). The Supreme Court ruled that segregation was unconstitutional (illegal), and declared that 'separate educational facilities are inherently unequal'. The following year the Court declared that public schools should be desegregated 'with all deliberate speed', but left it for the lower courts to implement this.

The NAACP protesting against school segregation, 1963

National Association for the Advancement of Colored People (NAACP)

The NAACP was set up in 1909 with the aim of promoting and defending the legal and constitutional rights of African Americans. It opposed the Ku Klux Klan, and lobbied local and national politicians to end racial discrimination.

During the 1950s, its main tactic was to work through the courts to fight racial discrimination. In 1952, the NAACP appealed to the Supreme Court to rule that segregated education was unconstitutional, and the landmark case *Brown v. Board of Education of Topeka* (see previous page) ensued.

The NAACP was also involved in the campaign to end segregation on public transport. It took a case against the Montgomery Bus Company to the Supreme Court and was again successful.

During the 1960s and 1970s, the NAACP continued to fight legal battles to end all forms of racial discrimination against African-American people in the USA. Many younger and more militant African-American groups rejected the legal approach of the NAACP and instead resorted to more violent action. However, the NAACP kept up its work as a pressure group and achieved notable success in advancing the cause of African-American civil rights.

The Process of Integration

Events in Mississippi during the summer of 1955 focused national attention on the issue of racial prejudice and proved to be a catalyst for the civil rights movement. Emmett Till, a 14-year-old African-American boy from Chicago, was visiting relations in Mississippi. After whistling at a white woman he was brutally murdered by the woman's husband and another man. An all-white jury found his murderers not guilty. The prosecution lawyers argued that the incident had been a NAACP plot. The injustice of the case outraged African Americans and many white liberals.

Eisenhower believed that laws could not change people's attitudes; change would only come, he said, 'by appealing to reason, by prayer and by constantly working at it through our own efforts'. However, in 1957, he was forced to act when the Governor of Arkansas tried to prevent nine African-American students from attending a white school in Little Rock. Federal troops were sent to protect the black students and ensure that desegregation laws were upheld. The troops remained at the school for the rest of the school year.

By the end of the 1950s fewer than 1 per cent of African-American children in the south attended school with white children. In 1969, this figure had increased to 20 per cent.

In 1962, **James Meredith**, an African-American student, tried to enrol in the all-white University of Mississippi. The Governor of Mississippi and an angry mob tried to prevent him registering. The NAACP brought the case to the courts and won the right for Meredith to enrol. President Kennedy sent in troops to protect Meredith when he went to register, but riots broke out, leaving two dead and 375 injured. Gradually, over the next few years, the rest of the state universities in the south were integrated, but it was a slow process.

QUESTIONS

1 What kinds of discrimination were brought in against African Americans in the south at the end of the nineteenth century?

2 What were the Jim Crow laws?

3 How did World War II affect African Americans?

4 What was the NAACP?

5 What decision was made by the Supreme Court in 1954?

6 What was the reaction of southern whites to *Brown v. Board of Education of Topeka*?

7 What happened at Little Rock, Arkansas in 1957?

School segregation was not confined to the south. In the cities of the north and west, local schools were segregated because African Americans and whites lived in different zones of the cities. In 1971, the Supreme Court, in *Swann v. Charlotte-Mecklenburg Board*, upheld **bussing** as a way of ensuring racial balance in the public schools. The Court order was resisted in many northern cities, particularly in Detroit and Boston. In Denver and Michigan, school buses were firebombed. Many saw bussing as a step too far.

In 1972 Nixon tried unsuccessfully to pass anti-bussing laws in Congress. During the 1980s a more conservative Supreme Court backed down on the bussing issue. In both the north and the south, the white middle classes got around the segregation laws by sending their children to private schools, and for economic reasons it was mainly African-American students who attended the public schools.

Bussing meant bringing, by bus, African-American students out of the inner-city ghettoes to suburban (white) schools and white students to inner-city (African-American) schools.

Public Facilities

Jim Crow laws enforced racial segregation in public transport in the south: African Americans were required to sit at the back of the buses, whites at the front. In 1955, an event in Montgomery, Alabama sparked off a year-long bus boycott (see Chapter 5) which resulted in a Supreme Court decision that overturned the 'separate but equal' doctrine and outlawed racial segregation on public buses. The **Montgomery bus boycott** began a new phase of African-American **activism**. It marked a shift away from legal struggles in the courts to non-violent protests on the streets. This became known as the civil rights movement.

In 1960, another unplanned African-American protest began. Inspired by the success of Montgomery, four African-American students defied the segregation laws by sitting at a whites-only lunch counter in Greensboro, North Carolina. When they were not served, they refused to leave and began a 'sit-in'. Other students all over the south followed their example. By the end of the year the peaceful sit-in campaign by over 50,000 young people had succeeded in desegregating public facilities in more than one hundred cities in the south.

The following year, 1961, African-American and white civil rights activists organised a '**Freedom Ride**'. Travelling through the south by bus, they wanted to test the 1960 Supreme Court ruling outlawing segregation in all bus and train stations.

They were assaulted, threatened and intimidated by white mobs. They appealed to the Justice Department to protect them. The Attorney General (Robert F. Kennedy, brother of the president) sent in federal marshals to escort them, and the desegregation laws were enforced. More Freedom Riders joined the protest over the next twelve months, and the campaign received national media attention.

Voting

African Americans in the south who wanted to vote faced many obstacles: poll taxes and literacy tests (see page 48); economic pressure from white employers – African Americans would lose their jobs if they voted; and intimidation and violence from the KKK. As a result, in 1955 only 4 per cent of African Americans in the south were registered to vote.

During the 1960s, the African-American civil rights movement gained momentum. Under the leadership of **Martin Luther King** (see Chapter 5) peaceful protests were organised throughout the south. In 1963, a massive campaign was launched to get African-American voting rights. The NAACP's slogan was 'Free by '63' (1963 was the 100th anniversary of the Emancipation Proclamation). King, a powerful and charismatic speaker, managed to bring together all the elements of African-

American activism, the new **Student Non-Violent Coordinating Committee** (SNCC), the **Congress On Racial Equality** (CORE), his own **Southern Christian Leadership Conference** (SCLC) and the NAACP. Whites in the north were impressed with King, and found his doctrine of non-violence 'safe'.

In April 1963, King organised a protest march in Birmingham, Alabama – a big industrial city known for its racial prejudice. The marchers filled the streets day after day, singing 'We Shall Overcome'. When the marchers were arrested, they were replaced by others, some as young as 6 years old. King himself was arrested, and his '**Letter from Birmingham Jail**' was one of the most effective documents of the civil rights movement.

On 8 May, six thousand African-American children marched through Birmingham. The police arrested thousands of them. On the following day, the police chief, Eugene (Bull) O'Connor, ordered his men to use water hoses, electric cattle prods and dogs against the protestors. Crucially, the events in Birmingham were broadcast live on national television to shocked audiences, winning widespread white support for King. The President sent officials to negotiate with the city authorities. The violence ended and the protestors were granted most of their demands. Kennedy brought in a Civil Rights Bill providing for an end to all

discrimination and an extension of voting rights for African Americans. The Bill was delayed by Congress.

In August 1963, King organised a rally in Washington, DC to demonstrate for 'jobs and freedom', and show support for the Civil Rights Bill going through Congress. Over 200,000 African-American and white civil rights supporters marched to the Lincoln Memorial, where King delivered his famous **'I Have a Dream'** speech (see page 61). Many white Americans were moved by his vision of a racially integrated America. Kennedy feared that the march would make it difficult to get his Civil Rights Bill passed, but the rally was peaceful and ordered, and in fact helped to get the Bill passed a year later. By that time Kennedy was dead, but under his successor, L.B. Johnson, a comprehensive new **Civil Rights Act** was passed in 1964. This law banned discrimination in all public accommodation, outlawed job discrimination and reduced the power of local voter registration boards to disqualify African Americans from voting.

Also in 1964, the **24th Amendment to the Constitution** was passed. This outlawed using non-payment of the poll tax as a method of blocking people from voting in elections.

In the summer of 1964, the SNCC and CORE began a campaign to get African-American voters to register in the south. Two civil rights volunteers (one white, one black) were murdered in Selma, Alabama during the campaign. The governor, George Wallace, and local police tried to prevent the young civil rights organisers from getting African Americans to register. The KKK burned several African-American churches, and three young civil rights workers (one African American from Mississippi and two whites from New York) were also murdered.

The white racists who were brought to trial for the murders of the three young civil rights workers were acquitted by a white Mississippi jury – this was the subject of the 1988 film *Mississippi Burning*.

In 1964, over 80 per cent of eligible African-American voters in Alabama were still not registered. In January 1965, King decided to lead a protest march from Selma to Montgomery. The police used teargas and clubs against the peaceful demonstrators. Seventeen marchers were seriously injured and forty others were hospitalised. Again, television brought scenes of violence into many Americans' homes, helping to win over white liberals to the cause of civil rights. Johnson sent the Alabama National Guard to protect the marchers.

In August 1965, Johnson signed the **Voting Rights Act**. This was the last major civil rights act of the 1960s, and finally gave African-American southerners the equal voting rights that had been promised a century earlier after the Civil War.

As a result of these legislative and judicial actions, there was a dramatic rise in southern African-American voter registration. By 1968, 60 per cent of African Americans were registered, the same figure as for whites. In addition, more African Americans were elected to public office in the south.

HOW DID AFRICAN-AMERICAN MILITANCY ARISE?

For a growing number of African-American militants, civil rights reforms were 'too little, too late'. The movement, and Martin Luther King's leadership of it, began to show signs of disunity. By 1965, all the legal barriers to equality were gone, but serious prejudices still remained. African Americans were the poorest, most illiterate, most badly housed and most unemployed racial group in America. The gap between promises and fulfilment was particularly felt by young urban African Americans in the northern cities, who came to reject both white liberalism and King's civil rights campaign.

By 1964, the SNCC was openly critical of inter-racial co-operation. In 1966, its chairman, Stokely Carmichael, said the time had come for African Americans to take control of the civil rights movement themselves and that there was no room for white involvement. He rejected King's faith in white reforms and in non-violence. Many young African-American radicals agreed with him and soon 'Black Power' became their slogan. They felt disillusioned with the slow pace of reform and believed that whites would only respond to violence.

In 1966, a more extreme group, the **Black Panthers**, was set up. They were a paramilitary force, and their leader, Huey Newton, called on African Americans to defend themselves against the police by collecting weapons. The Panthers targeted the police, and their campaign did indeed frighten many whites.

In the African-American ghettoes in northern cities, a group called the **Nation of Islam** won much popular support. They called Christianity a 'slave religion', and proclaimed African-American superiority. Their leader, Elijah Muhammad, advocated separatism and racial pride. He urged African Americans to have no associations with whites and denounced King as a tool of white society. The great boxing world champion, Cassius Clay, became a Muslim, changing his name to Muhammad Ali (see page 192). By the mid-1960s, **Malcolm X** had become the main spokesman for the Nation of Islam. He was a charismatic leader

Black power – the Black Panthers march in militant fashion, 1968

and his message of **black nationalism** appealed to many urban African Americans in the north. He expressed their discontent and anger more fully than King's moderate and peaceful approach did. In 1965, Malcolm X was assassinated by an African-American gunman and he was quickly seen as a martyr by thousands of African Americans.

QUESTIONS

1 Explain how African Americans were legally prevented from voting in the south.

2 What happened in Birmingham, Alabama in 1963?

3 How did white southerners react to the campaign to get African Americans to register to vote?

4 Why did the Nation of Islam appeal to African Americans in northern ghettoes?

5 What were the results of the rise in African-American militancy?

In 1964, small-scale racial violence erupted in Harlem. In August 1965, five days after the Civil Rights Bill was signed by the President, a huge riot broke out in Watts, an African-American ghetto in Los Angeles (see page 44). For six days, looting and fighting between African-American youths and police raged. Thirty-four people were killed, including twenty-eight African Americans, and the damage to property was estimated at $30 million. The riot greatly upset King and he moved the SCLC headquarters to Chicago, determined to shift his focus from the south to the northern ghettoes and the problems of jobs and housing.

During the summers of 1966 and 1967, further rioting took place in New York, Detroit, Chicago, Newark and other cities. In 1967, 83 people were killed in 164 different riots, causing over $100 million in damages to property. The civil rights movement became deeply divided. King and other moderate leaders appealed for calm and denounced the violence. Fearing a white backlash, they insisted that the militants represented only a minority of African Americans.

In April 1968, King was assassinated in Memphis. His death seemed to destroy any hope of resolving the race problem. Riots, driven by people's grief and anger, broke out in ghettoes in 125 cities following his death. A week after King's assassination a new **Civil Rights Act** was passed, outlawing racial discrimination in housing.

Post-Militancy

During the late 1960s and early 1970s, the country was preoccupied with the Vietnam War and the economy. The protests of the 1960s had brought many positive changes for African Americans. A new African-American middle class emerged, growing numbers of African-American students were attending university, African-American incomes were rising, and African-American voters were now an important factor in elections.

But discrimination still existed. Some civil rights activists called for 'affirmative action' as a temporary measure to give preferential treatment to minority groups in jobs, training and promotions at work. Under Nixon, the government introduced this policy for African Americans. Firms with government contracts had to hire a required number (a **quota**) of African Americans and other minorities. This helped middle-class African Americans, who were educated and able to improve their status, career opportunities and incomes.

Without strong leadership, many poor African Americans sank into apathy. Poverty, drugs and crime became major problems in the ghettoes. There was an expanding African-American 'under-class' of unemployed people who lived in ghettoes and depended on welfare, and a growing number of single-parent African-American families, headed by women. By the end of the 1970s, the average African-American family was still only 60 per cent as rich as the average white family. During the 1980s, unemployment rates for African Americans (over 10 per cent) were more than double those for whites. A staggering 40 per cent of African-American teenagers were unemployed in this decade.

Nixon, elected by the 'silent majority' or 'white backlash', tried to cut welfare programmes and enforce law and order. He moved the responsibility for social problems away from the federal government and on to state and local authorities. In terms of civil rights, he shifted responsibility to the courts. When Earl Warren (see page 52) retired as Chief Justice, Nixon replaced him with the more conservative Warren Burger, and appointed conservative judges to the Supreme Court. The Court did not overturn the decisions made on segregation, but the pro-civil rights approach taken under Earl Warren did not continue.

Reagan cut many welfare programmes, forcing poor African Americans further into poverty. A supporter of reduced government involvement in social and economic affairs, his government gave control of welfare spending to the states. By 1984, over 14 per cent of Americans were living below the poverty line, the majority of them African Americans. In 1990, African Americans made up over 12 per cent of the US population. The vast majority of them lived in the south or in crowded urban ghettoes in the north-east, in the midwest and on the Pacific coast. In 1989 (when Reagan left office), the issue of poverty was still very real for most African Americans.

QUESTIONS

1 What is *affirmative action*?

2 What were the main problems affecting African Americans at the end of the 1980s?

Results of Racial Conflict

- At first, the movement for civil rights was an inter-racial movement, involving African-American and white supporters. Growing militancy led to divisions in the movement and increased tensions between the races. In the end, violence took over, resulting in racial conflict and serious urban warfare. Many moderate whites saw African Americans as ungrateful: having been given so many reforms by government and the Supreme Court, they repaid society by rioting and destroying property. This led many white voters to demand tougher laws and welfare cuts and to reject civil rights reforms.

- Inspired by the African-American civil rights movement, other racial and minority groups

Homeless men in New York City, 1989

began to demonstrate. Chicanos (Mexican-Americans) and Native Americans called for 'Brown Power' and 'Red Power'. Following the example of the civil rights movement, they organised boycotts and marches. Women, too, were encouraged by the African-American civil rights movement, and began imitating some of its tactics and policies to win equal rights for women (see Chapter 3).

- African Americans found a genuine self-awareness and pride in being black, replacing an older attitude of inferiority and deference to whites. The 'Black is Beautiful' idea led to a decline in sales of hair straighteners, dyes and bleaches and other cosmetics that African Americans had used to hide their racial characteristics. African Americans began to wear **afro** hair styles and colourful clothes with pride. Courses in African-American history were taught in colleges, and there was a growth in interest in African-American art and literature.

- The increased racial tensions from the mid-1960s onwards moved the focus of racism away from the south to northern cities, where a combination of social problems led to racial conflict. Many cities had areas where no white person could safely walk or drive through the streets.

- The brutality of the police against the early civil rights marchers alienated many northern African Americans. The race riots in the mid-1960s were primarily directed against the police, and urban African-American youths became particularly hostile towards officers of the law. Many whites became alarmed by the heavy-handed tactics used by the police against civil rights marchers and urban rioters. America's image abroad also suffered.

CIVIL RIGHTS ERA TIMELINE 1948–1968

1948	President Truman desegregates the military.
1954	In *Brown v. Board of Education of Topeka*, the Supreme Court rules unanimously that separate educational facilities are unconstitutional.
1955	In Mississippi, 14-year-old **Emmett Till** is murdered. All-white jury acquits the two men accused of beating and shooting him. **Rosa Parks** refuses to give up her bus seat to a white person in Montgomery (see page 65). Leads to successful year-long boycott of buses. **Martin Luther King** emerges as a major figure.
1956	Supreme Court rules that the segregation of Montgomery buses is unconstitutional.
1957	President Eisenhower orders the military to escort nine African-American students to school in **Little Rock, Arkansas**.
1960	Four African-American college students hold a **sit-in** at a lunch counter in Greensboro, North Carolina, launching a wave of similar protests across the south.
1961	**Congress of Racial Equality** (CORE) begins to organise **Freedom Rides** throughout the south to try to desegregate interstate public bus travel.
1962	Nation of Islam leader **Malcolm X** rejects the non-violent civil rights movement and integration, becoming a champion of African-American separatism and black pride. President Kennedy sends federal troops to the University of Mississippi so that James Meredith, the school's first African-American student, can attend. The Supreme Court rules that segregation is unconstitutional in all transportation facilities such as bus stations.
1963	200,000 people march on Washington; Martin Luther King gives his 'I Have a Dream' speech. King is arrested after a march in Birmingham, Alabama. While in jail he writes 'Letter from a Birmingham Jail', his famous statement about the civil rights movement.

1964	Three civil rights workers are murdered in Mississippi.
	President Lyndon Johnson signs the **Civil Rights Act**, outlawing discrimination in employment, voting and education. African Americans can no longer be excluded from restaurants, hotels and other public facilities.
1965	Malcolm X is assassinated in New York by gunmen from the Nation of Islam.
	King organises a protest march for voting rights from Selma to Montgomery. Police club and teargas protesters.
	The **Voting Rights Act** outlaws the practices used to stop African Americans voting, such as literacy tests and poll taxes.
	Race riots break out in the Watts area of Los Angeles, leaving 34 dead and a thousand injured.
1966	Huey P. Newton and Bobby Seales found the **Black Panther Party**, a radical African-American power group.
1967	In the 'Long Hot Summer' race riots erupt in many cities, including Detroit, Newark, Atlanta, Boston and New York.
1968	Martin Luther King is assassinated in Memphis, Tennessee. His murder sparks a week of rioting across the country.

END-OF-CHAPTER REVIEW

DOCUMENT A

Excerpt from a speech by Martin Luther King, Washington, DC, 28 August 1963

... I say to you today, my friends, that in spite of all the difficulties and frustrations of the moment I still have a dream. It is a dream deeply rooted in the American Dream.

I have a dream that one day this great nation will rise up and live out the true meaning of its creed: We hold these truths to be self-evident; that all men are created equal ...

I have a dream that my four little children will one day live in a nation where they will not be judged by the color of their skin but by the content of their character.

I have a dream today ...

1 DOCUMENT A QUESTIONS

a) What were the difficulties and frustrations King is referring to in this document?

b) Who is he addressing in his speech and where did he make it?

c) What creed does he quote and where does it come from?

d) What is his dream for his children?

DOCUMENT B

(1) Unemployment by Race, 1950–1970

Year	All People	Whites	African Americans
1950	5.3%	4.9%	9.0%
1960	5.5%	4.9%	10.2%
1970	4.9%	4.5%	8.2%

(2) African-American Families in Poverty and Education of Head of Household

Education	1978	1987
At least one year in college	12.6%	11.2%
High school graduate	18.7%	27.8%
High school dropout	34.2%	39.4%

(3) Income Distribution by Race, 1990

Income	White Families	African-American Families
Over $50,000	32.5%	14.5%
$35–$50,000	20.8%	15.0%
$25–$35,000	16.5%	14.0%
$15–$25,000	16.0%	19.5%
Under $15,000	14.2%	37.0%

2 DOCUMENT B QUESTIONS

a) What do the unemployment figures tell us about inequality between African Americans and whites?

b) What changes in education are shown in table (2)?

c) What percentage of African Americans earned less than $15,000 in 1990?

3 ORDINARY LEVEL QUESTIONS

Write a paragraph on the following:

a) Martin Luther King.

b) The main events in the Civil Rights movement.

c) The Civil Rights Act 1964.

4 HIGHER LEVEL ESSAYS

a) What was the contribution of Martin Luther King to US affairs? (Leaving Cert 2011)

b) What were the main developments in race relations in the USA, 1945–68? (Leaving Cert 2013)

c) Why did race relations remain a major issue in the USA, 1945–89? (Leaving Cert 2014)

⑤ The Montgomery Bus Boycott 1955–1956 (Case Study)

HOW WERE AFRICAN AMERICANS DISCRIMINATED AGAINST IN MONTGOMERY?

In 1954, the US Supreme Court decision in *Brown v. Board of Education of Topeka* (see page 52) removed the legal basis for segregation in education. However, in the southern states of the USA Jim Crow laws (see page 49) continued to enforce segregation and discrimination against African Americans in housing, transport and various public facilities.

Montgomery, the state capital of Alabama, a state with a long tradition of racial tension, was one of the most racially segregated cities in the USA in the 1950s. At that time, Montgomery had a population of 120,000, of whom over 40 per cent were African American (around 50,000 people).

In 1952, a white woman in Montgomery accused an African-American teenage boy, Jeremiah Reeves, of rape. He was tried and convicted by an all-white jury and sentenced to death. The National Association for the Advancement of Colored People (NAACP – see page 53) appealed the decision, but after a bitter legal battle that went on for five years, Reeves was executed. The case caused great resentment among Montgomery's African-American community, who saw it as an example of legal double standards. They knew of many cases of sexual abuse and murder of African-American women by white men, but no one was ever arrested or tried for these crimes. Therefore, many people concluded, the justice system in Montgomery discriminated against African Americans.

In Montgomery a black person was not allowed to hold public office. Thousands of African

The majority of African-American women in the south were employed as domestic servants in white people's homes

Americans were denied voting rights because of poll taxes, literacy tests and intimidation (see page 55). The vast majority of African-American people worked in low-paid unskilled jobs in the city: 63 per cent of African-American women were employed as domestic workers, and 48 per cent of African-American males worked as domestics or labourers. The average annual income of an African-American worker in Montgomery in 1950 was $970, half the income of the average white worker.

For African Americans in Montgomery, segregation was a fact of everyday living. By law, they had to use separate facilities from whites in public places such as parks, theatres, restaurants, and on buses. A local law even forbade black and white people from playing cards, dice or dominos together.

There were over fifty churches catering for African-American congregations in and around Montgomery. Most African-American church leaders preached acceptance of the system. They focused on the spiritual needs of the congregations and not on social or political reform.

Towards the end of 1955, however, an event occurred in Montgomery which would become the starting point of the first organised and mass movement of African Americans in twentieth-century America.

This event involved segregation on the city's buses and was led by the NAACP and some progressive African-American religious leaders.

Segregation on the Buses

In Montgomery, it was the law that African-American people travelling on the buses could not sit at the front, even if the seats there were not occupied. The first four rows of seats were reserved for whites only. If all the seats at the front were occupied and more white passengers got on the bus, African Americans sitting at the back had to give up their seats to the whites. Furthermore, if a white person sat beside an African American at the back of the bus, the African American had to stand.

All the bus drivers were white. Seventy per cent of the people using the buses were African American. The drivers often humiliated and harassed African-American passengers, calling them names such as 'nigger' or 'ape'. Women, in particular, were singled out for abuse.

Drivers made African-American passengers pay their fare at the front of the bus, then get off and re-board the bus at a back door; sometimes the driver would take off before the person could get back on the bus, leaving them stranded on the street. This activity was a source of amusement for bus drivers and white passengers, but caused deep resentment among African Americans.

African Americans who did not obey the segregation laws on buses were fined and jailed. In March 1955, a black teenager, Claudette Colvin, was arrested because she refused to give up her seat to a white person on a bus in Montgomery. She was tried and ordered to pay a fine. In October of that year, 18-year-old Mary Louise Smith refused to move out of her seat for a white person. Like Colvin, she was arrested and fined. The mood of African-American citizens in Montgomery was becoming increasingly angry about the segregation policy on buses.

WHAT WAS THE BUS BOYCOTT?

Rosa Parks

On the evening of 1 December 1955, an African-American seamstress, **Rosa Parks**, got on a bus in downtown Montgomery. She was tired after her day's work. When asked to move to let a white passenger sit down, she refused. She did not argue with the driver, but remained in her seat. The police were called and minutes later Parks was arrested.

Parks was well known and respected in the African-American community in Montgomery, and the 43-year-old had been secretary of the Montgomery NAACP. From jail she phoned her friend Edgar Daniel Nixon, leader of the NAACP in Alabama. He agreed to pay her bail and then contacted other African-American community leaders. He told Parks, 'We can go to the Supreme Court with this ... and boycott the bus line at the same time.'

The NAACP had been following a policy of using the courts to end discrimination against African Americans in the USA. Nixon knew that challenging racism in the courts would require the support of other African-American leaders. He also knew that organising a bus boycott would need the full backing of the entire African-American community in Montgomery. He contacted the Reverend Ralph Abernathy and the Reverend **Martin Luther King** (see page 189), a popular young Baptist minister, to organise a meeting.

Rosa Parks sitting in the front of a bus in Montgomery, Alabama, after the Supreme Court ruled that segregation on the city's buses was illegal

The African-American community in Montgomery was outraged when they heard about the arrest of Rosa Parks. Jo-Ann Robinson, the leader of the **Women's Political Committee**, organised a one-day bus boycott for Monday, 5 December 1955, the day Parks was due in court.

Meanwhile, Nixon and some African-American religious leaders were becoming alarmed by the mood in the African-American community. There were rumours that some members of the community wanted to confront the bus drivers, threatening to 'beat the hell' out of them. In order to prevent violence, on 2 December Nixon, Abernathy and King called a meeting in King's church. Over forty religious and civic leaders from the African-American community attended this meeting. They agreed to support the boycott. They would take a stand against racial segregation, using non-violent methods.

Their message was one of non-co-operation with the bus company. Montgomery's African-American community would walk, drive or use any other form of transport rather than use segregated buses.

Thousands of leaflets were distributed in African-American areas of the city, informing citizens of the boycott on Monday 5 December. Taxi companies run by African Americans agreed to charge African-American passengers the same fare as buses – 10 cents.

The organisers hoped that 60 per cent of the African-American population would back the boycott. On a normal working day the early morning buses would be packed with African-American workers; on Monday 5 December, the first bus was empty. So was the second bus. All over the city African Americans walked, thumbed lifts, used cabs or drove private cars to work. By evening it was clear that the boycott had received almost 100 per cent support. King later wrote: 'A miracle had taken place ... The once dormant and quiescent Negro community was now fully awake' (*Stride Toward Freedom: The Montgomery Story*, New York, 1958).

King and Abernathy attended Rosa Parks' trial at 9 a.m. the same day. The judge found her guilty and fined her $14. Nixon called for an appeal. So began the legal battle against segregation on public transport in Montgomery.

African-American students wave at an empty bus during the boycott

HOW DID MARTIN LUTHER KING EMERGE AS LEADER OF THE BOYCOTT?

The leaders of the boycott met that afternoon and set up a permanent organisation to run the boycott – they had already decided that the boycott should last for more than one day. They called it the **Montgomery Improvement Association** (MIA). Martin Luther King (see page 189) was unanimously elected leader of this new group. That evening he addressed a huge crowd at a meeting called by the MIA.

He urged them to follow non-violent Christian principles, to use persuasion, not coercion. Abernathy read out the MIA demands:

1   Blacks must be treated with courtesy by bus drivers.

2   Segregation on the buses must end.

3   Black drivers must be employed on the buses.

The African-American citizens of Montgomery would not travel on the buses until these demands were met. King closed the meeting by calling on all in favour of the MIA proposal to stand. Everyone stood and applauded. The boycott would continue.

The task now facing the MIA was to ensure that the boycott worked, and worked peacefully.

However, the leaders knew that the boycott would only be a temporary measure. The real business was to use the Parks case to win a legal battle against segregation. It was the intention of the MIA to combine the legal action of the NAACP with the peaceful protest of thousands of African-American boycotters in Montgomery.

King was a dedicated and popular minister at the Dexter Avenue Baptist Church in Montgomery. He was also active in the local branch of the NAACP. He was young, energetic and a brilliant public speaker.

King and other African-American leaders wanted to give the boycotters a sense of involvement. They held meetings to plan strategy and set up a Transportation Committee to raise funds and organise alternative transport for African Americans to get to work. Ministers, labourers, business people, teachers and even some white supporters collected money, organised carpools and set up taxi services to ensure that workers had transport to and from work. Many white housewives in Montgomery were unwilling to do without their domestic servants, and arranged to have them driven to and from work.

On 8 December, King and representatives of the MIA met the Mayor, W.A. 'Tacky' Gayle, and

Minister Martin Luther King – a brilliant and energetic speaker, 1964

representatives of the bus company. King was optimistic that a compromise would be found. The boycott was now receiving widespread, national media attention. Reporters and television camera crews were present for this meeting at City Hall. The bus company refused to change the segregated seating arrangement on the buses. The Mayor joked about the boycott and said, 'Comes the first rainy day and the Negros will be back on the buses.' He was not going to take the side of the boycotters. It did rain the next day, but African Americans continued the boycott. The Mayor then announced that communists were behind the boycott.

QUESTIONS

1 What were Jim Crow laws? List some examples of how they operated in Montgomery before 1956.

2 Who was Rosa Parks?

3 Who called a meeting on 2 December 1955, and why did they take this action?

4 What decision was made at this meeting?

5 Why was Martin Luther King chosen as leader of the MIA?

White Reaction

After Christmas 1955, when it became clear that the African-American community in Montgomery was determined to continue the boycott until their demands were met, some whites began to use measures aimed at forcing them to give up. These included:

- **Psychological pressure:** Rumours were spread that King was misusing MIA funds. It was claimed that he had bought himself and his wife new cars. Attempts were made to stir up criticism of King among African-American church leaders. Aware of this, King offered to

resign. The MIA, however, assured him that he had their unanimous support and urged him to remain as leader.

- **False media reports:** On 22 January the city authorities announced that the boycott was over, and that a settlement had been reached with its leaders. King responded quickly. He told African Americans to ignore these false reports and assured them that no agreement had been made with the bus company or the city government.

- **Police harassment:** Carpool drivers were arrested for giving lifts to African-American workers. The police threatened to take away their driving licences and cancel their insurance policies. African-American people waiting on the streets for lifts to work were arrested for loitering. King was arrested for speeding – he was doing 30 miles per hour in a 25 mph zone. He was taken to jail, fingerprinted and only released when a crowd of African Americans gathered outside the jail. At his trial he was found guilty.

In February, 89 African-American leaders, including 24 ministers and all the carpool drivers, were arrested for breaking an old law which prohibited boycotts. At the time King was in Nashville giving lectures at a university. When he returned to Montgomery a few days later, he joined the others in jail. His arrest and trial made the headlines in the national and international news.

Violence and Intimidation

The Ku Klux Klan roamed the streets, attacking African Americans and wrecking cars used in the carpool. African-American churches were attacked. On the night of 30 January 1956, King's home was bombed, while his wife and baby daughter were home. They escaped unhurt. African-American leaders received threatening phone calls and letters.

One night a caller phoned King and told him: 'Nigger, if you aren't out of this town in three days we gonna blow your brains out and blow up your house.' He did not leave.

The KKK were deeply angered by the boycott and attacked and threatened ordinary African-American citizens, 1956

WHAT WAS INVOLVED IN THE LEGAL STRUGGLE TO END SEGREGATION?

Despite these challenges, the African-American community continued to boycott the buses. Meanwhile, the NAACP was working through the legal process to end segregation on the buses. In June, a panel of three federal judges ruled that the bus laws in Alabama were unconstitutional. Lawyers for the City of Montgomery filed an appeal with the US Supreme Court to overturn this decision.

Before the Supreme Court had reached its decision on the appeal, the authorities in Montgomery decided to take the leaders of the boycott to court. On 30 October 1956, they declared that the carpool was 'a public nuisance' and an illegal 'private enterprise'. They sued the MIA for damages and demanded an end to the boycott. African-American leaders knew that if the carpool was stopped the boycott would be under extreme pressure. African Americans would now be forced to use the buses to get to work. On 13 November, the case against the MIA was heard. The City was looking for $15,000 in compensation for the loss caused by the boycott.

While the court was sitting in Montgomery, word came through that the US Supreme Court had declared that segregated seating on public buses was unconstitutional. In other words, the City of Montgomery had lost its appeal case. The issue before the court in Montgomery on that same day was now irrelevant. The Supreme Court's decision was to come into operation on 20 December 1956, just over one year after the boycott had begun.

On 14 November, the MIA called off the boycott. However, they asked the African-American citizens of Montgomery to stay off the buses until the Supreme Court ruling came into effect. As carpooling was now illegal, African-American workers walked to work for a further few weeks.

On 21 December, in a symbolic gesture, King and a white minister, Glenn Smiley, sat together in what was previously a white-only section of a Montgomery bus. The boycott was officially over.

WHAT WERE THE RESULTS OF THE MONTGOMERY BUS BOYCOTT?

The Montgomery bus boycott lasted for 381 days. It cost the MIA $225,000 (for providing transport, court and legal fees, and other expenses), and the

Worker removing a segregated seating sign from the rear of a bus in Dallas, Texas

bus company over $250,000 in lost revenue. The City of Montgomery lost thousands of dollars in tax earnings. Businesses in the city also lost millions of dollars.

The human cost was high too. African-American people had endured great hardship in getting to and from work during the year-long boycott. They had also suffered intimidation and violence from both the city authorities and white racists.

The ending of the boycott did not bring an end to white opposition in Montgomery. A group of segregationists tried to set up a white-only bus company. They were not successful, but their attempt showed how ingrained racism was in Montgomery.

The violence also continued. On the night of the Supreme Court ruling on 13 November 1956, forty carloads of whites wearing KKK robes and hoods drove into African-American areas threatening residents. On 28 December, armed whites fired into buses, where seating was now mixed. Later, in January 1957, white people opposed to desegregation distributed leaflets attacking King and other leaders. African-American homes and churches were bombed.

A turning point came after Reverend Abernathy's house and church were destroyed by a bomb. Many whites were appalled and condemned the bombings. The media and the city's businessmen denounced the extremists who were breaking the

law. White church ministers called the bombings unchristian. In the face of this white support for the rule of law, and for the African-American community, the KKK and other white racists backed down. The violence stopped.

The boycott was successful in ending segregation on the buses, but many African Americans were slow to change their habits. Older people, in particular, continued to sit at the back of the buses, as they had always done. It would take time for the African-American community to become accustomed to its new status of equality when travelling on the buses.

The struggle to end segregation in Montgomery, and the south in general, was not over when buses became integrated. All other public institutions remained segregated. The success of the boycott inspired further action to remove Jim Crow laws from every aspect of life and to achieve full civil rights for African Americans throughout the USA. It was an important milestone in American history.

WHY WAS THE BOYCOTT IMPORTANT FOR THE CIVIL RIGHTS MOVEMENT?

- It was the first organised mass movement of African Americans in the twentieth century.

- It succeeded in ending segregation on the buses in the state of Alabama.

- It proved that direct non-violent action could work in modern-day America. These tactics would be adopted in later campaigns against discrimination.

- It inspired hope for change among African Americans, who had lost faith in the justice system in the USA, and gave ordinary African Americans a sense of participation and community involvement.

- It focused the attention of the nation on the issue of civil rights and provided a model of protest and African-American activism in the 1960s and 1970s.

- It provided white liberals and supporters of civil rights the opportunity to work with African Americans to end racial discrimination.

- It gave Martin Luther King, and other leaders, a national platform and a chance to display their leadership skills in mobilising a successful campaign. King's road to fame began in Montgomery.

- It led to a new sense of pride in the African-American community throughout the USA.

The success of the boycott is reflected in the words of an African-American janitor (maintenance man) in Montgomery, 'We got our heads up now, and we won't ever bow down again – no sir – except before God!'

- It highlighted the central role of the churches, and of Christian values, in African-American communities and in the struggle to end segregation.

MONTGOMERY BUS BOYCOTT TIMELINE 1955–1956

1955

1 December Rosa Parks refuses to give her seat to a white passenger on a bus in Montgomery, sparking the Montgomery bus boycott.

5 December The boycott begins. It is supported by over 90% of African-Americans in the town.

Montgomery Improvement Association is set up to run the boycott. It elects **Dr Martin Luther King**, pastor of Dexter Avenue Baptist Church, as president to lead the boycott.

A carpooling system is developed to transport African Americans to work; others walk.

1956

January and February Four African-American churches and the homes of civil rights leaders Martin Luther King and Edgar D. Nixon are attacked.

February A suit is filed in a federal court challenging the bus segregation law.

King and other leaders are arrested for organising a boycott.

June The federal court rules that segregation on buses is unconstitutional – the decision is appealed to the Supreme Court.

13 November The **Supreme Court** upholds the federal court ruling outlawing segregation on buses.

20 December The Montgomery bus boycott ends successfully after 381 days.

QUESTIONS

1 List some of the measures taken to force an end to the bus boycott.

2 What was the result of the City of Montgomery's appeal case to the Supreme Court?

3 What were the main results of the Montgomery bus boycott?

DOCUMENT A

This document contains two sections of the Montgomery City Code (Chapter 6, Sections 10 and 11) relating to segregation laws on the buses.

Sec. 10. Separation of races – Required

Every person operating a bus line in the city shall provide equal but separate accommodations for white people and Negroes on his buses, by requiring the employees in charge thereof to assign passengers seats on the vehicles under their charge in such manner as to separate the white people from the Negroes, where there are both white and Negroes on the same car; provided, however, that Negro nurses having in charge white children or sick or infirm white persons, may be assigned seats among white people.

Nothing in this section shall be construed as prohibiting the operators of such bus lines from separating the races by means of separate vehicles if they see fit. (Code 1938, 608, 606)

Sec. 11. Same – Powers of person in charge of vehicle; passengers to obey directions.

Any employee in charge of a bus operated in the city shall have the powers of a police officer of the city while in actual charge of any bus, for the purpose of carrying out the provisions of the preceding section, and it shall be unlawful for any passenger to refuse or fail to take a seat among those assigned to the race to which he belongs, at the request of any such employee in charge, if there is a seat vacant. (Code 1938, 604)

1 DOCUMENT A QUESTIONS

a) Who was responsible for separating black and white people on the buses?

b) Which black people were exempt from the segregation rule on the buses?

c) What powers did bus drivers have?

DOCUMENT B

In this document Rosa Parks gives her own account of what happened to her on
1 December 1955.

> *Having to take a certain section (on the bus) because of your race was
> humiliating, but having to stand up because a particular driver wanted to keep a
> white person from having to stand was, to my mind, most inhumane.*
>
> *Over the years, I had had my own problems with the bus drivers. In fact, some
> did tell me not to ride their buses if I felt that I was too important to go to the
> back door to get on. One had evicted me from the bus in 1943.*
>
> *On December 1, 1955, I had finished my day's work as a tailor's assistant and I
> was on my way home. There was one vacant seat on the Cleveland Avenue bus,
> which I took alongside a man and two women. On the third (stop), the front seats
> were occupied and this one man, a white man, was standing. The driver asked us
> to stand up and let him have those seats, and when none of us moved at his first
> words, he said, 'You all make it light on yourselves and let him have those seats.'*
>
> *When the driver saw me still sitting, he asked if I was going to stand up and I
> said, 'No, I'm not.' And he said, 'Well, if you don't stand up, I'm going to call the
> police and have you arrested.'*
>
> *I said, 'You may do that.'*
>
> *He did get off the bus, and I still stayed where I was. Two policemen came on the
> bus. One policeman asked me if the bus driver had asked me to stand and I said yes.*
>
> *He said, 'Why don't you stand up?'*
>
> *And I asked him, 'Why do you push us around?'*
>
> *He said, 'I don't know, but the law is the law and you're under arrest'.*
>
> Source: Henry Hampton and Steve Fayer, *Voices of Freedom*

2 DOCUMENT B QUESTIONS

a) What was Rosa Parks' job at the time
of her arrest?

b) What happened at the third stop?

c) What did the bus driver do when
Rosa Parks refused to stand up?

3 ORDINARY LEVEL QUESTIONS

a) What did the Montgomery bus boycott (1956) contribute to the civil rights movement? (Leaving Cert 2010)

b) Why was the Montgomery bus boycott (1956) so important in the story of the civil rights movement? (Leaving Cert 2006)

c) Write an account of the part played by one or more of the following in the Montgomery bus boycott: (i) Rosa Parks; (ii) Martin Luther King; (iii) the NAACP; (iv) the Ku Klux Klan

4 HIGHER LEVEL ESSAYS

a) In what ways did the Montgomery bus boycott, 1956, advance the cause of the civil rights movement? (Leaving Cert 2007)

b) What were the origins and significance of the Montgomery bus boycott?

c) Martin Luther King believed in a policy of non-violence. How did he implement this policy during the Montgomery bus boycott and why was it successful?

Martin Luther King and Glenn Smiley sit side by side among many other African-American passengers on a public bus, 21 December 1956. They are all sitting in the previously whites-only section.

What can we learn from this picture? Give reasons for your answer.

KEY QUESTIONS

The key issue that dominated US foreign policy after World War II was the rivalry with the USSR known as the **Cold War**. The term 'cold' was used to describe this conflict because it fell short of a 'hot' war with actual fighting between the two powers.

The USA and the USSR were the world's two most powerful countries and they had very different economic and political systems (see the table on page 77). Their rivalry began in the ruins of defeated Germany and soon spread throughout the world.

The Cold War had a major impact on relations between the two countries. It led to an arms race (see Chapter 11) and a space race (Chapter 12) and resulted in a number of crises that threatened

world peace. Propaganda played a key role as each side, convinced of its own superiority, attempted to spread its influence throughout the world. The Cold War also saw a growth in the USA of domestic anti-communist hysteria, often referred to as **McCarthyism**.

Competition between powerful countries was not new, but what made the Cold War different was nuclear weapons and with them the threat of the destruction of the human race.

The main aim of successive US administrations was stopping the spread of communism. As a result the USA abandoned its traditional **isolationism** and committed itself to the defence of Western Europe. Throughout the world the USA gave economic support and military aid to countries that were threatened by communist revolution. As successive US governments prioritised the struggle against communism this sometimes led them to support governments that had poor human rights records.

> ### Note
>
> Throughout the text the USSR will also be called the Soviet Union or Russia, and citizens of the USSR will be described as Soviets or Russians. Though the terms Russia and Russian are not strictly accurate, they were used in sources from the period.
>
> The terms **Soviet/Soviets/Soviet Union** come from the official name for the USSR: the Union of Soviet Socialist Republics. A soviet was a workers' and soldiers' council set up to control the cities during the political turbulence in Russia in 1905 and 1917.
>
> In 1991 the Soviet Union broke up into 15 independent countries including Russia, Ukraine and the Baltic republics.

HOW DID THE COLD WAR BEGIN?

Why Did the USA Fear the Spread of Communism?

Before examining American foreign policy we need to look at the reasons why the majority of Americans were opposed to communism. As you can see from the table on the opposite page, the USA and the USSR had very **different political systems**. To most Americans the communist system represented a threat to civilisation and personal freedom everywhere in the world. They pointed to the brutality of Stalin's regime and the establishment of communist regimes in Eastern Europe after World War II. It seemed as if the Soviet Union was intent on worldwide revolution. Powerful business interests were also worried about communism. They feared the loss of markets abroad if communism continued to spread.

During the Cold War the overwhelming majority of Americans saw the role of the USA as defending freedom against the spread of communist tyranny. Domestic debates about US policy were over **how**, not **whether**, to oppose the spread of communism.

The Impact of the Defeat of Germany on Relations between the Superpowers

Hostility to communism was not new in the USA. Prior to World War II, the Americans had been strongly opposed to communism. The USA did not establish diplomatic relations with the government of the USSR until 1933 – 16 years after the communists came to power. However, in December 1941 both nations became allies against Hitler's Germany. The USA supplied vast amounts of war material to the USSR, including aviation fuel and vehicles that were essential for the Russian army.

There were divisions and suspicions between the two nations but as long as the war lasted they were united in their determination to defeat Nazi Germany. The Soviet leader Josef Stalin became quite a popular figure in the USA, where he was referred to as 'Uncle Joe'. In 1945, when it was clear that Germany had been beaten, differences between the two nations began to emerge.

Divisions Develop at the Yalta and Potsdam Conferences

Yalta

In February 1945, Stalin, the British Prime Minister Winston Churchill, and US President Roosevelt met at **Yalta in the USSR** to plan what should happen when the war ended. It was clear that the Germans were on the verge of defeat. The three leaders agreed on the following:

- The **United Nations** (UN) would be established to preserve world peace.

- **Germany** was to be divided into four zones to be administered by the four victorious allies (America, Britain, France and the USSR). Germany's capital, Berlin, would also be divided into four zones.

- Free elections were to be held in the states of Eastern Europe, including Poland.

- Russia agreed to join the war against Japan after Germany was defeated.

There were a number of areas of tension, though. The leaders could not agree about what should happen to Poland. Spreading communist control

USA	USSR
Democratic – free elections in which people could vote for different political parties.	**Dictatorship** – no free elections. Only one party allowed.
Capitalism – business and property owned by private individuals. Private enterprise encouraged.	**Communism** – businesses owned and managed by the government. The state decided what was produced. Supporters argued that this created a fairer and more equal society.
Human rights – individual rights protected. Citizens free to express opinions and practise religious beliefs.	**Human rights** – no freedom of expression, censorship was enforced and individual rights were not protected.

there angered the USA. The USSR did not carry out its pledge to hold free elections in Poland and instead installed a communist government. There were also disagreements about what to do with a defeated Germany. Despite these disputes, Stalin and Roosevelt got on well and relations between the two countries were still good.

> **internationalism** A belief that the USA must play a role in European and world affairs, especially to halt the spread of communism. In a sense, it is the view that because of its superpower status the USA has to exercise a role as the world's policeman. This is in contrast to the **isolationism** of the 1920s and 1930s, when America stayed out of events in Europe.

Potsdam Conference

By the time of Germany's surrender in May 1945, the USA was the world's strongest economic power, while the USSR had the largest army. Significantly, Russia was effectively in control on the ground throughout Eastern Europe. **President Roosevelt** had died in April, just before the end of the war, and he was replaced by his vice-president **Harry Truman**. Inexperienced in foreign relations, Truman was determined to defend American interests in the world. He believed in taking a tough line in negotiations with the Soviets, especially over Poland.

In July, Stalin, Truman and Winston Churchill (who was replaced during the conference by the new prime minister, Clement Attlee) met at the **Potsdam Conference** near Berlin to draw up a

Winston Churchill, Harold Truman and Josef Stalin at the Potsdam Conference

post-war peace treaty. Truman had hoped that face-to-face negotiations with Stalin would help to moderate Soviet policies in Eastern Europe. He did not want a total breakdown in relations between the two countries. There was agreement on a number of issues: Germany and Austria would be divided into four zones; Nazi leaders were to be tried for their crimes; and land was to be transferred from Germany to Poland. Stalin also confirmed Soviet support in the war against Japan.

During the conference Truman learned that the atomic bomb tests had been successful. On 6 August the USA dropped the new atomic bomb on Hiroshima; a few days later Nagasaki was also bombed. As a result of the destruction of the two cites the Japanese surrendered unconditionally. The atomic bomb added a dramatic new element to traditional great power rivalry: the threat of total destruction in the event of war.

However, there was little progress on the issues that had been divisive at Yalta: future German reunification and the political future of Poland.

Nonetheless the conference was a personal success for Truman and there seemed to have been an improvement in relations between the USSR and the USA.

This brief improvement in relations was not to last. By the end of 1945 relations between the two World War II allies had cooled considerably. One cause of concern for Truman was the unfolding events in Eastern Europe.

Soviet Control Strengthens in Eastern Europe

During the war, the USSR had suffered enormous destruction, with the loss of 25 million lives. In order to prevent a future invasion Stalin was determined to dominate Eastern Europe by installing communist governments. This would ensure that the USSR would control these countries' foreign policy and that they remained 'friendly' to the USSR.

Under Stalin's direction, communist governments took control throughout Eastern Europe. Elections were rigged, opposition leaders arrested and non-communist parties banned. By 1948 there were communist governments in **Poland**, **Hungary**, **Bulgaria**, **Albania**, **Romania** and **Czechoslovakia** (see the map below).

Stalin's actions in Eastern Europe caused great alarm in the USA. His claim that his actions were justified by the need for self-defence was not accepted by the USA or its allies. It appeared to Western commentators that Russia was intent on

The division of Europe as a result of the Cold War. The countries in red saw communist governments installed at the end of the war. Yugoslavia was also communist, but its ruler, Marshal Tito, fell out with Stalin in 1948 and the country was not controlled by Moscow

dominating the whole of Europe. The Communist take-over in Czechoslovakia in 1948 had a particularly strong impact because this was the country that the West had abandoned to Hitler at Munich in 1938. Memories of appeasement haunted Western policymakers, including Truman, and they were determined to stand up to Soviet aggression.

Women scavenge for food and cigarette ends near a British barracks in post-war Berlin

Already in 1946 **Winston Churchill** had coined a new phrase to describe the division between Western and Eastern Europe – the **Iron Curtain**. During a speech made at **Fulton, Missouri**, he said, 'From Stettin in the Baltic to Trieste in the Adriatic an **iron curtain** has descended across the continent.'

Reaction in the USA

Truman and his advisers were worried by the spread of communism outside Eastern Europe as well. While the USA experienced a post-war boom, conditions were very different in Europe. In 1947 the continent was still devastated economically, and poor weather made matters worse. These conditions helped the French and Italian

communist parties become stronger. As these parties were controlled by Stalin, their increasing support alarmed the USA.

In **Greece**, communist guerrillas were involved in a bitter civil war against the UK-backed Greek government. The USSR was also putting pressure on the weak government of Turkey to share control of the strategic **Dardanelle Straits** – the entrance to the Black Sea. There were fears that the USSR intended to invade Turkey and seize control of the Straits.

The growing communist support in Western Europe, allied with events in Greece and Turkey, led the USA to take action against communism. The USA decided to reverse a key part of its foreign policy – avoiding alliances in peacetime – and commit itself to the defence of Western Europe.

This action took two forms:

1 **Political** – to stop the spread of communism: the **Truman Doctrine**

2 **Economic** – to improve economic conditions for ordinary people: **Marshall Aid**.

The Truman Doctrine

Traditionally Britain had been one of the dominant powers in the **Mediterranean** region, but Britain was in severe economic difficulties after the war. In February 1947, the British told the United States that they could no longer supply economic and military aid to Greece or Turkey. The USA decided that it had to stop the spread of communism. This became known as the **Truman Doctrine**. It led to direct military assistance and support for anti-communist governments in Europe and later throughout the world.

On 12 March 1947 Truman announced aid to Greece and Turkey in the context of a general war against communism. America promised it 'would support free peoples who are resisting subjugation (domination) by armed minorities or by outside pressures'. Congress approved $400 million in military aid for Greece and Turkey. Greece received large amounts of arms and supplies, which helped the Greek government defeat the communists. The Truman Doctrine clearly stated what was to become the main policy of the United States for the next forty years: **containment**.

General George C. Marshall

The Marshall Plan

The Americans also realised that a prosperous Europe would be better able to resist the spread of communism. A European recovery would also provide markets for American goods, which would benefit American industry. Central to this recovery would be reviving the German economy – an aim opposed by the Soviets.

In 1947 the American Secretary of State, **General George Marshall**, announced the **European Recovery Programme**, which became known as the **Marshall Plan.** This was an offer of massive economic aid to Europe to help it recover from the damage caused by the war.

Marshall Aid was also offered to the countries of Eastern Europe. Some were tempted, but Stalin told them not to accept the aid, which he saw as an attempt by the Americans to buy control of Western

Europe, and to interfere in Eastern Europe. Stalin was also opposed to German economic recovery as he wanted to keep the country as weak as possible.

Meanwhile, as the Marshall Plan pumped billions of US dollars into Europe, the West German economic recovery triggered a general European economic recovery. The assistance grew to $20 billion by 1951. The plan hardened divisions between the superpowers and led directly to a crisis over Berlin.

WHY WAS THE BERLIN BLOCKADE IMPORTANT FOR US FOREIGN POLICY?

The introduction of Marshall Aid to Germany caused the first real conflict between the superpowers during the Cold War and led to the first test of US resolve to resist the spread of communism: the **Berlin Blockade**.

Background to the Crisis

The future status of Germany and its former capital was a major area of disagreement between the USA and the USSR. During the war US opinion was divided on the best approach to a defeated Germany, but now Truman realised that German economic recovery was needed for a Europe-wide economic improvement. He also felt that a restored democratic Germany could be an ally against Stalin.

The USA, Britain and France – somewhat reluctantly – joined their zones together to facilitate economic reform. The aim was that this would lead to eventual unification. As we have seen, Stalin wanted to keep Germany weak and divided. He opposed this move and he established a communist state in the Soviet zone.

Berlin had also been split into four occupation zones after the surrender of Germany. As you can see from the map on the next page, the location of Berlin was very problematic as it was deep inside the Soviet zone. The Allies enjoyed right of access to their zones by road, rail and along specified air corridors. For Stalin, Berlin was an island of democracy that he wanted removed. He was worried that this outpost of capitalism would be

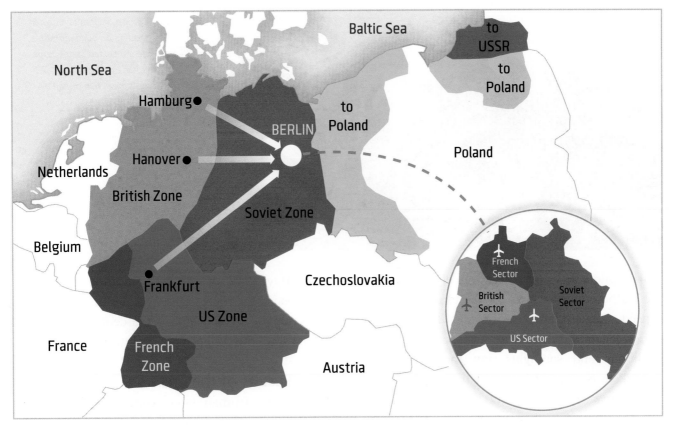

The Berlin Blockade. Note that Berlin, located inside the Soviet-controlled part of Germany, was itself divided into four zones, which were controlled by Britain, France, the USA and the USSR. The arrows indicate the air corridors into Berlin

much wealthier than the Russian zone that surrounded it.

The Blockade Begins

In June 1948, as part of the Marshall Plan, a new currency – the **deutschmark** – was introduced into West Germany. Stalin strongly opposed its introduction into the Western zones of Berlin. When the Allies ignored Soviet warnings and introduced the currency into Berlin, Stalin acted.

On 27 June he ordered the blockade of West Berlin's roads and railways. There was no way of travelling by land into the city. Berlin faced starvation. The only access to West Berlin was through an air corridor about 30 kilometres wide. Stalin thought that the West could not remain in Berlin if the land access was cut. The American response caught him by surprise.

US Reaction

In keeping with the policy of containment, Truman was determined that America would not be driven from West Berlin. He could do nothing to stop communist control spreading in Eastern Europe, but American troops were on the ground in Berlin.

He worried what a Western retreat from the city would do to American prestige. Fearing that American troops forcing their way by land into Berlin might lead to war, on 28 June he approved a plan to fly supplies into the city. Truman commented, 'we would stay, period.' He was determined to see the airlift through until a diplomatic solution was found. He was supported in his decision by the USA's closest ally, Britain, which supplied planes to help the Americans. France could offer little practical support as it was heavily involved in the fighting in one of its colonies, Vietnam.

The operation was given the codename **Operation Vittles**. To ensure that the Soviets did not act militarily Truman moved B-29 bombers to bases in Britain. These planes were capable of carrying nuclear bombs and were intended to send Stalin a clear warning.

The Berlin Airlift moved enough goods into West Berlin over 320 days to entirely support the economy of the city. On average planes were landing every three minutes throughout the siege. The 2.5 million citizens of West Berlin survived on the supplies sent during the Berlin Airlift.

A group of German children, standing on building rubble, cheer a United States cargo airplane as it flies over a western section of Berlin

Airlift pilots flew under an extremely strict system of traffic control which set the exact height and speed of each plane. The US and British aircraft often encountered Soviet obstructions such as balloons and spotlights, but they were never attacked. Stalin did not want to provoke a third world war. The high point of the airlift was at Easter 1949 when there were 1,398 flights, with a plane landing every 90 seconds. One humanitarian aspect of the airlift that caught the popular imagination in the USA was the actions of pilot Gail Halvorsen. He was nicknamed the Candy Bomber because he started dropping sweets for the children of Berlin.

In May 1949 the Soviets admitted defeat and reopened the routes into West Berlin. The city was to remain divided and at the centre of the Cold War until the collapse of Communism in 1989.

The Results of the Crisis

President Truman later wrote about the airlift: 'We demonstrated to the people of Europe that with their co-operation we would act, and act resolutely, when their freedom was threatened. Politically it brought the peoples of western Europe closer to us' (Nigel Hamilton, *American Caesars*, p. 66). His statement was reflected in the results of the crisis.

Propaganda

A feature of the Cold War was the use of **propaganda** by both sides to influence opinion both domestically and internationally. All types of media, e.g. radio, newspapers, TV and films, were used to get the message across. The message, put simply, was 'We are the good guys and they are the bad guys!'

The Cold War rivals stressed their successes, e.g. the Soviet launch of Sputnik, and downplayed defeats, e.g. the Berlin Blockade.

They particularly enjoyed emphasising events in which the other side was humiliated, e.g. the Bay of Pigs (see page 93).

Language was used by each side to portray the other in a bad light.

For example:

- The United States was an **aggressive imperialist** power dominated by **big business** that aimed to **enslave** the working class.
- The USSR was a **tyranny** and an enemy to **freedom-loving** people everywhere. (Famously, President Reagan described the USSR as an **evil empire**.)

Each superpower said its actions were always just, peaceful or in the interest of others, while the other side's actions were provocative, criminal, selfish, etc.

During the Cold War the USA was at a disadvantage in the control of information as it had an open society with a free media and it was difficult to keep bad news from people. The USSR was a closed society where it was often difficult for citizens to obtain accurate information (especially bad news!). Domestic criticism was not permitted.

The Berlin Blockade was the first major crisis of the Cold War and it had an important impact on both the Cold War and US foreign policy:

- The crisis had been a major victory for the USA. Containment had worked and the spread of communism had been halted. Truman's personal standing and that of the USA had been greatly strengthened throughout Western Europe. The actions of the USA were in stark contrast to the Soviets, who had shown communism at its worst. To this day many historians regard the blockade as Truman's finest hour.

- In 1949 the USA, Canada and most Western European nations formed the **North Atlantic Treaty Organization** (**NATO**) to co-ordinate their defence against Russia. Crucially, the USA was now committed to defending Europe against the spread of communism.

- The division of Germany was now permanent. In 1949 West Germany became the **Federal Republic of Germany**, while the East became the **German Democratic Republic**.

- The West Germans were very impressed by the aid that the Americans had sent to Berlin. It brought West Germany closer to the USA, and West Germany was to be a loyal ally of the USA during the Cold War. The USA encouraged German rearmament and West Germany joined NATO in 1955. The **Warsaw Pact** alliance of the communist countries of Eastern Europe was formed in response to this event. Two hostile alliances now faced each other in Europe.

- The Cold War dominated diplomacy. The USA and the USSR were now enemies and any dispute between them might lead to war – with terrible consequences for the human race.

The Arms Race

In August 1949 Russia tested its first atomic bomb (nicknamed Joe 1 by the Americans). America's nuclear monopoly was over. The USA responded by working on a more powerful **hydrogen bomb**. An arms race developed as sides increased their expenditure on nuclear and conventional weapons. Developments in rocket technology saw the introduction of intercontinental ballistic missiles (ICBMs). First tested by the Soviets in 1957, they could fly thousands of kilometres. By the late 1950s both sides had the capacity to destroy each other in the event of war. For more detail about developments in the arms race, see Chapter 11.

QUESTIONS

1 Explain why most Americans were opposed to communism.

2 What decisions were reached at the Yalta Conference and why did divisions emerge between the USA and the USSR?

3 What were the results of the Potsdam Conference?

4 What happened to the countries of Eastern Europe after World War II?

5 Explain the background to the Truman Doctrine.

6 What was 'containment'? Why was this policy so important?

7 Why did the USA propose Marshall Aid and what was the reaction of the Soviets?

8 Why did Stalin act to drive the Western powers out of Berlin?

9 How did Truman respond to the actions of the Soviets in Berlin?

10 Outline some of the main consequences of the Berlin Blockade.

WHAT IMPACT DID MCCARTHYISM HAVE ON US FOREIGN POLICY?

The Cold War not only shaped US foreign policy, it also had a major effect on domestic affairs. It led to the '**Second Red Scare**', also known as **McCarthyism**.

Growing Anti-Communist Feeling in the USA

There were a number of factors that contributed to the growth of anti-communist feeling in the USA:

- Anti-communist sentiment had been strong in the USA before the war. There had been a **Red Scare** in the years just after World War I. (This is often referred to as the 'First Red Scare'.) The Cold War revived this hostility.

- In 1949 news of the successful Soviet atomic test worried Americans. This alarm increased when communists, led by **Mao Zedong**, took control of **China** in the same year. The Chinese communists' **Nationalist** opponents fled to the island of **Taiwan**. The US government refused to recognise the new communist government and insisted that the Nationalists in Taiwan were the rightful government of China. One-third of the human race now lived under communism. Despite the success over Berlin it seemed as if communism was advancing throughout the world. Domestically Truman was attacked as the man who had 'lost China'.

- Many people believed that these communist advances could only be possible with the help of spies in America. A number of high-profile spy cases seemed to confirm fears that American communists indeed posed a threat to the USA. The government also uncovered a spy network that had passed atomic secrets to the Russians. In 1950 a British scientist who had worked on the Manhattan Project (the development of the atomic bomb) admitted passing information to the USSR. Later the same year four American communists, including Julius and Ethel Rosenberg, were accused of giving atomic secrets to the Soviets. The Rosenbergs were executed in 1953.

- Most Americans feared that home-grown communists were also undermining the 'American way of life'. They believed that communists were loyal to Moscow, not to the USA.

- Truman's political opponents, the Republicans, alleged that there were many communists working for the government.

Political Reaction to the Fear of Communism

In 1947, under pressure not to be seen as weak on communism, President Truman established a **Federal Employee Loyalty Programme**. This was designed to remove government employees considered a security risk. Its investigations led to the dismissal of about three hundred federal employees out of a total of three million. While the president may have helped fan the flames of political intolerance, it was Congress that was to turn it into a witch hunt. For the most part this came about through the activities of a committee called the House Un-American Activities Committee (HUAC) in the House of Representatives and, more famously, Senator Joseph McCarthy and his committee in the Senate.

The Role of HUAC

In 1947 the **House Un-American Activities Committee** (**HUAC**) was revived. It had been originally created in 1938 to investigate Americans with suspected links to the Nazis. It is best known for its investigation into communist influence in the film industry. HUAC pressurised actors, writers and producers to name names: they were asked, 'Are you now or have you ever been a member of the Communist Party?' Witnesses who answered yes would be expected to give information on other members of the Communist Party. If they refused they were added to a **blacklist** that was drawn up by the Hollywood studios. Anyone on the list was barred from working in Hollywood.

The blacklist had over 320 names, including Charlie Chaplin, Paul Robeson and Arthur Miller. When some writers (known as the **Hollywood Ten**) refused to testify in front of the committee they were sent to prison (see Chapter 9).

Although a number of communists were blacklisted, the careers of many innocent people were ruined.

In 1948 a senior State Department official, **Alger Hiss**, an adviser to President Roosevelt at Yalta, was accused by a former Soviet agent of being a spy. He was brought before HUAC, denied the allegations and was at first found not guilty. **Richard Nixon**, a member of the committee, made his name as an anti-communist crusader during his cross-examination of Hiss. Later Hiss was convicted of perjury (lying to Congress) and in 1950 he was sentenced to five years in prison. Today historians still debate his guilt or innocence.

Senator Joseph McCarthy during his second appearance before the Senate Foreign Relations Subcommittee, March 1950

McCarthyism

The most famous anti-communist crusader was **Senator Joseph McCarthy** from Wisconsin. In 1950 he faced defeat in upcoming Senate elections after a poor record as a senator. He decided to exploit the growing anti-communist paranoia for his own political advantage. He gained national attention by claiming that he had a list of 205 known communists in the US State Department. Though he failed to produce any real evidence, he struck a chord with Americans, and a great witch hunt against suspected communists was launched. McCarthy was encouraged by many figures in the Republican Party who saw his activities as a good way of undermining support for President Truman (see the cartoon). He was also supported by the FBI and its director, **Edgar Hoover**, and the FBI

gave him most of the material that he used in his Senate hearings.

Although one commentator noted that McCarthy could not tell the difference between Karl Marx and Groucho Marx, to millions of Americans he became the nation's defender against the communist menace. McCarthy greatly exaggerated the danger of domestic communism. His influence grew, and opinion polls showed that he had strong popular support. He used his position to attack his Democratic opponents and his intervention helped to ensure Eisenhower's victory in the 1952 election.

In 1953 he was appointed chairman of the Senate **Committee on Government Operations** and its **Subcommittee on Investigations.** He used this position to search for suspected communists throughout the US government.

"You Mean I'm Supposed To Stand On That?"

The term McCarthyism was first used in this 1950 cartoon by the famous political cartoonist Herbert Block. Leading Republicans were using McCarthy's actions to make the Republican Party more popular, which Block shows as the men dragging the elephant towards a platform made of buckets of tar, with 'McCarthyism' at the top. The symbol of the Republican Party is an elephant, and the men named in the cartoon were leading figures in the party

The Impact of the McCarthy Witch Hunt

Although there were communist spies in America, the vast majority of the victims of McCarthyism were innocent. Journalists, diplomats, authors, actors, trade unionists and scholars were called to testify in front of McCarthy's committee. Hundreds of 'little McCarthys' operated across the country. Government and business organisations called in experts to root out communists. People were fired and careers were ruined. Companies that refused to fire suspected communists could themselves be blacklisted. Little distinction was made between 'real' communists and people who held socialist or liberal views. It is difficult to estimate how many people were affected, but the number could be close to ten thousand. In 1954 the American Communist Party was declared illegal. The hysteria prevented much-needed social reforms in health and other areas as the country moved to the right.

McCarthy's attack had made him many enemies. Liberal Americans were worried that while the USA was defending freedom abroad it was being denied at home. Many in the Republican Party were annoyed at McCarthy's continuing attacks on the administration of President Eisenhower, a firm Republican. In 1954 McCarthy began an investigation into the army that was to lead to his political downfall. The army hit back with its own allegations and a Senate committee was set up to investigate the controversy. Watched by millions on TV, McCarthy was discredited as people saw his bullying tactics for the first time. He was becoming an embarrassment to the Republican Party. His political enemies acted and McCarthy was censured (criticised) by the Senate in December 1954. President Eisenhower, who detested McCarthy, referred to 'McCarthy*was*m' in conversation with a reporter.

Aside from the tragic domestic impact of the Second Red Scare, and especially McCarthyism, the anti-communist climate it created had a major influence on US foreign policy:

- Opposition to US policies in the Cold War left people open to the charge of supporting communism. It was now very difficult politically to challenge the basic assumptions of US foreign policy.

- It handed the USSR an excellent propaganda tool to use against the USA. It also made many Europeans critical of a country that had allowed this sort of hysteria to develop.

It was in this charged anti-communist atmosphere that the Korean War took place.

WHAT IMPACT DID THE KOREAN WAR (1950–1953) HAVE ON US FOREIGN POLICY?

Background

Korea had been ruled as a Japanese colony since 1910. At the end of World War II it was agreed that the Japanese would surrender the area south of the 38th Parallel to the USA and the area north of the 38th Parallel to the USSR. It had been intended that the division of the country would be temporary. Post-war elections, which would lead to reunification, were planned but they were not held in the North. After elections in the South, the US-backed **Republic of Korea**, led by **Syngman Rhee**, was established. The North became the Soviet-backed **Democratic People's Republic of Korea**, led by **Kim Il Sung**. With worsening relations between the superpowers, no agreement could be reached and the division became permanent.

In 1949, following a UN agreement, both the USA and the USSR pulled their troops out of the peninsula. Relations between North and South Korea were tense and there were frequent border clashes. In June 1950 troops from the North invaded the South in an attempt to reunify the country under communist control. Within weeks North Korea's forces controlled much of the peninsula except for an area around the city of **Pusan**.

The USA Intervenes

While historians still debate the role the Soviets played in the invasion, Truman and his administration were certain that the Soviets were behind the actions of the North Koreans.

After the 'loss' of China to communism, Truman took the view that the defeat of South Korea would be too great a blow to US prestige. It would also lead South Korea's allies to question the American commitment to resisting Soviet aggression. As far as the USA was concerned, communist aggression had to be resisted in Asia or the Soviets might be tempted to act in Europe. Truman decided to act to support the South Koreans.

The USA called for a meeting of the **UN Security Council**, which the Soviet Union was at the time boycotting over the issue of Chinese representation. With the Soviets absent the UN condemned the North Korean invasion.

Truman (left) with MacArthur during the Korean War. They were at odds about how the war should be fought. Truman later fired MacArthur for publicly opposing government policy

A UN military force was then sent to defend South Korea. This army contained men from sixteen nations, though most of the soldiers came from the USA, and was under the command of US World War II hero General **Douglas MacArthur**. In September 1950, MacArthur's forces made a daring landing at **Inchon** near the South Korean capital, Seoul. UN forces achieved complete success and routed the North Koreans.

China Intervenes

MacArthur then received permission from the Truman administration to cross the border to secure the final defeat of the North Koreans and the unification of the country. UN forces advanced

Troops of the US Army 31st Infantry Regiment land at Inchon Harbour, Korea, September 1950

quickly towards the border with China. The new communist Chinese government was worried about the American advance. It was also alarmed by the prospect of having US-controlled Korea on its border and feared an American-inspired attack from its defeated **Nationalist** enemies on **Taiwan**.

China had warned that it would intervene if the UN crossed the 38th Parallel. Truman was worried by the threat of Chinese intervention, but MacArthur dismissed the president's concerns. When UN troops were a few kilometres from **Yalu River**, which marked the border, China launched a massive counter-attack, driving the UN forces back across the 38th Parallel. After bitter fighting the front eventually stabilised near the original border.

MacArthur began publicly criticising the president's tactics of limiting the war to Korea. He called for expanding the war with attacks on China and enlisting the aid of the Nationalist Chinese. By criticising the president in this manner, MacArthur had challenged the principle of civilian control over the military: generals did not publicly criticise the president. Truman had no alternative but to replace him. In April 1951, ignoring the political risks of dismissing such a popular general, Truman replaced MacArthur with **General Matthew Ridgway**. MacArthur returned home to a hero's welcome and Truman's popularity plummeted. Against the backdrop of McCarthyism, the failure to achieve a military victory in Korea allowed the Republicans to attack Truman mercilessly.

The main events of the Korean War

1 *North Korean Offensive June– September 1950*
2 *UN Offensive September–October 1950*
3 *Chinese Offensive November– December 1950*
4 *The border in 1953*

The End of the Korean War

The hot summers and bitterly cold winters made fighting in Korea very difficult. Neither side was able to force the other to surrender. Trench conditions, similar to those of World War I, developed. The USA relied on air power to bomb North Korean targets, inflicting heavy civilian casualties.

In November 1951 peace talks began at **Panmunjon** but they dragged on for two years. The USSR did little to end the stalemate as Stalin was quite happy to see both the Chinese and the USA bogged down in Korea.

The victory of **Dwight D. Eisenhower** in the 1952 presidential election saw greater US urgency to end the war in Korea. In 1953 the new Eisenhower administration gave strong signals that the restrictions placed on US military actions, such as the unwillingness to attack China, might be lifted. There was even talk of the possibility of using nuclear weapons.

The crucial factor, though, was the death of Stalin in 1953. The new leadership in the USSR also wanted to end the war and it put pressure on the Chinese. On 27 July 1953 an armistice (ceasefire) was signed. A **Demilitarised Zone (DMZ)** was created along the 38th Parallel marking the border between South and North Korea.

Consequences of the Korean War

- Sandwiched between World War II and the Vietnam War, the Korean War is often referred to as the **Forgotten War** in the USA, but the war had been very costly in human lives. The total death toll was estimated to be about two and a half million people, most of whom were Korean civilians. US casualties, though far fewer, were proportionally far greater than in the Vietnam War. In three years over 33,000 US servicemen were killed and over 100,000 wounded.

- Because of the stalemate, dissatisfaction with the war grew in the USA. This, allied with his dismissal of MacArthur, contributed to the rising unpopularity of Truman. He did not stand for re-election in 1952. In the presidential campaign **Dwight D. Eisenhower** promised to end the deadlock and this pledge contributed to his victory. His first act as president was to visit Korea. The ending of the war in Korea made the new president very popular.

- Although unpopular at home, the war was another success for the American policy of **containment**. The USA had achieved its major aim – South Korea had been saved from a communist takeover.

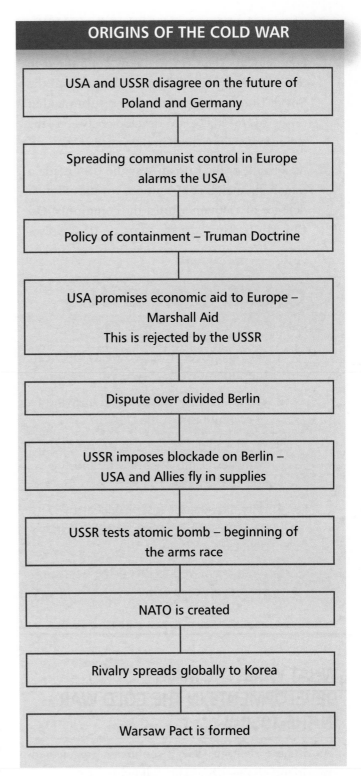

ORIGINS OF THE COLD WAR

USA and USSR disagree on the future of Poland and Germany

Spreading communist control in Europe alarms the USA

Policy of containment – Truman Doctrine

USA promises economic aid to Europe – Marshall Aid
This is rejected by the USSR

Dispute over divided Berlin

USSR imposes blockade on Berlin – USA and Allies fly in supplies

USSR tests atomic bomb – beginning of the arms race

NATO is created

Rivalry spreads globally to Korea

Warsaw Pact is formed

- The war had demonstrated that the Cold War was no longer confined to Europe – it had gone global. The USA was now committed to the defence of both Europe and Asia from the Soviet Union and its allies. The result was that crises were likely to develop between the superpowers anywhere in the world.

- As a result of the Korean War the USA made a major financial contribution to the French defence of Vietnam against the communist **Ho Chi Minh**. This was the start of US involve- ment in Vietnam, which we will read about in the next chapter.

- The war saw a massive rise in defence spending. Between 1950 and 1953, the USA's defence budget grew from $14 billion to $44 billion. This resulted in an economic boom that saw incomes rise and unemployment fall. The war also contributed greatly to the economies of both Japan and West Germany, which supplied war material to the Americans.

QUESTIONS

1 How did an arms race develop between the superpowers?

2 What factors contributed to growing fear of communism in the USA?

3 What role did the House Un-American Activities Committee play during the Red Scare?

4 Why did Senator Joseph McCarthy become such an important figure in US politics?

5 What events led to McCarthy's censure by the Senate in 1954?

6 Explain the origins of the Korean War.

7 Why did the Chinese intervene in the Korean War?

8 What caused Truman to remove MacArthur as commander?

9 What factors contributed to the end of the war in 1953?

10 What impact did the war have on the USA?

WHAT WERE THE MAIN DEVELOPMENTS IN THE COLD WAR IN THE 1950s?

As we have seen, in 1952 Eisenhower was elected president of the USA. The following year saw a change in the political leadership of the USSR: Stalin died and was succeeded by **Nikita Khrushchev**. Khrushchev's rule saw an easing of control over the lives of Soviet citizens. In 1956, at a Communist Party congress, Khrushchev denounced Stalin's brutal regime and called for reform. His new foreign policy approach talked of **peaceful co-existence** with the West, and he argued for non-violent competition between communism and capitalism.

This new attitude encouraged opposition groups to press for changes in the communist-controlled states of Eastern Europe (known to the Americans as **Soviet satellites**). However, a basic principle of Soviet foreign policy was the belief that the security of the USSR depended on '**friendly governments**' in Eastern Europe. 'Friendly' meant communist, and Khrushchev was not prepared to tolerate any reforms that might lead to political change away from communism. The most dramatic demonstration of this determination to maintain Soviet control occurred in **Hungary** where the Soviets intervened to crush an anti-communist revolt in 1956.

Despite appeals from the Hungarians for Western support, no help was forthcoming from the USA.

Nikita Khrushchev (1894–1971) was First Secretary of the Communist Party from 1953 to 1964. He had been one of Stalin's main advisers. In 1964, due partly to the Cuban Missile Crisis and failed economic reforms, he was removed from power and replaced by Leonid Brezhnev

President Eisenhower receives a replica of the Lunik II space probe from Khrushchev during the latter's state visit to the American capital, September 1959

Eisenhower was reluctant to intervene in the affairs of a Soviet satellite as to do so would lead to war. This established an unwritten rule of US policy during the Cold War that Eastern Europe was in the Soviet **sphere of influence**. While the USA might protest at the lack of democracy or Soviet actions there, it would not intervene to help countries resisting communism.

While opposing the spread of communism, especially in **Vietnam**, Eisenhower preferred to use diplomacy rather than confrontation in dealing with the Soviets. He met Khrushchev on a number of occasions and encouraged negotiations between the two countries.

His moderate policies and patient diplomacy left him open to criticism at home. Democrats accused Eisenhower of allowing a '**missile gap**' to develop with the USSR. This criticism grew after the launch of **Sputnik I** (see Chapter 12). But he refused to bow to demands for increased military spending. He made it clear that his goal was to end what he saw as a wasteful arms race, not to accelerate it. His cautious diplomacy led to a brief improvement in relations between the superpowers – or a **thaw** in the Cold War.

However, his policies received a severe blow in 1960 when a high-altitude **U-2** spy plane was shot down over the USSR. At first the USA denied any

knowledge of the flight, but in a major propaganda victory the Soviets presented evidence of the plane's wreckage as well as its pilot, **Francis Gary Powers**. The **U-2 incident** undermined a Paris summit between Khrushchev and Eisenhower several weeks later. Events in Berlin and Cuba were to make matters a lot worse.

Key Concept: The Military–Industrial Complex

This term refers to the combination of the US military, arms industry and politicians, which grew rapidly in scale and influence during the Cold War. The phrase was first used by **President Eisenhower** in his presidential farewell address in 1961.

He warned that the country 'must guard against the acquisition of unwarranted influence ... by the **military–industrial complex**. The potential for the disastrous rise of misplaced power exists and will persist.'

The term was commonly used by critics of US policy, especially during the **Vietnam War**. The allegation was that there was a conspiracy between the military, members of Congress and the defence industry to maintain tension and to create crises and even wars in order to increase defence spending and thereby profits. Politicians benefited through political donations from the defence industry.

WHY WAS THERE A SECOND CRISIS OVER BERLIN IN 1961?

During the 1950s West Germany had prospered under what became known as the '**economic miracle**'. In contrast, East Germany remained poor and nowhere was the difference between the two Germanies greater than in Berlin. The city was divided into West Berlin, under US, British and French control; and East Berlin, under Russian rule.

As it was easy to cross from East to West Berlin, thousands of East Germans took refuge in prosperous West Berlin and then travelled on to West Germany. Nearly three million people left between 1949 and 1961. The loss of these citizens, many of them skilled workers, undermined the economy of East Germany and damaged communist prestige.

Since 1958 Khrushchev had put pressure on the West to give up West Berlin, describing it as a '**hotbed of espionage**'. Eisenhower refused to budge and the matter was dropped.

In the 1960 presidential election, the Democrat **John F. Kennedy** defeated the Republican **Richard Nixon**. Khrushchev believed that the time was now ripe for a renewed campaign over Berlin. He thought that Kennedy was inexperienced and weak and would give in to pressure. He was also under pressure from the East Germans to stop the continued flow of people to the West.

In June 1961 a meeting between the two leaders in **Vienna** went badly. Khrushchev attempted to bully Kennedy, warning him that Warsaw Pact forces could invade West Berlin at any time. He issued an ultimatum – the issue of Berlin must be solved by December. Back in Moscow Khrushchev, confirmed in his impression of Kennedy, said that he didn't have 'the courage to stand up to a serious challenge'.

President Kennedy was shaken by the encounter with Khrushchev, but he was determined to stand firm and defend West Berlin. In July he announced that he could not 'permit the Communists to drive us out of Berlin, either gradually or by force'.

The Berlin Wall

As the crisis heated up during the summer of 1961, more and more East Germans fled to the West through Berlin. The East Germans put increased pressure on the Soviets to act, and on 13 August a barbed wire barrier was erected between East and West Berlin to stop the flight of people to the West. In the next few months a concrete wall 155 kilometres long was built around West Berlin. Anybody who tried to cross from East to West faced being shot on sight.

The building of the wall solved the crisis over Berlin. The flow of refugees stopped. The tension between the superpowers was defused as the USA signalled to the Soviets that they would not act to prevent the division of Berlin.

Nonetheless the Berlin Wall became the symbol of

President
Kennedy at
the Berlin
Wall in 1963.
US presidents
realised that
the Wall was
probably the
most effective
propaganda
weapon the
West had

East–West division. To the West it was seen as a prison (between 1961 and 1989 nearly two hundred people were killed trying to climb it). It represented the failure of the Communist system. It was also used by the USA as a major propaganda weapon during the Cold War.

WHY DID THE CUBAN MISSILE CRISIS BRING THE WORLD TO THE BRINK OF NUCLEAR WAR?

Events in Berlin heightened suspicions between the superpowers. This increased tension was to result in the most dangerous episode in the Cold War, the **Cuban Missile Crisis** of 1962. This thirteen-day crisis proved to be the biggest test of Kennedy's presidency as he struggled to find a peaceful solution with the Soviets.

Soviet Nuclear Weapons on Cuba

The island of Cuba is about 140 kilometres off the coast of Florida. It was a playground for rich Americans, and US companies controlled much of its economy. In 1959, **Fidel Castro** overthrew the military dictator, **General Batista**. A number of executions followed and thousands of Cubans fled to the USA. Castro's government nationalised American-owned companies. This led to considerable domestic pressure on the US government to act against Castro.

In response the **Eisenhower** administration introduced a trade embargo on Cuba. In 1961 President Kennedy approved a plan drawn up by Eisenhower's administration to help anti-Castro Cubans overthrow Castro. The CIA trained a force of 1,500 men who landed at the **Bay of Pigs**. The invasion was a complete failure and the US-backed forces were easily defeated. Kennedy, while approving the invasion, refused to offer any US military aid to help the invading force. This defeat was an embarrassing reverse for the Americans and for the president personally. Castro responded by declaring Cuba a socialist state.

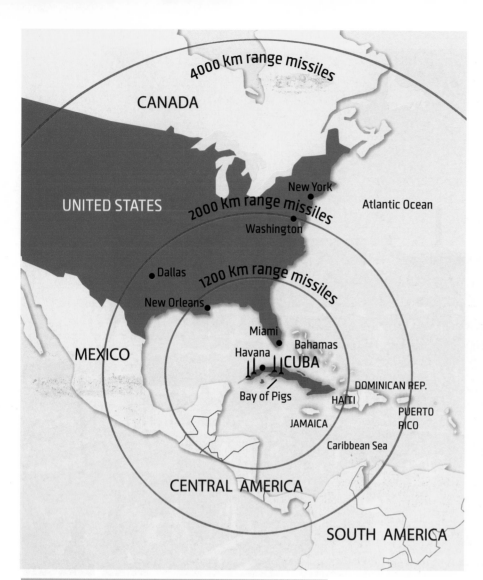

4000 km range missiles

CANADA

UNITED STATES

2000 km range missiles

New York

Atlantic Ocean

Washington

Dallas

1200 km range missiles

New Orleans

MEXICO

Miami

Havana

Bahamas

CUBA

Bay of Pigs

DOMINICAN REP.

HAITI

PUERTO RICO

JAMAICA

Caribbean Sea

CENTRAL AMERICA

SOUTH AMERICA

This map shows the full range of the nuclear missiles under construction in Cuba. It was used during the secret ExComm meetings on the Cuban crisis. Can you explain why the Americans saw the missiles as a threat?

- Intercontinental ballistic missiles (ICBMs) had a range of thousands of kilometres and could travel from one superpower to the other.
- Medium- or intermediate-range ballistic missiles (MRBMs or IRBMs) could travel about 2500 to 5000 kilometres (see Chapter 11).

The US government continued to work to over-throw Castro. He turned to the Soviet Union for military help. Khrushchev was delighted at the possibility of a communist ally in America's 'back-yard'. He decided to place medium-range nuclear missiles secretly on the island to defend it against

Fidel Castro in 1964. Castro was a controversial figure. To many he was a hero who stood up to the United States; to others he was a dictator and a dangerous communist revolutionary

US attack. The Soviets believed that unless they acted a US invasion was inevitable.

There was another reason for this decision. Khrushchev was conscious that the USA had far more ICBMs than the USSR. This left the USSR in a weak position. He saw a chance to catch up with the USA in the arms race. Medium-range missiles (of which the USSR had plenty) placed on Cuba would effectively become ICBMs. That would put most American cities, including Washington, within striking distance of Soviet missiles (see the map on the previous page). Castro reluctantly agreed to Khrushchev's proposal. Khrushchev thought he could keep the deployment secret until the missile bases became operational.

The Crisis Develops

The Americans quickly found out what was going on when the CIA monitored an increase in the number of Soviet ships heading for Cuba. On 14 October 1962 a U-2 spy plane took pictures of missile bases being constructed on the island.

The presence of Soviet missiles in the Caribbean less than 150km from its borders was completely unacceptable to the USA. To give them time to plan their response the Americans did not tell the USSR about their discovery. Kennedy formed a special cabinet of advisers – the Executive Committee of the National Security Council, or **ExComm** – to decide what action the USA would take. Kennedy was also aware that his popularity had sunk in the polls and he could not be seen to be weak on this threat to US security. For a week an intensive secret debate was held behind closed doors.

President Kennedy had **three** main options:
1   Bomb the missile sites
2   Invade Cuba
3   Blockade the island and prevent Soviet ships bringing weapons to Cuba.

At first he was tempted to launch an air strike but in the end he resisted calls from his generals for military action. He chose to blockade Cuba, or 'quarantine' it, as the Americans officially called their policy. In addition he moved troops to Florida and placed US forces around the world on alert. There were a number of reasons behind this decision:

- Quarantine put pressure on Khrushchev but it also allowed time for a diplomatic solution. Kennedy had decided that force would only be used as a last resort.

- Air strikes could lead to Soviet military retaliation that could quickly escalate into a full-scale nuclear war. The USA was also worried that the Soviets might lay siege to West Berlin.

An ExComm meeting in the White House during the Cuban Missile Crisis

- Military action could look like American bullying and lose the USA international diplomatic support.

On 22 October 1962, Kennedy told the world that the USSR was placing missiles on Cuba. He said that the US navy would stop and search all ships heading for Cuba, and he called on Khrushchev to 'halt and eliminate this clandestine [secret], reckless and provocative threat to world peace.'

The president's actions were strongly supported by both Britain and France. He also received unanimous support from the twenty members of the **Organization of American States**.

The End of the Crisis

The world held its breath as both superpowers seemed to be moving towards conflict. There was panic buying in the USA as people stocked up on food. On 24 October the crisis eased a little when on orders from Moscow the Soviet ships sailing to Cuba slowed down and stopped. The following day the UN Security Council debated the crisis in an emergency session.

Nonetheless, the missiles were still on Cuba and there was no sign of any willingness from the Soviets to remove them. On 26 October, a letter from the Russian leader offered to withdraw Soviet missiles from Cuba if the USA promised never to invade the island.

However, events were to get worse, and the following day, 27 October, was the worst day of the stand-off between the superpowers.

- That morning a second, more aggressive message was received from Khrushchev. It added another condition for the withdrawal of Soviet missiles: the USA was to publicly agree to remove all its missiles from **Turkey** (a US ally that bordered the Soviet Union).

- As Kennedy considered the options, a **U-2** spy plane was shot down over Cuba. The situation was so serious that **Robert McNamara**, the Secretary of Defence, later wrote: 'I walked out of the president's Oval Office and ... I thought I might never live to see another Saturday night.' The military wanted to bomb the missile sites but Kennedy wanted time to negotiate with Khrushchev.

The president's brother, Attorney General **Robert Kennedy**, met the Soviet Ambassador to the USA in secret. In return for Soviet missiles being removed from Cuba, the USA agreed not to invade Cuba and to withdraw their missiles from Turkey in six months. This US promise to withdraw missiles from Turkey was to be kept secret.

In a televised address on 22 October 1962, President Kennedy told the American people that there were missile sites on Cuba

Khrushchev was now extremely worried that the crisis was getting out of control. He agreed to pull Soviet missiles out of Cuba rather than risk war. On 28 October, the Soviets announced the withdrawal of their missiles from Cuba. The decision prompted Secretary of State **Dean Rusk** to comment, 'We are eyeball to eyeball, and the other fellow just blinked.' The crisis was over, but both sides were well aware how close they had come to nuclear annihilation.

The historian Arthur Schlesinger, who was an adviser to President Kennedy during the crisis, later wrote: 'This was not only the most dangerous moment in the Cold War. It was the most dangerous moment in history.'

The Impact of the Crisis

The ending of the crisis was a personal triumph for Kennedy and his approval ratings among the American public rose to well over 70 per cent.

In the words of historian Nigel Hamilton: 'In the greatest international crisis since World War II, Kennedy had shown firmness and great statesmanship ... ensuring the peaceful resolution of an extraordinary adventure' (Nigel Hamilton, *American Caesars*, p. 150).

Nonetheless, events in Cuba had shaken both Kennedy and Khrushchev as they both realised how close the world had come to nuclear war. Kennedy was determined to reduce the role of nuclear weapons in American foreign policy. Relations began to improve slowly as both men sought to improve relations. A feature of the crisis had been the absence of any direct means of communication between Kennedy and Khrushchev. Now a **hotline** was set up to facilitate direct communication between the Kremlin (the seat of Soviet government) and the White House during any future crisis.

Negotiations on limiting the testing of nuclear weapons were resumed. In 1961 the Soviet Union had exploded the largest bomb in history. Called the Tsar Bomba, its explosive power was 58 megatons – 4,000 times more powerful than the bomb dropped on Hiroshima. The environmental effect of the testing was an increasing cause of concern. To speed up agreement the USA dropped its demand for on-site inspections and permitted underground testing. After twelve days of negotiations a **Test Ban Treaty** was signed in 1963. The agreement banned testing in the atmosphere, underwater or in space. A start had been made on limiting the arms race between both countries.

COLD WAR RIVALS – LEADERS OF THE USA AND THE USSR			
USA		**USSR**	
Harry Truman	1945–53	Josef Stalin	1924–53
Dwight Eisenhower	1953–61	Nikita Khrushchev	1953–64
John F. Kennedy	1961–63		
Lyndon Johnson	1963–69	Leonid Brezhnev	1964–82
Richard Nixon	1969–74		
Gerald Ford	1974–77		
Jimmy Carter	1977–81		
Ronald Reagan	1981–89	Yuri Andropov	1982–84
		Konstantin Chernenko	1984–85
		Mikhail Gorbachev	1985–91

WHAT WERE THE MAIN DEVELOPMENTS IN US FOREIGN POLICY IN THE REST OF THE 1960s?

The USA was still as firmly committed to stopping the spread of communism, as was shown by events in Vietnam (see Chapter 7). A further area of rivalry between the superpowers developed. During the 1950s and 1960s the colonial empires of European countries in Asia and Africa, such as Britain's, gained their independence. This process, known as **decolonisation**, saw both sides look for allies among these new countries. The USA supported newly established governments that were anti-communist. However, some of these governments were very brutal and corrupt, especially in Africa.

In 1967 there was a renewal of the Arab–Israeli conflict when the **Six-Day War** erupted. The superpowers found themselves on opposite sides, with the USA strongly backing Israel and the USSR supporting the Arabs. This pattern was repeated in a renewal of hostilities between the Arabs and Israelis in 1973 that became known as the **Yom Kippur War**.

Eastern Europe, or the **Eastern Bloc**, remained firmly in the grip of the Soviets. Little freedom was allowed to the people there. This was clearly demonstrated in Czechoslovakia in 1968. A government led by **Alexander Dubček** brought in a number of reforms that became known as the **Prague Spring**. Alarmed, the Soviets sent in the tanks and removed Dubček. Apart from protesting at the Russian actions, the USA did nothing to help the Czechs.

However, during the 1960s the two superpowers had learned to tolerate each other and a new spirit of co-operation – **détente** – was to develop in the 1970s (see Chapter 8).

QUESTIONS

1 What was the USA's reaction to events in Hungary in 1956?

2 How did relations with the USSR develop under Eisenhower?

3 What was Khrushchev's attitude to the new US President, John F. Kennedy?

4 Why did a crisis erupt over Berlin in 1961?

5 What was the propaganda impact of the Berlin Wall?

6 What actions did the USA take against Fidel Castro and his government in Cuba?

7 Why did Kennedy decide to blockade Cuba rather than attack the island?

8 What evidence is there to show that the crisis over the Cuban missiles was very serious? How was the crisis resolved?

9 'President Kennedy showed great leadership during the crisis.' Do you agree? Support your answer with evidence.

10 Outline examples of improved USA–USSR relations after the crisis.

11 What happened in Czechoslovakia in 1968?

US FOREIGN POLICY 1945–1972 TIMELINE

Note: some of the events listed here are covered in Chapter 7.

1945	Yalta Conference
	Potsdam Conference
	Atomic bombs dropped on Japan
1945–48	Soviet Union establishes communist governments in Bulgaria, Romania,Hungary, Czechoslovakia, Poland
1946	Churchill's 'Iron Curtain' speech
1947	Truman Doctrine announced
	Marshall Plan proposed
1948	Eastern Europe under Communist control
	Berlin Blockade begins
1949	NATO established
	Berlin Blockade ends
	USSR tests its first atomic bomb
	Communists come to power in China: opponents flee to Taiwan
1950	Korean War begins when the North invades the South
	UN sends troops
1952	USA tests the first hydrogen bomb
1953	Death of Stalin
	Korean War ends
1954	French surrender at Dien Bien Phu
	Geneva Accords divide Vietnam into North and South
1955	West Germany joins NATO
	Warsaw Pact established
1956	Hungarian uprising crushed by Soviet troops
1957	USSR tests the first ICBM
	Sputnik I (the first satellite) launched
1961	Crisis over Berlin leads to the Berlin Wall being built around the Western Zones
1962	Cuban Missile Crisis
1963	US–Soviet hotline established
	Test Ban Treaty bans atmospheric testing of nuclear weapons
1964	Gulf of Tonkin incident
	Khrushchev removed as Soviet leader; succeeded by Leonid Brezhnev
1965	US combat troops sent to Vietnam
1968	Tet offensive in Vietnam
	Warsaw Pact forces invade Czechoslovakia

DOCUMENT

The following is an excerpt from a memo presented to President Eisenhower summarising opinion polls taken about the Korean War. Study it and answer the questions that follow.

Memorandum on Recent Polls on Korea

1. Truce Along Present Line

US Success or Failure (mid-May 1953)

'If we do get a truce in Korea along the present battle line, would it seem to you that we had generally succeeded or generally failed in our main purpose in going into Korea?'

Generally Succeeded	45%
Generally Failed	38%
No opinion	17%

2. Korea Worthwhile?

'As things stand now, do you feel that the war in Korea had been worth fighting, or not?'

	Oct 1952	Nov 1952	Jan 1953	April 1953
Worth fighting	32%	34%	39%	36%
Not worth fighting	56	58	52	55
No opinion	12	8	9	9

Source: Dwight D. Eisenhower Presidential Library, http://www.eisenhower.utexas.edu/research/online_documents/korean_war/Public_Opinion_1953_06_02.pdf

1 DOCUMENT QUESTIONS

a) What was the main purpose of the USA in going into Korea? Did people think the USA had succeeded?

b) From the polls, what was the attitude of the US people to whether the fighting in Korea was worthwhile? Give evidence to support your answer.

c) Given the results of the polls, what advice would you have given the president about the war in Korea? Support your answer with evidence.

2 ORDINARY LEVEL QUESTIONS

a) How did President Harry Truman conduct foreign affairs between 1945 and1953? (Leaving Cert 2012)

b) How did Senator Joe McCarthy influence the direction of foreign policy in the United States? (Leaving Cert 2007)

c) How did Joe McCarthy contribute to a 'red scare' in the USA? (Leaving Cert 2013)

d) What problems did one or more of the following pose for the USA: Berlin; Korea; Cuba? (Leaving Cert 2013)

e) How did President Kennedy deal with the Cuban Missile Crisis?

3 HIGHER LEVEL ESSAYS

a) How did McCarthyism affect US foreign policy? (Amended Leaving Cert 2007)

b) What was the importance for US foreign policy of one or more of the following: Berlin; Korea; Cuba? (Leaving Cert 2010)

c) What were the main international challenges facing the USA between 1945 and 1962?

d) How successfully did President Kennedy handle relations with the USSR?

e) How did relations between the superpowers develop during the 1960s?

L.B. Johnson and the Vietnam War 1963–1968 (Case Study)

KEY QUESTIONS

North and South Vietnam and south-east Asia. Can you suggest, with evidence from the map, why the USA was keen to stop the communists taking control of South Vietnam?

Vietnam is nearly 15,000 kilometres from the west coast of America. During Lyndon Johnson's term as president, the USA committed more and more ground troops to a struggle in this distant country. By 1968, over 500,000 American troops were helping South Vietnam try to defeat a communist guerrilla campaign. A conflict that devastated one nation and divided another, Vietnam brought a new dimension to the Cold War. It forced the United States to re-think its goals in that struggle.

WHY DID THE USA BECOME INVOLVED IN VIETNAM?

Colonial Background

Vietnam became a French colony in the 1860s. It was part of **French Indochina**, which also included **Cambodia** and **Laos**. The majority of the Vietnamese never accepted French rule.

By the 1930s, the anti-French resistance was led by the communists. Their leader, **Ho Chi Minh**, was a dedicated communist and nationalist who believed it was his duty to liberate Vietnam from French colonial rule.

When Japan occupied Vietnam during World War II, Ho Chi Minh and his organisation, the **Vietnam Independence League (Vietminh** for short), were soon fighting the Japanese. As he was opposing the Japanese he received aid from both the Chinese and the USA. The US president, **Franklin Roosevelt**, disliked European colonialism and opposed returning Indochina to French control after the war. The emergence of the Cold War would cause a shift in the US position.

Vietnam after World War II

In 1945, following Japan's surrender, the Vietminh seized control in the north of the country and declared an independent **Democratic Republic of Vietnam (DRV)**. The Vietminh then began brutally establishing a communist regime in areas under their control.

As France was a US ally in the emerging Cold War, US policy changed. It now supported the French attempt to recover their colony. Although the French succeeded in driving the Vietminh from the southern cities, France had been shattered by World War II and was simply not strong enough to restore control over its former subjects. The Vietminh were supported by China, which was under communist control from 1949.

US Support for France

In 1950, the USA started to support the French with financial aid. By 1954, the USA was paying 80 per cent of France's costs in the bitter struggle against the Vietminh. The USA also sent a number of advisers to help the French.

US actions were strongly influenced by the **Cold War**. As both France and the USA were members of NATO, the USA felt it had to support its ally. The **Eisenhower** administration viewed **Ho Chi Minh** and the Vietminh as part of the world communist bloc. The USA believed the French position that the Vietminh were simply another part of the

Ho Chi Minh

Ho Chi Minh (1890–1969) lived in France after World War I and was a founding member of the French Communist Party. His birth name was Nguyen Sinh Cung, but during the struggle against the Japanese he adopted the name Ho Chi Minh, which translates as 'bringer of light'.

Dedicated to the cause of Vietnamese independence, he was prepared to fight as long as it took, whatever the cost. The French and the USA both thought that their military superiority would defeat Ho Chi Minh quickly. They were to be proved wrong.

In 1946, when war with the French loomed, he warned them, 'You can kill ten of my men for every one I kill of yours, yet even at those odds, you will lose and I will win.'

international communist conspiracy, and tools of the Kremlin. Obsessed with the Cold War, US policy-makers did not understand that, as well as being a communist, Ho Chi Minh was also the leader of a nationalist movement.

The Americans concluded that preventing a communist takeover in Vietnam was vital for US interests in Asia. They feared that if Vietnam was lost, other non-communist states in the region – **Thailand**, **Burma**, **Indonesia**, **Malaysia**, **Laos**, **Cambodia** and **India** – would also be vulnerable to communist takeover. This belief became known as the '**domino theory**', a theory that was to influence US actions throughout its involvement in Vietnam.

The Division of Vietnam

Unfortunately for the USA, France was losing the war in Vietnam. In 1954, its army suffered a severe military setback when French forces surrounded at **Dien Bien Phu** were forced into a humiliating surrender. This defeat marked the end of France's involvement in Vietnam. France withdrew its forces from the country.

Negotiations led to the **Geneva Accords**, agreed in 1954. The country was divided along the **17th Parallel** into North and South Vietnam. This division was supposed to be temporary until elections leading to unification were held throughout Vietnam.

The elections were never held. They were opposed by the USA, which felt that the communists would win. Instead, the USA decided to convert South Vietnam into a fully functioning independent state. This policy resulted in growing US involvement in Vietnamese affairs.

Outbreak of Civil War in South Vietnam

The USA installed the Vietnamese nationalist **Ngo Dinh Diem** as ruler of South Vietnam. He had opposed French rule, but was also strongly anti-communist. His regime received massive financial support from the USA, which poured over $1 billion of aid into the country. Vietnam was soon the largest overseas recipient of US aid.

Despite US support, Diem's regime was unpopular among many Vietnamese. Backed by the Catholic minority, it discriminated against the Buddhist majority. It also postponed land reform, which lost it support among peasants.

In 1959, taking advantage of the unpopularity of Diem's government, the Northern government ordered the Vietminh in the south to resume guerrilla action. The aim was to reunify the country under communist control. Anti-Diem forces were

French prisoners of war march into captivity after their defeat at Dien Bien Phu, 1954

Ngo Dinh Diem (1901–1963) was an opponent of French colonial rule. The Americans hoped that he would help save Vietnam from communism. They did not listen to the French, who described him 'as not only incapable but mad'

reorganised into the **National Liberation Front for South Vietnam**. The Americans began calling this army the **Vietcong**. The Vietcong were soon launching guerrilla-style attacks on the **South Vietnamese Army** (also known as **ARVN**).

JFK and Vietnam

When **John F. Kennedy** became president in 1961, he accepted the Eisenhower administration's views on Vietnam. He agreed with the domino theory, and believed that the USA must contain communism in Asia. He ignored the unpopularity of the Diem regime. He saw the confrontation in the country in terms of 'Communism versus Democracy'. Like his predecessor, this led him to greatly underestimate the support for unity in both parts of Vietnam.

Kennedy increased the USA's financial and military commitment. In May 1961, he sent 400 of the elite **Green Berets** to help the South Vietnamese Army defeat the National Liberation Front. He also urged Diem to introduce reforms. Diem, refusing to be a puppet of the USA, declined. The USA was reluctant to be seen to force him and did not press the issue.

The Vietcong proved elusive and dangerous opponents. Their supply chain from the North was

A young Buddhist monk burns himself to death in protest at the policies of Diem's government

QUESTIONS

1 Explain why Ho Chi Minh came to prominence in Vietnam.

2 What happened in North Vietnam at the end of World War II?

3 Why did US policy towards Vietnam change after World War II?

4 Explain the domino theory.

5 What was the significance of the French defeat at Dien Bien Phu?

6 What peace deal was agreed concerning Vietnam at Geneva?

7 How did the USA support South Vietnam?

8 Why did Diem's regime prove unpopular?

9 What was the aim of the North in encouraging a communist revolt in South Vietnam?

10 What was Kennedy's attitude to the events in Vietnam?

11 Outline the events that led to the downfall of Diem's government.

---

along the **Ho Chi Minh trail**. This was a dirt track through neutral Laos and Cambodia that linked North and South Vietnam. Men, supplies and weapons passed along this trail to support the Vietcong in the South.

In 1963, the unpopularity of Diem's regime was clearly demonstrated when anti-Diem riots spread throughout South Vietnam. The mainly Buddhist demonstrators were demanding the removal of Diem and unification with the North. The army cracked down harshly and their leaders were arrested.

Kennedy was worried by the growing Diem–Buddhist confrontation, as it seemed to threaten the US objective of preserving South Vietnam as a pro-US state. The regime was so discredited that the USA urged army officers to overthrow Diem. Diem was subsequently murdered and a military government came to power in Saigon. This was the first of a series of military takeovers during the next ten years that were to increase instability in South Vietnam.

By the time of Kennedy's assassination in 1963, the USA was being drawn more deeply into the intensifying civil war in Vietnam. There were 16,500 US military advisers in Vietnam and this involvement was to escalate greatly under Kennedy's successor, Lyndon B. Johnson.

HOW DID US INVOLVEMENT IN VIETNAM ESCALATE?

Johnson's Attitude to Vietnam

Lyndon B. Johnson was not as experienced in international affairs as his predecessor John F. Kennedy. He had also been suddenly thrust into the job by Kennedy's assassination. He believed that he had to continue Kennedy's policies and accepted the domino theory. He retained most of Kennedy's advisers, including Secretary of Defense **Robert McNamara** and Secretary of State (foreign minister) **Dean Rusk**.

He turned to them for advice. Both were anti-communist and felt that South Vietnam had to be protected against a communist takeover. They worried about the damage to US prestige internationally if the USA were defeated or pulled out of Vietnam. They felt that the USSR would take advantage of such American weakness to make gains elsewhere. Not only could defeat in Vietnam trigger a collapse of non-communist governments in the region, but it might lead to communist attacks on other US interests in Asia, such as Taiwan or Japan. Therefore, by this logic, South Vietnam could not be abandoned. Johnson agreed with McNamara and Rusk's views. In a TV interview on 15 March 1964, given soon after becoming president, Johnson outlined his support of the domino theory. Here is an extract of what he said:

> **Mr Sevareid:** *'Mr Kennedy said, on the subject of Vietnam, I think, that he did believe in the "falling domino" theory, that if Vietnam were lost, other countries in the area would soon be lost.'*
>
> **The President:** *'I think it would be a very dangerous thing, and I share President Kennedy's view, and I think the whole of South-East Asia would be involved and that would involve hundreds of millions of people, and I think it's – it cannot be ignored, we must do everything that we can, we must be responsible, we must stay there and help them, and that is what we are going to do.'*
>
> Source: *The Pentagon Papers*, Gravel Edition, Vol. 3

Johnson also feared that any sign of weakness could be exploited by his Republican opponents in the forthcoming presidential election. He had to be seen to act tough.

Johnson did have deep misgivings, however. He was more interested in his domestic reforms. He did not want war in Vietnam – which he called 'that raggedy-ass little fourth-rate country' – to distract resources and energy from the **Great Society reforms** (see page 23) he hoped to introduce in the USA.

He decided to fight a limited war that would force the North Vietnamese to accept a negotiated peace and preserve the independence of South Vietnam. He ignored his more aggressive advisers and rejected any moves that might bring the Chinese, or even the Soviets, into the war. American military strength was so overwhelming that it seemed victory might not take so long to achieve.

However, Johnson found himself being drawn step by step into a full-scale war.

The Gulf of Tonkin Incident

The event that triggered this escalation was the **Gulf of Tonkin incident**. In August 1964, the USS *Maddox*, an American destroyer (warship) on patrol in the Gulf of Tonkin off the coast of Vietnam, exchanged fire with North Vietnamese torpedo boats. Two days later, in poor weather, the ship's captain reported that he was under attack again. Despite conflicting evidence, the USA insisted that

Johnson and his cabinet at a meeting in 1965

there had been a second unprovoked attack. It is widely accepted today that the second attack never happened and that faulty radar was to blame.

The next day, Johnson persuaded Congress to pass a resolution empowering him to protect American lives in Vietnam. The **Gulf of Tonkin Resolution** allowed the President to take 'all necessary steps' to defend the forces of the United States and its allies. As a result, US involvement in Vietnam grew – without a formal declaration of war. Johnson ordered bombing attacks on North Vietnamese military targets. The American bombings triggered a huge increase in the numbers joining the Vietcong.

At the time Johnson's actions were very popular. A poll taken on 10 August 1964 showed that 85 per cent of Americans supported his handling of the incident.

Johnson still did not want to commit ground forces to Vietnam. He sent more advisers to the country and put pressure on the South Vietnamese to make their regime more popular. During the 1964 presidential election, Johnson portrayed himself as a moderate, and labelled his Republican opponent **Barry Goldwater** an extremist. While Goldwater argued for increased US involvement in Vietnam, Johnson declared that he was not willing 'to send American boys nine or ten thousand miles away from home to do what Asian boys ought to be doing for themselves'.

Johnson won the election with a landslide, the largest ever achieved by a US president.

Operation Rolling Thunder

What the American people did not know was that Johnson was waiting until the election was over to implement the very policies his Republican opponent advocated. He and his military advisers had decided to escalate their efforts in Vietnam. More troops would be committed and they were secretly planning a massive bombing offensive to end communist attacks on the South. It was hoped that the attacks would stabilise the South and force the North to cease supporting the Vietcong and negotiate. Bombing was also seen as less likely to cost American lives and money.

The Americans had to be careful, though, not to provoke Chinese intervention or damage relations with the USSR. Bombing was prohibited within 40km of the Chinese border and 16km of Hanoi. Much to the annoyance of the military, air bases could not be attacked for fear of killing Soviet technicians who operated the anti-aircraft SAM (Surface to Air Missiles) sites.

In February 1965, Johnson authorised an aggressive bombing campaign against North Vietnam, which became known as **Operation Rolling Thunder**. Originally intended to last eight weeks, this operation continued for three years. Bombing raids rose from a hundred a month in March 1965 to 12,000 by September 1966. The

B52s bombing Vietnam. A B52D bomber carried 25,000kg of bombs. The planes were a particular object of hate for the anti-war movement in the USA

tonnage dropped exceeded that dropped on Germany, Japan and Italy during World War II.

The bombing failed to weaken Northern support for the communist guerrillas in the South. In fact it had the opposite effect, stiffening their will to fight. It did not disrupt the flow of men or material to the Vietcong. The bombing also provided the North with a massive propaganda weapon to use against the USA, as over 50,000 civilians were killed in the attacks.

The Soviets also took advantage of US actions in Vietnam to discredit the USA internationally. Although careful not to get dragged into the conflict, they supported North Vietnam throughout the war, supplying military aid, training and advisers as well as diplomatic support and economic aid.

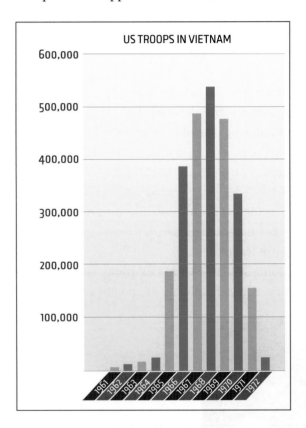

US TROOPS IN VIETNAM

The First US Troops Arrive

It soon became clear that bombing alone would not defeat the Vietcong and the North Vietnamese. Johnson became convinced that US soldiers would be needed on the ground if the South was to survive. In March 1965 a request was received from the US commander in Vietnam, **General William Westmoreland**, to protect **Da Nang** air-base. In response, marines were sent there.

There were requests for more troops and the following month a further 20,000 were sent. By the end of the year there were 200,000 American soldiers in Vietnam. In 1968, the number stationed in Vietnam reached over 500,000. These troops would form part of the estimated 2.7 million soldiers who served in Vietnam on a revolving basis.

While two-thirds of the troops in Vietnam were volunteers, one-third of the soldiers were conscripted or **drafted** for a one-year tour of duty. The draft system was seen by many to be unfair. It was relatively easy for the wealthy to avoid the draft by going to university, leaving the country or enlisting in the **National Guard** (a reserve force). Out of the ten recent presidential candidates who were eligible for the draft, eight managed to avoid it, including **Bill Clinton** and **George Bush Jr**. This meant that the majority of US troops in Vietnam were working-class whites, or members of the African-American or Hispanic communities.

WHAT WAS THE NATURE OF THE FIGHTING IN VIETNAM?

Difficult Conditions

After suffering tremendous losses fighting US troops in open pitched battles, the communists were forced to change tactics. The Americans now found the **Vietcong** and the **North Vietnamese Army** very elusive enemies.

The Vietcong attacked the South Vietnamese Army and retreated into the jungle or the mountains before the US forces arrived. Trails through the countryside and villages were booby-trapped or mined. Guerrillas disguised as peasants launched surprise attacks or attacked from tunnels.

This made fighting for the American soldiers very difficult. They went on 'search and destroy' missions to defeat the Vietcong. However, these missions often resulted in the deaths of innocent civilians as well as Vietcong guerrillas. As one marine captain explained, 'You never knew who the enemy was and who the friend was. They all looked alike. They all dressed alike.' One marine officer admitted that **civilians** 'were usually

American troops relied heavily on helicopters during the fighting in Vietnam. These allowed for rapid movement of troops to where they were needed, allowing soldiers to ride into battle (like aerial cavalry). They could also attack the enemy on the ground with rocket and gun fire

counted as enemy dead, under the unwritten rule "If he's dead and Vietnamese, he's VC [Vietcong].'"

To remove the dense jungle cover used by the Vietcong guerrillas, the USA decided to destroy vegetation by using **herbicides** (toxic substances). They also targeted crops that were used to feed the Vietcong. The most famous of these herbicides was **Agent Orange**. During the war, about 10 per cent of the land area of Vietnam was sprayed with chemicals, of which 66 per cent was Agent Orange. The use of these chemicals was very controversial and they have had harmful long-term effects on both Vietnamese civilians and US army veterans.

Controversially, the USA also made use of **napalm** and **phosphorous bombs** against the Vietcong guerrillas. These weapons caused terrible burn injuries and they often killed or wounded civilians.

Falling Morale

Far away from home, fighting an unseen enemy and unable to distinguish friend from foe, the soldiers' morale began to crack. Matters were made worse by the weather. It was hot and humid during the day, and night time brought swarms of mosquitoes which attacked the sleeping soldiers.

Clear evidence of this collapse in morale could be seen in increased desertion from the army and drug use by soldiers.

- Going AWOL (Absent Without Official Leave) rose dramatically. At the height of the war, on

A wounded Marine being led past his comrade after a fierce firefight

The Ho Chi Minh trail

US troops interrogate a Vietcong prisoner. Note that he is not wearing a uniform

average one soldier went AWOL every three minutes.

- Surveys suggested that over 30 per cent of American troops had tried hard drugs (heroin or cocaine), and over 60 per cent had smoked marijuana. Vietcong spies often sold marijuana cigarettes laced with heroin in the hope of making US soldiers addicted.

Many soldiers now had only one aim: to survive their one-year term in Vietnam. They tried to minimise their contact with the enemy. '**Fragging**', the practice of using fragmentation grenades to kill unpopular officers, became common (see slang phrases, page 113). During the war an estimated 600 officers were murdered by their own men. There was also considerable racial tension between white and black troops that sometimes led to racially motivated gun battles.

Opposition to the war was growing at home too.

WHAT FACTORS LED TO THE GROWTH OF THE ANTI-WAR MOVEMENT?

Anti-War Protests

Opposition to the war began in America's universities as a reaction to the bombing of North Vietnam. In the 1960s, there was a new mood in society and students were unwilling to readily accept the 'establishment position' (see Chapter 9). This was clearly shown in their attitude to the war. Marathon '**teach-ins**' began throughout American universities, stressing the errors of US policy. The action escalated with rallies and the burning of draft cards. Angry students chanted, '**Hell, no, we won't go!**'

The first protests were organised by socialists and pacifists, but as US involvement escalated, more and more people, alarmed about their government's policies, began to support the anti-war movement.

The Media and the War

A very important source of anti-war feeling was the media. Some historians suggest that the negative media image of the war in many ways caused the American defeat in Vietnam.

The press had always reported on wars, but rarely had it been given such unrestricted access to the battle zones as in Vietnam. There was no censorship of news reports from the battle fronts. Reporting the war was dangerous and 75 journalists were killed while working on the war in Vietnam.

At first, most journalists accepted the government's view of the conflict. As the war dragged on,

however, a growing number began to doubt the official line. They felt that they had been fooled by government assurances that the war was being won. Influential newspapers and magazines, such as the *New York Times*, the *Washington Post*, *Newsweek*, *Time* and *Life* started to criticise the government, as did many programmes on television and radio.

TV played a crucial role in changing popular opinion. It brought the war into nearly every living room in the USA. Viewing the war and the slaughter every evening turned many viewers against the conflict. **Dean Rusk** pointed out at the time: 'This was the first struggle fought on television in everybody's living room every day ... whether ordinary people can sustain a war effort under that kind of daily hammering is a very large question.'

Growing Opposition

Martin Luther King (see page 189), **Norman Mailer** (page 191) and a host of other prominent figures condemned the war. King said that the war wasted lives and misused American resources. **Muhammad Ali** (see page 192) refused to serve in the army. Stripped of his heavyweight title as a result, he became one of the most prominent figures in the anti-war movement. Many in the civil rights movement protested at what they alleged were the disproportionate number of black Americans in the US army in Vietnam (statistically this was not the case). They saw it as a 'white man's war but the black man's fight'. One popular quote at the time was: 'No Vietcong ever called me Nigger.'

Divisions began to emerge in the president's own Democratic Party. A growing number of congressmen were doubtful of the president's assurances that everything was going to plan. Johnson's popularity sank.

Events on the battlefield reinforced this growing disillusionment. While US forces frequently defeated their foes in open battle, final victory was proving very difficult to achieve.

Furthermore, the tactics that were being used by the US army shocked many people. Civilian casualties mounted as American troops reacted indiscriminately to attacks. 'In order to save the village, it was necessary to destroy it,' one officer told a reporter. The public were appalled by the **My Lai massacre** of March 1968, in which 347 men, women and children were murdered by troops under the command of **Lieutenant William Calley**. He was later tried and imprisoned for the massacre.

Diplomacy

While the fighting went on, both sides looked to diplomacy to advance their aims. Scores of diplomatic initiatives were taken between 1964 and 1968, but all failed. Both sides had completely different aims:

- Johnson insisted on an independent South Vietnam.
- North Vietnam demanded a Vietnam unified under its control.

Johnson ordered reductions or suspensions of the bombing while discussions took place. The longest pause took place over Christmas 1965. These gestures made no difference.

The communists took advantage of the lulls in the bombing to improve their position on the battlefield – a policy they called '**talking while fighting**'. Johnson later estimated that he had been involved in seventy efforts at negotiation with the Hanoi government during his term of office.

WHAT WAS THE IMPORTANCE OF THE TET OFFENSIVE?

The turning point of the war came in 1968. The view of the majority of Americans that they were winning the war was shattered by events in Vietnam. On 30 January, the Vietcong and the North Vietnamese Army launched an offensive against cities throughout the South. As the attack was launched during the **Vietnamese New Year** celebration, or **Tet** holiday period, it became known as the **Tet Offensive**. It was hoped that the timing would achieve maximum surprise.

Dramatically, during the fighting in **Saigon**, the US embassy was attacked. The ancient royal capital of **Hue**, which was temporarily captured by the communists, was also the scene of heavy fighting. However, there was no general uprising against the USA, and the South Vietnamese Army fought back strongly. After a few weeks the Americans and their allies regained control.

American soldiers developed their own slang during the fighting in Vietnam. Here are some examples:

gung ho	enthusiastic or committed (Chinese phrase)
fragging	assassination of an unpopular officer by his own men (usually using a fragmentation grenade)
Charlie/Gook/VC	slang terms for a Vietnamese
grunt	nickname for an American soldier in Vietnam

A US marine drags a wounded comrade from the ruins of the Citadel at Hue during the Tet Offensive

- In strictly military terms the USA had won an overwhelming victory. The Tet Offensive was a total military defeat for the North. It is estimated that about 70 per cent of the men committed to the battle, about 58,000 men, were killed.

- However, politically it was a spectacular defeat for the USA. Images of the fighting in Vietnam were to have a profound effect on opinion in the USA. The sight of Vietcong guerrillas in the US embassy shocked Americans. The Vietcong had penetrated the very heart of US power in Vietnam. The American people had also seen the fighting in all its gory detail.

Many agreed with respected TV reporter Walter Cronkite of CBS, who said, 'What the hell is going on? I thought we were winning the war.' In a broadcast watched by nine million people, he argued that the USA should seek an honourable way out of the conflict, 'not as victors, but as an honourable people who lived up to their pledge to defend democracy and did the best they could'. Johnson, watching the programme, commented that if he had lost Cronkite he had lost Middle (moderate) America.

Some leading officials in the administration lost faith in their own policy in Vietnam. Secretary of Defense McNamara, disillusioned by the progress of the war, resigned to take a job as head of the World Bank. The new Secretary of Defense, **Clark Clifford**, advised Johnson to reconsider US policy on Vietnam. He gathered a group of distinguished elder statesmen and former Generals to advise on future US policy. Known as the '**Wise Men**', they recommended that the USA withdraw from Vietnam.

Walter Cronkite reports on Tet Offensive, Vietnam, 1968

Public Support and the Vietnam War

The Tet Offensive of 1968 had undermined support for both the war and the president (see the table).

Johnson was very conscious of this change in popular opinion and it influenced his decision not to seek re-election.

Johnson's Resignation

Demonstrations against the war intensified after the Tet Offensive. The war had damaged Johnson's personal reputation and he was unable to travel anywhere without chants of, 'Hey, hey, LBJ, how many kids did you kill today?'

EFFECT OF THE TET OFFENSIVE			
Question	Pre-Tet	Post-Tet	Change
Approves Johnson's handling of job as president	48%	36%	−12
Approves Johnson's handling of Vietnam	39%	26%	−13

Source: www.digitalhistory.uh.edu/

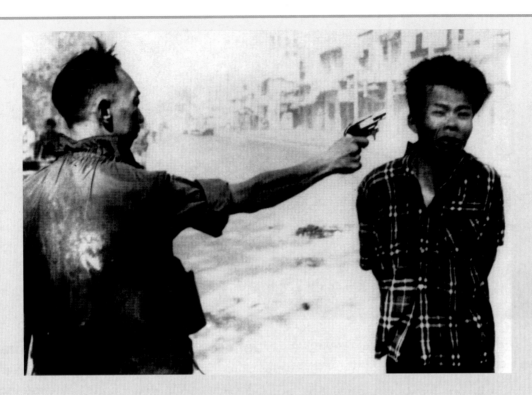

A Defining Anti-War Photograph

This is a very famous award-winning picture taken during the Tet Offensive. It shows Vietcong guerrilla captain Nguyen Van Lem being executed without trial by the chief of police General Nguyen Ngoc Loan.

This single picture caused many Americans to question why they were supporting South Vietnam. If this was happening on camera, what was happening off camera? It greatly strengthened the anti-war movement and became an anti-war icon. The general's action seemed to justify opposition to the war.

However, throughout the war both sides were guilty of massacres and acts of brutality. During the occupation of Hue in 1968, the communists had killed an estimated 5,000 civilians suspected of being supporters of the South Vietnamese regime. Lem was shot because the General believed he had been involved in the massacre of a number of civilians.

The photographer Eddie Adams regretted that the photograph had turned people against the war. He later defended the execution and wrote in *Time* magazine:

'What the photograph didn't say was, "What would you do if you were the general at that time and place on that hot day, and you caught the so-called bad guy after he blew away one, two or three American people?" How do you know you wouldn't have pulled the trigger yourself?'

Eddie Adams later apologised in person to General Nguyen and his family for the damage the picture did to his reputation. When General Nguyen died, Adams praised him as a hero of a 'just cause'.

The 1968 presidential election was shaping into a major battle over the war. During the primaries (the selection of candidates for the election), Johnson faced a challenge within his own party from the anti-war senator **Eugene McCarthy**. It was very unusual for a sitting president to be opposed from within his own party in the primaries. **Bobby Kennedy**, the brother of John Kennedy, then announced that he would enter the race for the Democratic nomination. Polls showed that he was more popular than Johnson.

Johnson lost heart and decided not to seek another term. He acknowledged that the war had destroyed his presidency. It had weakened his cherished domestic reforms (the Great Society), forcing him to cut back on their funding. He was also worried about his health. He had suffered

a massive heart attack in 1955 and doubted whether he would survive another four years in office.

On the night of 31 March 1968, Johnson appeared on TV to make the dramatic announcement that he would not be seeking re-election as President. He also announced a partial bombing pause and the start of peace negotiations with North Vietnam. The negotiations opened in Paris in May amid great hope, but they were to drag on for years before a settlement was reached.

Johnson and Vietnam: an Assessment

Johnson's presidency was fatally damaged by the Vietnam War. His successful domestic reform programme and civil rights legislation were over-shadowed by events in Vietnam. He committed hundreds of thousands of US troops to the struggle against the North Vietnamese. By the end of his presidency over 220,000 US servicemen had been killed or wounded.

He found himself in a bitter struggle which he could not end either by military victory or by negotiations. He wanted to limit the war, but the

QUESTIONS

1 Give three reasons why Johnson agreed with US aid to South Vietnam.

2 What was the significance of the Gulf of Tonkin incident?

3 Explain why the USA began Operation Rolling Thunder.

4 How could men avoid the draft?

5 Why was the fighting in Vietnam difficult for American soldiers?

6 Do you agree with the view that the morale of US troops in Vietnam deteriorated during the war?

7 What role did the media play in contributing to opposition to the war?

8 Explain why diplomatic efforts failed to secure peace in Vietnam.

9 How was the Tet offensive a military failure, but a propaganda success, for North Vietnam?

10 Explain why Lyndon B. Johnson decided not to stand for re-election in 1968.

harder he struggled to find a solution the more deeply he became involved.

The war diverted resources from his ambitious programme of domestic reforms (the Great Society). Johnson refused to raise taxes to pay for the war and this created inflation that took years to control.

The Vietnam War divided the nation, made Johnson unpopular and ultimately led to his decision to stand down as president. Many Americans became suspicious of all government activities and less likely to support future ambitious liberal reform programmes such as Johnson's Great Society.

The historian Robert Dallek wrote this about Johnson and the Vietnam War: 'His assumption that a combination of bombing, ground forces and aid to the Saigon government would assure the independence of South Vietnam proved to be false.' In 1968, despite his domestic gains, Johnson faced an America so divided that he had to announce his withdrawal from that year's presidential campaign. He will be remembered as a larger-than-life figure with great accomplishments and great failings.

WHAT EVENTS LED TO US WITHDRAWAL FROM VIETNAM?

President Nixon's Policies

The 1968 presidential election resulted in a victory for the Republican Richard Nixon. He wanted an exit strategy from Vietnam that would leave US credibility intact. His **'Vietnamisation'** policy involved strengthening the South Vietnamese Army to take on most of the fighting and cope without US support. He wished to shift the burden of their defence to the South Vietnamese. This policy would lead to a phased withdrawal of US forces and result in a reduction of US casualties.

In 1969, the first major withdrawals took place and they continued on a gradual basis. By April 1972, there were 69,000 US troops in Vietnam – in 1968 there had been 543,000. Despite this shift in policy, the president had no intention of abandoning

South Vietnam and allowing a communist victory. Supply trails to the Vietcong that ran through neutral Laos and Cambodia were bombed.

The Anti-war Movement

Nixon's Vietnamisation policy had succeeded in weakening the anti-war movement. As the troops came home, there were fewer protests. Most US middle-class activists lost interest, while a small group of extremists launched a wave of bombings. These bombings discredited the anti-war movement. Nixon particularly disliked the anti-war movement, as he believed that it undermined the US determination to win in Vietnam and challenged his ability to conduct foreign policy. Nixon and other officials used the extremist violence to discredit the whole anti-war movement. They called it 'pro-communist' and 'anti-American'. Nixon argued that the majority of Americans – the great silent majority – supported US policy in Vietnam. However, opinion polls showed that a slim majority were opposed to the war.

Most Americans, while opposing US involvement in Vietnam, were also suspicious of the anti-war movement. Class divisions were beginning to emerge on the issue. Many working-class Americans were incensed at the anti-war demonstrations they saw on TV. The images of wealthy middle-class college students defying authority, burning the US flag and denouncing the United States angered them, especially as many of these same students were exempt from the draft. Speeches from administration figures fuelled working-class anger. In 1970, this antagonism was shown very dramatically when New York construction workers attacked an anti-war demonstration in the city. The term 'hard hats' was coined to describe working-class resentment to the anti-war movement.

Anti-war Protests Intensify

The extension of the war to Cambodia outraged the anti-war movement and gave it a new lease of life. As was the case earlier in the war, universities saw most of the protests. In May 1970, at Kent State University in Ohio, inexperienced National Guardsmen, responding to stone throwing from some students, opened fire. Four students were killed (two of whom were not even involved in any protest) and nine wounded. This event shocked the nation.

In the same month two students at Jackson State University in Mississippi were shot during protests. A wave of outrage swept through the peace movement and sections of the media. However, reaction to the killings highlighted the divisions in US society as the outrage was not shared by all Americans. Opinion polls showed that the majority of Americans sympathised with the guardsmen and not the demonstrators.

By 1971, the war was still the most important political issue in the USA. Many members of Congress increasingly questioned US involvement. The trial of Lieutenant William Calley for the My Lai massacre of Vietnamese villagers in 1968 (see page 112) provoked a national debate on the morality of US involvement in Vietnam.

Vietnam Veterans Against the War was formed to oppose US involvement in Vietnam. It claimed that brutality against Vietnamese civilians was part of the everyday conduct of the war. The future US presidential candidate **John Kerry** was a member of this group and he testified before Congress opposing the war. The publication of the **Pentagon Papers** by the *New York Times* further outraged anti-war opinion. Leaked by an administration official, they showed that the Johnson administration had consistently deceived the people about the reality of the war in Vietnam. Pressure was mounting on Nixon to find an end to the war.

The End of US Involvement

Negotiations continued slowly between the North Vietnamese and the USA to find a compromise solution. In 1972, hoping to take advantage of reduced US troop levels, the North launched an offensive. The South Vietnamese Army was now a much more formidable fighting force and defeated the offensive.

To force the North Vietnamese to agree to a ceasefire, Nixon ordered the bombing of North Vietnamese cities. Called **Operation Linebacker**, it was the heaviest bombing campaign in history. During the operation the USA made 41,500 attacks on North Vietnam. B52 bombers attacked **Hanoi** and the main port of **Haiphong**. The attacks, along with the failed offensive, weakened the North and it agreed to revive the peace negotiations.

The USA promised a fearful South Vietnam that it would not abandon it, if it signed a peace

A wounded student is helped after the shootings at Kent State University. A Presidential Commission later concluded that 'the indiscriminate firing of rifles into a crowd of students and the deaths that followed were unnecessary, unwarranted, and inexcusable'

agreement with the North. In January 1973, an agreement was swiftly reached.

The **Paris Peace Accords**, signed on 27 January 1973, ended hostilities between the USA and North Vietnam. Under the terms of the accords, the USA agreed to halt all military activities immediately and withdraw all remaining military personnel within 60 days. The North Vietnamese agreed to an immediate ceasefire and the release of all American prisoners of war within 60 days. Crucially, the agreement allowed North Vietnamese troops to remain in the South. As a result this left North Vietnam in control of 40 per cent of South Vietnam. President Nixon commented at the time that the agreement 'brings peace with honor in Vietnam and Southeast Asia'. By the end of March the last American troops left Vietnam and America's longest war was over.

The Collapse of South Vietnam

The Paris Peace Accords did not end the war between North and South Vietnam. Both North and South accused each other of breaking the agreement signed in Paris. At the time it was described as a 'post-war war'. In March 1975, the North launched an offensive that led to the quick collapse of the South. Weary of its involvement in Vietnam, the USA did not help and left South Vietnam to its fate.

Chaotic scenes broke out as a fleet of US helicopters evacuated US personnel and desperate

CASUALTIES DURING THE VIETNAM WAR 1965–1973		
Country	Dead	Wounded/Missing
USA	58,000	300,000
US allies (South Korea, Australia)	5,500	14,000
South Vietnamese Army	224,000	500,000
North Vietnamese and the Vietcong	1,100,000	900,000
Civilians	c.1,500,000	Unknown

Americans and South Vietnamese board a helicopter inside the US Embassy just before the fall of Saigon – a symbol of US defeat in Vietnam

South Vietnamese officials and civilians from Saigon. On 30 April, Saigon fell to the North Vietnamese. It was renamed **Ho Chi Minh City**. Vietnam was now unified as one country.

The new regime proved brutal and cruel. Thousands of people were executed and over the next few years more than one million refugees were forced to flee Vietnam.

WHAT WERE THE RESULTS OF THE WAR FOR THE USA?

- As the table on the previous page shows, the human cost of the war was appalling. More than 2.5 million Vietnamese perished in these years, while 58,000 US soldiers were killed and over 300,000 wounded.

- Financially the war had cost the USA $112 billion and diverted resources that could have been spent on domestic reforms.

- To many, it was a defeat for the US policy of containment. Not only had Vietnam become communist, but so had the rest of Indochina – Laos and Cambodia (under the murderous Khmer Rouge).

- Throughout the rest of the 1970s and during the 1980s, the USA became wary of international involvement for fear of another Vietnam.

- It damaged the morale and prestige of the US military. At the close of the war morale was at its lowest point ever.

- Domestically it was very divisive. The war contributed enormously to the disenchantment felt by many young people about their government and its traditional institutions, a disenchantment that became very evident in the late 1960s.

- It weakened the Democratic Party, as many working-class voters switched to the Republicans. This was mainly because they felt that the Democratic Party was dominated by its anti-war faction, who in their view were anti-patriotic.

North Vietnamese troops enter Saigon

The Killing Fields

In 1975, the Communist Khmer Rouge seized power in Cambodia under the leadership of Pol Pot. It began a brutal and tragic reformation of Cambodian society, murdering political opponents and the educated classes, emptying cities and forcing the population on to collective farms.

Historians dispute the death toll, but it is estimated that between 20 and 30 per cent of the population died in this communist experiment. Most of these people starved, while the rest were executed. The site of the executions became known as 'the killing fields', where the victims were buried in mass graves.

1941–45	French colony of Vietnam controlled by Japan. Resistance to occupation led by Ho Chi Minh.
1945	Ho Chi Min declares Vietnamese independence.
1946–54	France attempts to re-conquer Vietnam, backed by the USA; French defeated at Dien Bien Phu in 1954. Country divided into two, communist North and capitalist South, by the Geneva Accords.
1955–63	USA supports unpopular southern government, which is attacked by communist rebels (the Vietcong) backed by the North. President Kennedy sends US military advisers to support the South.
1964	Gulf of Tonkin incident, resulting in US involvement escalating with bombing of North Vietnam. Johnson re-elected president.
1965	Johnson orders Operation Rolling Thunder, the bombing of North Vietnam. First ground troops committed to the country. Beginning of opposition to the war in the USA.
1965–68	US troop numbers grow to over 500,000. Bombing of North Vietnam and the Ho Chi Minh trail continues. No breakthrough in peace efforts.
1968	Vietcong and North Vietnamese launch the Tet Offensive and suffer massive military defeat, but many Americans turn against the war. Johnson announces he will not seek re-election.
1969	President Richard Nixon announces a policy of 'Vietnamisation' – training and equipping the South Vietnamese military to fight the Vietcong. This would enable the USA to reduce troop numbers. Peace talks begin in Paris.
1970–73	US forces are gradually reduced. Bombing of the North continues. Massive anti-war protests in the USA.
1973	Paris Peace Accords signed. Last US troops leave Vietnam.
1975	South Vietnam conquered by North Vietnam. Vietnam unified under communist control. The other states in French Indochina – Laos and Cambodia – also become communist.

QUESTIONS

1 Explain what President Nixon's 'Vietnamisation' policy involved.

2 Why were Cambodia and Laos bombed? What was the reaction in the USA?

3 What evidence is there to suggest that most Americans supported their government's actions in Vietnam?

4 Why did Nixon order the bombing of North Vietnam in 1972? What were the effects of that bombing?

5 What was agreed in Paris in January 1973?

6 Outline the main events leading to the defeat of South Vietnam in 1975.

7 What consequences did the war have for the USA?

DOCUMENT

Read this extract from President Johnson's broadcast to the nation, 31 March 1968.

For 37 years in the service of the nation ... I have put the unity of the people first. There is division in the American house now. So I would ask all Americans, whatever their personal interests or concerns, to guard against divisiveness and all its ugly consequences.

I have concluded that I should not permit the presidency to become involved in the political divisions that are developing in this political year.

With America's sons in the fields far away, with America's future under challenge right here at home, with our hopes and the world's hopes for peace in the balance every day, I do not believe that I should devote an hour or a day of my time to any personal political causes or to any duties other than the awesome duties of this office – the Presidency of your country.

Accordingly, I shall not seek, and I will not accept, the nomination of my party for another term as your President.

Source: American Experience http://www.pbs.org

1 DOCUMENT QUESTIONS

a) What does Johnson ask of all Americans?

b) What does he not want to permit the presidency to become involved in?

c) According to the extract, why does Johnson not believe that he should devote any time to 'any personal political causes'?

d) Do you think political speeches such as the document are reliable sources of evidence for a historian?

2 ORDINARY LEVEL QUESTIONS

a) How did the USA become involved in Vietnam?

b) What problems did President Johnson encounter in dealing with Vietnam? (Leaving Cert 2012)

c) Describe what fighting was like in Vietnam.

d) What was the Tet Offensive?

e) Describe the US withdrawal from Vietnam. (Leaving Cert 2014)

f) What policies did President Johnson follow in relation to the war in Vietnam? (Leaving Cert 2006)

3 HIGHER LEVEL ESSAYS

a) Which had the greater impact on the United States: involvement in Korea or involvement in Vietnam? Argue your case, referring to both. (Leaving Cert 2006)

b) What were the successes and failures of the presidency of Lyndon Johnson? (Leaving Cert 2010)

c) Why did the USA lose the Vietnam War? (Amended Leaving Cert 2011)

d) Which president was more successful in his handling of US foreign policy: Harry Truman or Lyndon Johnson? Argue your case, referring to both. (Leaving Cert 2013)

e) What was the impact of the Tet Offensive (1968) on the presidency of Lyndon B. Johnson?

f) What impact did domestic opposition have on American involvement in Vietnam?

g) How successfully did Richard Nixon handle the war in Vietnam?

8 Decline of Cold War Certainties 1973–1989

The withdrawal of the United States from Vietnam (see pages 118–120) had been helped by the improving climate in relations between the USA and the USSR in the 1970s. Commentators referred to a warming of relations, or **détente**, between the superpowers. However, this warming of relations did not last, as the political divisions between the two nations were too great. By the mid-1980s, relations were as poor as they had been at any time during the Cold War.

WHAT WAS DÉTENTE?

Richard Nixon and Détente

The **Cuban Missile Crisis** (see pages 93–97) had made both superpowers realise that they faced a choice: slow down or continue the arms race which could result in all-out war. A partial **Test Ban Treaty** (see page 97) was signed in 1963, and a Nuclear **Non-Proliferation Treaty** in 1968 limited the number of countries allowed to have nuclear weapons.

In 1968, Richard Nixon won the presidential election, defeating the Democratic challenger **Hubert Humphrey**. Nixon and his very influential national security adviser, **Henry Kissinger**, were the architects of a new US approach to the Cold War. Absorbed at the time by events in Vietnam, they were reluctant to embark on new policies, but they felt they needed to improve relations with the USSR. Both were ready to accept the Soviet Union as America's nuclear equal. Kissinger argued that the USSR was now less interested in the spread of communism, and that both countries could negotiate as issues arose. This flexible approach was to yield results.

Soviet leader **Leonid Brezhnev** also wanted to relax Cold War tensions with America, as Russian relations with China worsened. The Soviet economy was also in trouble. The arms race was placing a massive strain on Russia's resources.

> **Mutual assured destruction (MAD)** was a theory developed in the 1960s by the US Secretary of Defense Robert McNamara. He hoped that neither side would ever consider using nuclear weapons and argued that both sides needed to have the ability to respond in a devastating manner to a nuclear attack. This would deter the other side from ever using nuclear weapons in a crisis or a surprise attack. This was called **nuclear deterrence**. As both sides could destroy each other, that would provide good reason for caution during a crisis.
>
> Defensive weapons such as anti-ballistic missiles were regarded as dangerous because they could encourage one side to attack without fear of response.

On the other hand, Nixon wanted to develop US–Chinese relations, partly to put pressure on the USSR. Soviet relations with China were poor. For example, there was a bitter border dispute between the two countries.

Nixon with the Chinese Prime Minister, Chou En-Lai, during his ground-breaking visit to China in 1972. The Chinese were beginning to take a greater role in international affairs. In 1964, they had successfully tested their own atomic bomb

WHAT WERE THE SALT AGREEMENTS?

The superpowers began to work together in areas of common interest. The most important area was limiting the arms race. Responding to a Soviet offer, Nixon agreed to start arms control talks. In 1969, the **Strategic Arms Limitation Talks** (**SALT**) began at Helsinki in Finland. The discussions proceeded slowly as the issues were very complicated and there was an absence of any real trust between the two sides. However, largely due to the work of **Henry Kissinger**, a number of agreements were reached.

Nixon Visits Moscow

In 1972, despite tension over US actions in Vietnam, Nixon flew to **Moscow** to formally sign the results of the SALT negotiations. This was a momentous occasion as it was the first peacetime visit of an American president to the USSR and it marked the onset of détente (spirit of co-operation). Two agreements, known as **SALT I**, were signed:

- The **Anti-Ballistic Missile (ABM) Treaty** restricted the use of defensive anti-ballistic missiles systems to two sites for each country.

- The second agreement froze at 1972 levels the number of intercontinental ballistic missiles (ICBMs) that each side could hold. It was intended that this agreement would be replaced by a more comprehensive treaty.

In the USA, détente was politically popular, as the American people were critical of the Vietnam War and the effort and expenditure associated with the Cold War.

> ### Leonid Brezhnev (1906–1982)
>
> In 1964 Brezhnev helped force Khrushchev from power. He defended the Soviet decision in 1968 to invade Czechoslovakia, in what became known as the 'Brezhnev Doctrine'. This was the policy of intervention to prevent reform (or political change) in socialist countries. In 1981, he put pressure on the Polish government to crush Solidarity. His invasion of Afghanistan in 1979 cost the USSR dearly, both militarily and economically. His rule of the USSR became known as the era of stagnation.

Further Progress

The warming in relations between the USA and the USSR was confirmed when Brezhnev visited Washington in 1973, although there were still deep tensions between the nations. In October 1973, the **Yom Kippur War** between the Israelis and the Arabs caused tensions between the superpowers, as the USA assisted the Israelis and the USSR supplied the Arabs.

However, it was in their common interests that détente continued. A new round of arms negotiations, **SALT II**, began, which aimed to reduce the number of nuclear weapons. Nixon visited Moscow again in 1974, when further treaties were signed. One of these treaties limited underground nuclear testing.

Détente continued under Nixon's successor, **Gerald Ford**. In 1974, at a successful summit at **Vladivostok**, progress was made on some of the issues holding up arms control talks. A framework for a future SALT II treaty was agreed.

In 1975, another concrete result of détente was agreed at **Helsinki** in Finland. This wide-ranging agreement, signed by 35 countries, was called the **Helsinki Final Act**. The frontiers of Europe set up after World War II were recognised and agreement was reached on future European security,

Gerald Ford (left) and Leonid Brezhnev meet for the first time, Vladivostok, 1974

Q U E S T I O N S

1 Explain why both the USA and the USSR were in favour of an improvement in relations in the early 1970s.

2 Explain the theory of mutual assured destruction.

3 Why did Nixon want to develop US–Chinese relations?

4 Outline what was agreed between the USA and the USSR in Moscow in 1972.

5 Why was détente politically popular in the USA?

6 Give other examples of agreement between the superpowers between 1973 and 1976.

economic co-operation and the protection of human rights.

The most public symbol of the new relationship between the superpowers was the joint **Apollo–Soyuz project** launched the same year. In space, co-operation was replacing years of Cold War confrontation (see Chapter 11).

SALT II

In the 1976 election, Democrat **Jimmy Carter** defeated **Gerald Ford**. He continued the policy of détente with the USSR. His overriding aim was to maintain world peace by negotiating arms control with the USSR. Negotiations went at a slow pace due to the worsening international climate and the complex issues involved. As a result agreement was not reached until 1979.

SALT II was signed by Carter and Brezhnev in Vienna in 1979. This agreement limited, but did not reduce, the number of nuclear missiles each side could possess, but it did continue the progress made under SALT I. The SALT II Treaty marked the end of détente, as a number of factors had caused relations between the two superpowers to worsen.

WHAT LED TO THE DECLINE OF DÉTENTE?

Détente Under Pressure

Nixon and Ford had not allowed idealism interfere with the practical realities of dealing with the USSR. On the other hand, Carter viewed human rights as a central plank in his dealings with other countries; he saw issues of human rights not as

Carter (centre left) and Brezhnev (centre right) in Vienna, 1979, before the negotiation of the SALT II treaty

'idealism' but as vital to the functioning of a civilised society. His pleas on behalf of **dissidents** (critics of communism), and of Jews who wished to leave the Soviet Union, angered the Soviet leadership. They viewed his statements as interference in their internal affairs.

In the USA, voices were being raised against détente. It was seen as harming US interests. Strong criticism was directed at Carter, who was accused of being weak in dealing with the threat posed by communism. Opponents pointed to communist advances in Africa. A large number of senators opposed the SALT II agreement, which they felt left the USA at a military disadvantage to the USSR.

Not willing to be seen as weak, the Carter administration increased military spending and approved the new **Trident** missile system. The president's attention was also diverted from the Cold War by events in Iran.

The brutal regime of the pro-US Shah of Iran had been overthrown by an Islamic revolution. A crisis developed when US embassy staff in the capital, Tehran, were seized in late 1979. The ensuing **Iran Hostage Crisis** lasted 444 days and completely overshadowed the remainder of Carter's presidency (until 1981).

The End of Détente

The 'death blow' for détente came in December 1979 with the Soviet invasion of **Afghanistan**. Carter felt betrayed by the invasion and commented that events in Afghanistan had caused him to rethink his entire attitude towards the USSR. He was worried that the invasion was part of a Soviet attempt to control the oil-rich **Persian Gulf**.

He announced that any attempt by the Soviet Union to gain control of the Persian Gulf would be viewed as an assault on the vital interests of the USA and would be resisted. This became known as the **Carter Doctrine**.

A number of other measures were taken by the USA to put pressure on the Soviets to leave Afghanistan:

- Trade restrictions were placed on the export of goods to the USSR, e.g. grain, technology.

- Ratification of the SALT II agreement was suspended.

- The USA announced a **boycott** of the Olympic Games that were to be held in Moscow in 1980.

The Cold War was to intensify further in the early 1980s when **Ronald Reagan** became president.

A US helicopter that crashed during a secret mission to rescue US hostages in Iran. The crisis over the hostages severely damaged Carter's chance of re-election in 1980

In 1979, American policymakers were worried that the invasion of Afghanistan was only the beginning of a Soviet plot to dominate the oil-rich Persian Gulf. The region has continued to dominate American foreign policy, as witnessed by two wars with Iraq in 1991 and 2003

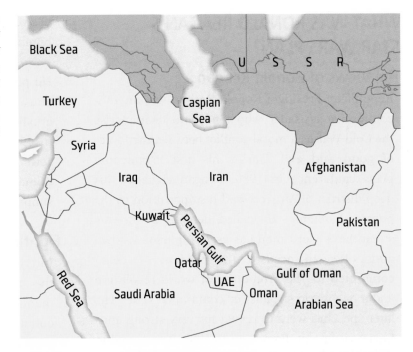

The invasion of Afghanistan was to prove disastrous for the Russians, who met fierce resistance from Afghan guerrillas called the Mujahideen. The guerrilla fighters received financial and military aid from the USA. Casualties rose and the Soviets withdrew in 1989, as shown here. That war has been called the 'Soviet Vietnam'

QUESTIONS

1 Why did it take so long to agree to SALT II in 1979?

2 What domestic criticism was there of Carter's policies?

3 How did the USSR react to Carter's emphasis on human rights?

4 Why did events in Iran become so important for the Carter administration?

5 What was the Carter Doctrine?

6 What measures did the USA take to put pressure on the USSR to leave Afghanistan?

WHAT WAS RONALD REAGAN'S STAR WARS PLAN?

The Views of Ronald Reagan

Republican President Ronald Reagan was an anti-communist crusader who tended to characterise the Cold War as a moral conflict between the forces of **good and evil**. During his first Presidential press conference in 1980, Reagan signalled his deep distrust of Moscow and his opposition to the policy of détente. He called détente 'a one-way street the Soviet Union has used to pursue its own aims'. Reagan accused the **Soviets** of being committed to 'the promotion of world revolution and a one-world socialist or communist state'. His later speeches were to repeat his very strong anti-Soviet viewpoint. Famously, in 1983, he referred to the USSR as an 'evil empire' and the 'focus of evil in the modern world'.

Reagan believed that the only way to deal with the Kremlin was from a position of strength. Unlike his immediate predecessors, he seemed to have little interest in diplomacy with the Soviets. His policies received strong support from the British prime minister, **Margaret Thatcher**.

The Renewal of the Cold War

SALT II was not ratified by the US Senate and Reagan began a new phase of rearmament. He was confident that the Soviet economy could not keep pace with the USA in a new arms race. He increased the defence budget by more than 50 per cent over five years. He approved production of the costly **B-1** bomber, a project President Carter had scrapped.

He put pressure on the USSR over human rights abuses in Eastern Europe, especially after the crushing of the **Solidarity Movement** in Poland in 1981, and the refusal of the Soviets to allow Jews to emigrate. These, and other examples of human rights abuses, saw increased public support for Reagan's policies.

Fighting the Spread of Communism

Internationally, Reagan decided to do more to stop the spread of communism. The Americans increased economic and military assistance to countries fighting left-wing revolutions, especially in South and Central America. The USA gave $4 billion to the government of **El Salvador** to crush a left-wing revolt, despite the regime's appalling human rights record.

The **Reagan Doctrine** promised US support for anti-communist movements in countries with left-wing regimes. Aid was sent to **Afghan** guerrillas fighting the Soviets. Secret aid was also sent to help the **Contra** guerrillas who were fighting against the left-wing government of **Nicaragua**. In 1985, high-ranking members from the Reagan administration persuaded Israel to sell US arms to Iran (at war with Iraq 1983–88) and used the profits to fund the Contras. This was illegal and when this secret funding was exposed there was uproar in the USA. The investigations into the

Reagan at his 70th birthday celebrations. Note his relaxed style – which earned him the nickname the 'Great Communicator'. Portrayed by his enemies as a warmonger, he pushed hard to end the Cold War. He was not a hard worker – setting the broad outline of policy, he left his officials to do most of the work. He once joked, 'It's true that hard work never killed anyone, but I figured why take the chance!'

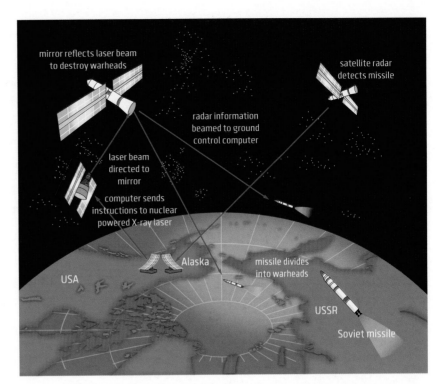

mirror reflects laser beam to destroy warheads

satellite radar detects missile

radar information beamed to ground control computer

laser beam directed to mirror

computer sends instructions to nuclear powered X-ray laser

Alaska

missile divides into warheads

USA

USSR

Soviet missile

Iran–Contra affair were to dominate the closing years of Reagan's presidency.

The Strategic Defense Initiative

In March 1983, Reagan announced that he intended to spend billions of dollars exploring the possibility of blocking Soviet missiles travelling to the USA. This defensive shield would use satellites, space-based lasers and other methods to stop the missiles in space. Called the **Strategic Defense Initiative** (SDI), its opponents soon labelled it **Star Wars** (after the film).

Reagan saw his proposal as a defensive strategy, but the Soviets saw it differently. To them it seemed like a serious attempt to escalate the arms race. They believed that it increased the possibility that the USA might launch an attack on the USSR, as it would not fear retaliation.

The Soviet leader, **Yuri Andropov** (who had replaced Brezhnev in 1982), attacked Reagan's 'Star Wars' plan. 'All attempts at achieving military superiority over the USSR are futile,' he said. Privately, the Soviets realised that they could never match the financial cost of the programme.

The Impact of SDI

However, there were all sorts of problems with the SDI. Much of the technology needed had not been developed, and some appeared to challenge the

laws of physics. The cost of producing it would be extremely high. Nevertheless, the SDI remained an article of faith for Reagan for the rest of his presidency, which complicated arms control negotiations. Some commentators have suggested that Reagan knew that the SDI would never work, but that he cleverly began the project to bankrupt the USSR as they tried to develop their own version.

The renewed arms race and Reagan's anti-Soviet speeches led to many Americans and Europeans portraying him as a warmonger. There were many protests and demonstrations against his policies. Later, Reagan claimed he was just as much against nuclear arms as the protestors were.

The announcement of SDI in 1983 contributed to international tension. In August 1983, a South Korean airliner was shot down over Soviet airspace, an event Reagan called an 'act of barbarism'. The USSR walked out of arms control talks in Geneva when **Cruise** and **Pershing** missiles were introduced into Western Europe.

The Soviet leadership believed that an attack by the West was imminent (see page 132). Reagan was surprised when he learned of Soviet fears. This was a turning point. Washington began to send reassuring signals to the Soviets. It was time, Reagan told his advisers, for a face-to-face meeting with Soviet leaders. The advent of a new leader in 1985 was to make this meeting possible.

There were two occasions during the Cold War when the Soviet Union was convinced it was on the brink of nuclear war with the USA: the Cuban Missile Crisis; and again in late 1983. But unlike the Cuban crisis, the 1983 escalation of nuclear tensions took place without the USA or much of the world knowing. As with Cuba, the lack of any real trust between both sides resulted in this crisis.

The anti-Soviet actions of the Reagan administration had led to increased Soviet monitoring of any signs of a US attack. The Soviets feared that the NATO Able Archer 83 exercise planned for November 1983 was a cover for a NATO invasion of Eastern Europe. Their fears were based on the following events:

1. An increase in coded messages between London and Washington in October. The USSR saw this as planning for an offensive.

    Explanation: In fact it was the UK protesting at the invasion of Grenada (a Commonwealth country) without consultation.

2. Flash that US bases were put on alert. Seen as preparation for an attack.

    Explanation: In reality it was heightened security in response to a terrorist attack on a US base in Lebanon.

3. Absence of top officials, such as the president, at the exercise.

    Explanation: The US president and his leading generals were originally supposed to attend the exercise, but it was decided that top officials would not attend as it could be seen as provocative by the Soviets. The Soviets took the opposite interpretation. In response they raised the alert level of their forces.

The USA realised how dangerous the situation had been only when the director of the CIA interrogated a Soviet defector. News of the war scare is said to have changed Reagan's view of the Soviets. He realised that they were genuinely fearful of US actions. It saw him pursue a policy of negotiation rather than confrontation.

HOW DID THE COLD WAR END?

Mikhail Gorbachev

In 1985, Mikhail Gorbachev came to power in the USSR. His policies were to have a dramatic effect on the USSR, Eastern Europe and the Cold War.

He saw that without reform the communist system could collapse. Gorbachev was determined to modernise the Soviet economy – a process he called **perestroika** (restructuring). He also promised greater freedom in Soviet society – a policy known as **glasnost** (openness).

Along with his domestic reforms, Gorbachev wanted to improve relations with the USA. He did not believe that the USA was a threat to the USSR, despite some of Reagan's speeches. He needed to end the arms race because military expenditure was placing a massive burden on the Soviet economy. Now in his second term, Reagan wanted to be remembered as a statesman who had done something effective to end the Cold War. Both sides were ready to negotiate. The result was a

Mikhail Gorbachev was general secretary of the Communist Party of the Soviet Union from 1985 to 1991. His reforms helped open up Soviet society in the late 1980s, but contributed to the downfall of communism and the break-up of the Soviet Union in 1991

Reagan and Gorbachev at the Geneva Summit

remarkable diplomatic process that ended the Cold War between the two countries.

In November 1985, Reagan and Gorbachev met in **Geneva** for the first superpower summit in six years. Though the two leaders remained divided by Reagan's 'Star Wars' initiative, the atmosphere was warm. The United States and the Soviet Union were talking again.

The following year Reagan and Gorbachev went to **Reykjavik** in Iceland for their second summit. Over the next few days, the two leaders took a series of bold steps aimed at reducing the threat of nuclear war. Reagan stunned Gorbachev and his own advisers by offering to eliminate all nuclear weapons within ten years. But Gorbachev continued to press Reagan on 'Star Wars'. Reagan would not budge.

The summit ended without an agreement – but each delegation realised that the discussions had crossed a historic line. The negotiations soon saw results.

In 1987, Reagan and Gorbachev met in Washington to sign the **Intermediate-range Nuclear Forces** (INF) Treaty. Soviet SS20 and US Cruise and Pershing missiles were eliminated. This was the first agreement between the superpowers that actually reduced the number of nuclear weapons. The Cold War warrior, Ronald Reagan, had displayed a remarkable willingness to negotiate with the USSR.

The End of Communism in Eastern Europe

Meanwhile, demands for reform were growing in Eastern Europe. In a major shift of Soviet policy, Gorbachev promised not to interfere if the people of Eastern Europe took their futures into their own hands. In 1989, **Hungary** quietly restored democracy and opened its border with Austria. Crucially, there was now a hole in the Iron Curtain. Thousands of East Germans flocked to Hungary to cross into the West. In **Poland**, elections brought a landslide victory for **Solidarity** and complete humiliation for the ruling communists.

Then, on 9 November, in a hugely symbolic act, the rulers of East Germany were forced to open the Berlin Wall after mass demonstrations and the flight of many of its citizens. The destruction of the Berlin Wall symbolised to many the end of the Cold War and within a year Germany was reunited as one country.

The following month the communist government in **Czechoslovakia** was overthrown in the peaceful 'Velvet Revolution'. Communism collapsed quietly in **Bulgaria** and **Albania** as well.

Only in **Romania** was there violence. The communist dictator **Nicolae Ceausescu** was removed in a bloody revolution that saw the deaths of over a thousand people.

The USA watched the unfolding events quietly, refraining from gloating or interfering. It

promised support to the new governments but avoided doing anything that could be seen as provocative to the Soviets.

In December, at a superpower summit at Malta, Gorbachev told **George Bush Sr** (elected as president in 1988) that the Soviets wanted the United States to remain a force in Europe. Then he decisively announced: 'We don't consider you an enemy any more.' One of Gorbachev's advisers said that the Cold War had lasted from '**Yalta to Malta**'.

Gorbachev's unwillingness to intervene to stop the spread of democracy in Eastern Europe was jokingly called the Sinatra doctrine, after the Frank Sinatra song 'My Way'. Coined by a Soviet official, it meant that the USSR was allowing the countries of Eastern Europe go their own way and decide their own political systems.

The End of the USSR

By 1991 the USSR itself was no more. Glasnost had given the Soviet people freedoms they had not

QUESTIONS

1 How did Reagan show through his speeches that he was opposed to communism?

2 What policies did Reagan pursue in Latin America?

3 What was the Strategic Defense Initiative? What impact did it have on relations between the USA and the USSR?

4 Show why the USSR thought it was going to be attacked in 1983. What effect did the crisis have on the Reagan administration?

5 What new policies did Gorbachev introduce to the Soviet Union?

6 Outline the events that led to the signing of the INF Treaty in 1987.

7 What major change in policy did Gorbachev make in regard to Eastern Europe?

8 Outline the main events in Eastern Europe in 1989.

9 How did the USA react to the unfolding events in Eastern Europe in 1989?

10 Outline the events that led to the collapse of the USSR.

enjoyed since 1917. It led to strong criticism of communism, open elections and a rise in nationalism among the non-Russian people in the USSR. The Baltic republics (taken over by Stalin in 1940) demanded independence. They were followed by Georgia and Ukraine. Gorbachev was also facing a power struggle with the anti-communist **Boris Yeltsin**. Yeltsin was president of the largest and most powerful republic, **Russia**, and he was no longer prepared to take orders from Gorbachev.

Gorbachev failed to cope with these problems and was losing control of events. In August 1991, communist hardliners, alarmed at the turn of events, staged an attempted military takeover. This takeover failed, largely through the actions of Boris Yeltsin. Gorbachev was sidelined and in December 1991 the USSR dissolved into its different republics. To many commentators America had won the Cold War.

END-OF-CHAPTER REVIEW

DOCUMENT

Look at the cartoon and answer the questions below.

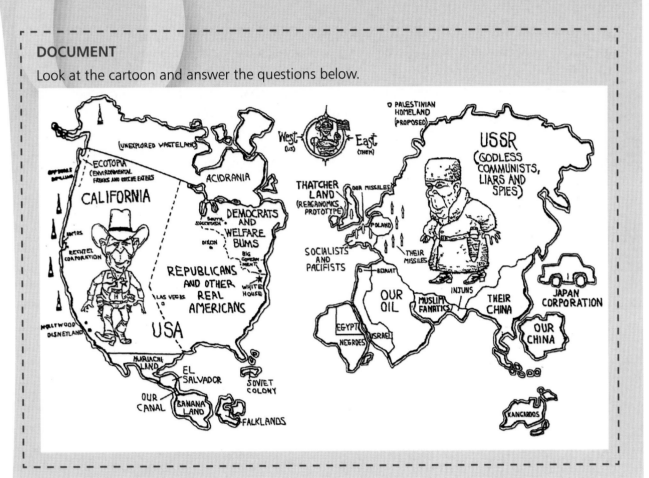

1 DOCUMENT QUESTIONS

a) What description is given to the USSR in the cartoon?

b) Who is the Russian leader in the cartoon?

c) What does the cartoon suggest was Reagan's attitude to Democrats in the USA?

d) How is Reagan portrayed in the cartoon?

e) Would you say this cartoon is pro- or anti-Reagan? Comment, giving evidence from the cartoon.

f) How effective do you think this cartoon is in getting its message across?

2 ORDINARY LEVEL QUESTIONS

Write an account of the following:

a) Détente, SALT and Star Wars. (Leaving Cert 2011)

b) The policies of Ronald Reagan.

c) The end of the Cold War.

3 HIGHER LEVEL ESSAYS

a) What were the successes and failures of the political career of Ronald Reagan? (Leaving Cert 2006)

b) What were the significant developments in US foreign policy, 1973–89? (Leaving Cert 2007)

c) What part did one or more of the following play in US foreign policy: Korea; Cuba; SALT and Star Wars? (Leaving Cert 2012)

d) How successful was Richard Nixon in handling relations with the Soviet Union?

e) What were the main developments in US–USSR relations during the presidency of Ronald Reagan?

4 Do you agree with the following statements about the Cold War?

a) Nuclear weapons prevented war breaking out between the superpowers during the Cold War.

b) The USA won the Cold War.

Write a short essay (one A4 page) outlining your views on each statement. You can either be for or against the statement, but you must back up your arguments with facts.

⑨ Consensus 1945–1989

WHAT FACTORS CONTRIBUTED TO THE AGE OF CONSENSUS 1945–1968?

As discussed in Chapter 2, the dominant mood in the USA in 1945 was one of optimism and confidence about the future. During the years of economic boom in the 1950s and early 1960s, most Americans wanted to be allowed to enjoy their new-found affluence. Although the Cold War, Korea and McCarthyism made news headlines in the early 1950s, opinion polls showed that most Americans were preoccupied with their own lives and were largely uninterested in politics.

The 1950s are often referred to as 'the age of consensus': a time when the majority of Americans focused on things that united them. They seemed to switch off issues that caused conflict and to embrace agreement and co-operation. In 1954, *McCalls* magazine coined the word '**togetherness**', celebrating Americans' commitment to domestic happiness and social uniformity. In this chapter we will examine the cultural impact of consensus in the 1950s and early 1960s and the causes and effects of its collapse after 1968.

> **culture** A range of customs and beliefs relating to the general interests and tastes of the people (low culture/mass culture/pop culture) and of artists/intellectuals (high culture).

The post-war generation in the USA had lived through the Great Depression of the early 1930s, and World War II. After 1945, the majority of them wanted to settle down to a quiet life, free from the anxieties of social, economic and political problems at home and abroad. The booming economy allowed very many Americans to enjoy the 'good life'. They buried their differences and looked for a middle ground when it came to issues that might divide them. This led to a mood of consensus and conformity.

Conformity in the workplace in the early 1950s – all white men, all wearing suits and with short hair

A number of factors contributed to the general atmosphere of cultural consensus after 1945 and into the 1960s, including the following:

- The war and victory encouraged a sense of **patriotism** among Americans. This feeling continued during the 1950s, when the USA claimed to be the leader of the 'free world' in the fight against communism (the Cold War). Most Americans supported their government and believed that being critical of its policies was un-American.

- The growth of the middle class led to uniformity. Between 1947 and the early 1960s, the number of middle-class families grew from 5.7 million to over 12 million (one-third of the population). As they became more prosperous, middle-class Americans became more **culturally homogeneous** (uniform or the same).

- The customs, beliefs and tastes of the middle class set the standards for the vast majority of Americans in the 1950s. They were prosperous, successful and very American. Everyone wanted to have what the middle class had.

- The rising incomes of blue-collar workers allowed them to share in middle-class affluence and cultural activities previously denied to them – sports, arts, etc.

- The percentage of immigrants in the population declined in the 1950s. By the mid-1960s, 95 per cent of Americans were native-born.

Ethnic differences seemed to be declining a most people wanted to be 100 per cer American. Schools reinforced the process Americanisation and cultural conformity.

- Interest in religion revived after the wa Membership of churches and churc attendance increased during the 1950s, at

A group of students leaving school, 1950

time when 95 per cent of Americans believed in God and over 50 per cent belonged to a church. Religion spread cultural consensus and acted as a unifying force in post-war America.

- Most Americans trusted their politicians during the 1950s. President Eisenhower appeared to many to be the embodiment of consensus. He won a landslide victory in the 1952 presidential election, with 34 million votes. Popular and calm, he followed moderate conservative politics. Like the American public, he avoided controversial issues.

WHAT WAS THE AMERICAN DREAM?

The idea of the '**American Dream**' had important effects on cultural attitudes and beliefs during the period 1945 to 1968. Central to the idea of the American Dream is a belief that the USA offers opportunities to everyone, regardless of class or background. Unlike the 'old world' (Europe), the USA saw itself as an open society where people can move up and improve their status in the world. Most Americans believed that America was the **land of opportunity** during this time, a place in which parents could expect their children to do better in life than they themselves had done. Success would come to those who worked hard and made the most of the opportunities life gave them.

Belief in the American Dream inspired a great sense of optimism and confidence – a belief in America and its unlimited power and resources.

Hollywood and the American Dream

During and after World War II, visual imagery played an important role in shaping public attitudes in the USA. Hollywood, the home of the American film industry, became a powerful influence on national thinking. During the war it released a number of patriotic films portraying American heroism and glorifying 'American' values of loyalty, courage and sacrifice. In contrast, Japanese and German characters were presented as cowardly, cruel and dishonourable. The US war ally, the USSR, and its leader, Stalin, were given favourable treatment in films made during the war.

However, allegiances changed during the Cold War and Hollywood reflected the growing rift with the USSR. The Russians became the 'bad guys'.

In the 1950s, Hollywood films also promoted the American Dream. The most popular movies were westerns and love stories, often with a simple moral tale involving the triumph of good over evil and always with a happy ending. American cinema viewers wanted entertainment, and by and large Hollywood gave them 'feel-good' movies (notable exceptions were films like *On the Waterfront*, starring the young **Marlon Brando**, and *Rebel Without a Cause*, starring **James Dean**).

A romantic Hollywood view of the pioneers who populated the West

Hollywood represented the American success story, and many actors were hugely successful. Marilyn Monroe (see page 193) became a Hollywood icon, featuring in a number of popular movies. In the 1950s, she represented the 'rags to riches' story, and seemed to show how in America there were opportunities and it was always possible to succeed.

During the 1940s and 1950s the Red Scare and McCarthyism had a profound effect on Hollywood.

The Red Scare

After 1945 the wartime alliance between the USA and the USSR fell apart, and the Cold War emerged. As we have seen in earlier chapters, a number of events led to a growing fear of a communist threat at home.

Anti-communist hysteria gripped the American public, who became convinced that communists were active inside America, particularly in the State Department and other government agencies. In 1947, Truman began ordering security checks on government employees to root out communists, and the following year set up loyalty boards which required a loyalty oath from all federal employees.

In 1950, the **Internal Security Act** required all communists to register with the Attorney General.

Also in 1950, Senator Joe McCarthy began his witch hunt against communists at home. The Red Scare lasted from 1946 to 1954, and when it ended thousands of suspected communists had lost their jobs, some had spent time in jail, more than fifty were deported and two were executed for spying.

Hollywood came into contact with the Red Scare through the investigations of the House Un-American Activities Committee (HUAC).

HUAC and Hollywood

HUAC had been set up by Congress in 1938. It was made permanent in 1947.

In the 1930s, many Hollywood actors and screen writers were drawn to the American Communist Party (which was critical of appeasement of Hitler and sympathetic to the Republican cause in the Spanish Civil War). During World War II many pro-Soviet films were released by Hollywood. Ronald Reagan, who was head of the Screen Actors Guild, was staunchly anti-communist and kept a close eye on communists in the Guild.

Film stars protest communism allegations. Shown listening to testimony before HUAC, front row, left to right: actors June Havoc, Humphrey Bogart and Lauren Bacall

In 1947, HUAC began investigating the film industry, believing that it was a hotbed of communism. It interviewed 41 people working in Hollywood. When called to testify before HUAC, they each co-operated with the investigation by attending voluntarily and by naming 19 fellow workers whom they suspected of being communists. For this, the 41 became known as 'friendly witnesses'. Of the 19 people they named, ten refused to appear before HUAC. Known as the 'Hollywood Ten', they claimed they had a constitutional right to freedom of speech (the **1st Amendment**). HUAC found them guilty of contempt of Congress and sentenced them to jail.

Pleading the 5th

A group of Hollywood stars protested at the Capitol in October 1947 and the Hollywood Ten appealed to the Supreme Court, but in 1948 that Court turned down the appeal on grounds of national security. Some of the Ten then pleaded the 5th Amendment (the right to remain silent), but this was taken as proof that they were hiding something and thus guilty.

As the HUAC investigations hit the newspaper headlines, Hollywood producers began publishing blacklists prohibiting anyone who refused to testify before HUAC from working in the film industry. The list had over 320 names, including Charlie Chaplin, Paul Robeson, Orson Welles and Arthur Miller. (Miller, who was sentenced to jail and fined $500, later wrote *The Crucible*, a play whose theme was seventeenth-century witch hunts at Salem and which had echoes of the contemporary anti-communist witch hunts.) Ronald Reagan co-operated with HUAC and supported the blacklisting of communists in Hollywood.

The public at first supported Hollywood, but as the hearings progressed they lost sympathy for the Ten.

The HUAC investigations continued in Hollywood until 1954. The committee cited over three hundred Hollywood employees as communists, either following their testimonies or because they pleaded the 5th. They were all blacklisted and many talented and innocent people's careers were ruined.

Cultural Effects of the Red Scare

- Hollywood lost its progressive edge. Controversy and dissent were silenced. Social problems were no longer given attention in movies. Many **anti-communist** (and anti-USSR) films were released. Entertainment and escapism dominated movie themes in the 1950s.

- In general, popular literature was dominated by books that had entertainment value, promoted anti-communism, and avoided social issues. However, **J.D. Salinger**, one of the most widely read authors in the 1950s (his *Catcher in the Rye* was published in 1951), won many literary awards, although he wrote about people who were wrapped up in their own lives.

- Education became a focus for anti-communism. Parents were warned to keep a close watch on what their children were being taught at school for fear that teachers might encourage communism. Hundreds of teachers lost their jobs and were blacklisted. **Loyalty oaths** were introduced into universities. Professors with liberal and communist sympathies were dismissed from their jobs. Many intellectuals and academics had communist sympathies in the 1930s, but during the Cold War things changed. The mood in universities generally was conservative and lecturers conformed to the anti-communist line in teaching. The study of history and social science offered an uncritical view of the USA and rejected Marxism.

- Influenced by teachers and educational courses, young people and students became increasingly conformist in the 1950s. Lacking concern about social and political issues, most students concentrated more on exams, jobs and sports. They became known as the '**Silent Generation**'.

- The media were controlled by anti-communist publishers. Reporters were often badly paid and lacked resources to follow up investigations. They needed to sell newspapers and keep their jobs in TV and radio. The Red Scare atmosphere of fear and intimidation encouraged them to go for sensational stories and hunt for '**reds**' (communists).

- Civil liberties came under attack as government extended its powers to investigate people's private lives. J. Edgar Hoover, head of the FBI, was a determined anti-communist. He used **phone-tapping** and **electronic surveillance** to compile detailed records on communist 'suspects'. Freedom of speech was severely restricted during the Red Scare.

Cultural Critics of the Consensus

During the troubled years that followed the 1950s, many people looked back on that decade with nostalgia. It was seen as a time of calm and national unity. However, critics saw it as bland and culturally sterile. The journalist William Shannon said, 'The Eisenhower years have been years of flabbiness and self-satisfaction and gross materialism ... It has been the age of the slob.' Novelist **Norman Mailer** (see page 191) called the 1950s 'one of the worst decades in the history of man'.

WHAT LED TO THE COLLAPSE OF CONSENSUS 1968–1989?

By the mid-1960s, consensus was being replaced by discord and conflict in the USA. Three sources of conflict in particular stand out:

1 Racial unrest and urban riots

2 Escalation of the war in Vietnam

3 Growth of radical protest movements among minorities and ethnic groups.

Together these forces produced levels of domesti turmoil unheard of since 1945. They divide Americans and caused widespread disillusionmer with traditional American beliefs. To th **disaffected**, the nation seemed incapable c confronting its many problems. They felt that the were shut out of the democratic process, and tha their individual voices had no effect on politica leaders. Many of them resorted to violence an law-breaking as the only method of getting th 'system' to listen to their demands.

Youth Culture

Many of the 'baby boomers' were in their mic teens by the 1960s. The term '**teenager**' was firs used in the USA during the 1940s to describe th 13–19 age group.

Educational reforms and the expansion of acces to third-level training (the GI Bill) after 194 enabled most young people to stay in full-tim education longer than any previous generatior Coming from comfortable middle-class home: they enjoyed the benefits of the affluent societ The economic boom provided them with part-tim jobs. With their increased numbers and thei spending power they created a new market. Fc the first time in history young people becam mass consumers of products designed to cater fc them as a distinct group – fashion, musi cosmetics, magazines and books. Young peopl themselves became aware of their uniqueness as group, and developed their own cultural identity.

A young couple at a New York discotheque, 1966

Anti-Vietnam War demonstration, San Franscisco, California

The Sexual Revolution

A new, more permissive attitude towards sex emerged in the 1960s. Studies by **Dr Alfred Kinsey** in the late 1940s and early 1950s showed that Americans were less traditional in their sexual behaviour than most people assumed. The contraceptive **pill** was invented in the 1950s and became widely available during the 1960s. Besides reducing the birth rate, the pill allowed risk-free sex, including extra-marital sex. More **permissive sexual values** were also encouraged by the decline in censorship when the Supreme Court ruled that a book, play or film had to be 'utterly without redeeming social value' to be regarded as obscene. The women's movement promoted a more liberal attitude to sex. By the mid-1960s, conventional attitudes about premarital sex, contraception and abortion, homosexuality and pornography were being openly challenged, particularly by the younger generation.

By the late 1970s, the growing rate of sexually transmitted diseases led many young people to question the benefits of the sexual revolution. In the 1980s, young people became more cautious about sex, particularly with the advent of AIDS.

The Generation Gap

The emergence of youth culture created a **generation gap**. Parents and the older generations became alarmed by what they saw: unacceptable tastes in dress, music and general attitudes and behaviour among the younger generation. They were particularly critical of rock'n'roll, calling it 'the devil's music'. Rock'n'roll had begun in the 1950s with Elvis Presley and Chuck Berry (but the music itself had its roots in the African-American Baptist harmonies of the Deep South from earlier in the century – the music of Elvis's childhood). During the 1960s, two British bands, the Beatles and the Rolling Stones, gained huge popularity with American youth. Rock was not just about music – it was also about fashion and lifestyle. Fans wore long hair and colourful clothes. Illegal drug use became popular around the rock scene and many middle-class white youths experimented with drugs such as marijuana and LSD (known as acid).

Permissive sexual attitudes and sexual behaviour was another feature of the rock scene. The older generation who grew up in the Depression years had worked hard for their new-found economic successes, and they failed to understand young people's rejection of materialism and American values.

The younger generation blamed older people for failing to address the social and political problems the USA faced in the 1960s. They accused them of hypocrisy, of preaching one thing and doing the opposite. They rejected the advice and 'wisdom' their parents offered, and many scorned the whole 'straight' world (the world of the traditional establishment).

The Counter-Culture

As the 1960s unfolded, a mood of rebellion became the norm among young people. Behaviour and attitudes that had previously been forbidden were no longer so.

During the 1960s, some youth groups went on to become involved in political protest movements. Many joined the **anti-war** and **civil rights** movements. Others, less politically motivated, formed a counter-culture, a new sub-culture within the youth movement. This group largely chose to turn its back on American society.

The followers of the counter-culture became known as **hippies**. The term comes from 'hip' – a jazz music expression meaning knowledgeable or 'with it'. They showed their contempt for middle-class values by wearing long hair, love beads, faded patched jeans and sandals. Hippies culti-vated their own way of speaking, often using slang and phrases borrowed from black ghetto youth ('Hey, man', 'groovy', etc.). They craved a life more in tune with nature and peace, and wore flowers in their hair and around their necks, referring to themselves as 'flower children'. Many of them lived in rural **communes**, or in urban areas like the Haight-Ashbury district in San Francisco or Greenwich Village in New York. There they practised **free love** and used drugs. **Timothy Leary**, a young Harvard professor, called on hippies to 'Tune in, turn on and drop out.'

In August 1969, over 400,000 young people attended the **Woodstock** Music and Art Festival in upstate New York. Over three chaotic days, most of them immersed themselves in a frenzy of 'drugs and sex and rock'n'roll'. Media reports on the festival outraged many older Americans.

The hippy movement did not last long. By 1970, sharp differences began to divide the movement. Most of them wanted nothing to do with violence, but a militant element who called themselves **Yippies** began to emerge. The leaders of this group were Jerry Rubin and Abbie Hoffman. Rubin advocated violence and law-breaking, saying, 'When in doubt BURN ... Fire is the revolutionary's god ... Burn the flag, burn churches. Burn, Burn, Burn.'

Many members of the counter-culture became victims of their own excesses. They suffered the physical and psychological effects of drug-taking, broken relationships and abuse. They attracted unfavourable media attention, and their liberal attitudes led to a conservative backlash in politics over the next two decades.

By the mid-1980s a new mood emerged among young Americans. This generation was less interested in challenging the system and wanted to leave the social and political unrest of the 1960s and 1970s behind them.

Probably the most enduring legacy of the counter-culture movement was its contribution to raising

Hippies at Woodstock Music and Art Festival, 1969

awareness about the **environment**. Flower power and the hippies wanted harmony with nature and were opposed to the destruction of the natural environment to make way for the demands of the consumer society.

The two oil crises in the 1970s had highlighted the need for **conservation** and the American public came to realise that their dependence on imported oil needed to be reduced. Opinion polls indicated that the main issue of concern for Americans in the 1970s was the environment, and this led to the emergence of an **environmental movement** that attracted widespread support. Young people dominated this new movement throughout the 1980s and 1990s, many of them taking their inspiration from the 1960s generation of hippies.

WHAT IS MULTICULTURALISM IN THE USA?

The growth of protest movements, and particularly the emergence of Black Power (see page 57), promoted the development of ethnic pride in the 1960s.

The children and grandchildren of earlier European immigrants began to look for their roots, seeking to express their own national identity. Seeking to express their culture in food, many people opened ethnic restaurants in large cities in the USA. Irish bars, Italian pizza places, Jewish bakeries, etc. promoted the traditions and customs of the home country. Various ethnic groups demanded that their history be included in school textbooks and catered for in university courses. German studies, Spanish studies, Polish studies and Irish studies programmes were offered in most colleges. Ethnic festivals were organised, promoting the music, dance and culture of the different ethnic groups.

Mexican Americans were at the forefront of this revival in ethnic consciousness (being aware of one's own culture, its traditions and values). The civil rights activist Cesar Chavez inspired an outburst of ethnic consciousness among Mexican Americans. They campaigned for bilingual programmes and better educational opportunities. Calling themselves Chicanos, a previously

derogatory term, young activists started to take pride in their cultural heritage.

Native Americans also began to demand recognition for their culture. They set up the **American Indian Movement** (**AIM**) and put pressure on the government to provide social and economic justice for their people. Red Power succeeded in changing Native American attitudes; they no longer felt inferior to whites and were proud to express their cultural differences.

The **Immigration and Nationality Act** (1965) abolished the old national quota system (for entering the country and for residency or citizenship rights) which favoured Western Europeans. Instead of national quotas, people with job skills and who had immediate family living in the USA were given preference. Immigration in the 1970s and 1980s grew dramatically, bringing a new wave of mainly Latin American and Asian immigrants into the USA. They were less willing than earlier immigrants to be assimilated into mainstream American culture, and tended to maintain their own cultural difference.

Critics of Multiculturalism

Many white native-born Americans opposed these multicultural trends. They argued that America was a **melting pot** that worked well when immigrants accepted the customs and traditions of their adopted country. They said that multiculturalism would lead to racial tensions and cause unnecessary divisions between different ethnic groups. Furthermore, ethnic difference would pose a threat to traditional American values. Their position implied stripping immigrants of their own culture and moulding them into 'good Americans', all of whom live in the 'melting pot'.

Other critics complained that American educational standards would suffer if school and college courses and curricula were changed to suit the needs of immigrants who lacked English language skills.

Some critics believed that multiculturalism led to social problems. Haunted by the ghetto riots of the 1960s, they saw new immigrants settling in urban areas where many of them turned to crime. If immigrants were converted to the 'American

way of life' and abandoned their own cultures this could be avoided, they claimed.

Many of the opponents of multiculturalism formed part of the New Right (supporters of traditional/ conservative social and political views) in the 1980s, and supported President Reagan.

In 1986, of the 601,000 new immigrants who came to the USA, nearly 500,000 were from Asia and Latin America. In addition, thousands of undocumented illegal immigrants, mainly from Mexico, also arrived. The Spanish language was more frequently heard than English in parts of Los Angeles, Miami, New York and many other cities. The debate between the supporters of multi-culturalism and the proponents of the melting pot continued throughout the 1980s.

END-OF-CHAPTER REVIEW

DOCUMENT

The following extract recounts the experiences of a Hollywood actor, Lee J. Cobb, who was called to testify before the HUAC.

> *When the facilities of the government of the United States are drawn on an individual it can be terrifying. The blacklist is just the opening gambit – being deprived of work. Your passport is confiscated. That's minor. But not being able to move without being tailed is something else. After a certain point it grows to implied as well as articulated threats, and people succumb. My wife did, and she was institutionalised.*

Source: *Naming Names* by Victor Navasky

1 DOCUMENT QUESTIONS

a) What does the author say is 'terrifying'?

b) What happened to his wife?

c) What kind of source is this? Give one reason for your answer.

d) Do you think this is an objective source? Explain your answer.

2 ORDINARY LEVEL QUESTIONS

Write a paragraph on the following:

a) The Red Scare and Hollywood.

b) Youth culture in modern America. (Leaving Cert 2006)

c) Marilyn Monroe. (Leaving Cert 2007)

3 HIGHER LEVEL ESSAYS

a) What factors contributed to the emergence of cultural consensus in post-war USA?

b) How did the emergence of the counter-culture and multiculturalism lead to a collapse of consensus 1968–89?

c) What was the significance of Hollywood in US history 1945–68? (Amended Leaving Cert 2012)

⑩ Religion in Modern US Culture

Religious Terms Explained

In this chapter you will meet some possibly unfamiliar terms relating to religion in the United States. Here is a brief explanation of these terms:

born again Phrase used by many Americans who claim to have rediscovered their personal faith in God

conservative In a religious sense, a person who puts great importance on traditional moral values

denomination Religious group (or strand of a particular group)

evangelical/fundamentalist Christians with a strong belief in the Bible as the source of all truth. Usually very conservative, and unhappy at developments in US society

liberal On religious matters, a liberal would feel that religion should take account of the changing values in society and would favour the separation of Church and State

Moral Majority Coalition of Christian groups who wanted to influence the political agenda by promoting what they saw as traditional values

organised religion Traditional view of religion, judged by church attendance

religious right/Christian right Movement that developed among evangelical Protestants to reverse or stop liberal reforms in matters such as morals, women's rights and education

secular state A country that does not support or favour one religion. Religion is seen as a personal matter

traditional values Respect for your neighbours, importance of the family, sexual restraint, patriotism, hard work, etc.

Baptist Church congregation with pastor, 1979

Religious freedom and the separation of Church and State are enshrined in the American Constitution. The 1st Amendment states: 'Congress shall make no law respecting an establishment of religion, or prohibiting the free exercise thereof ...'

This means that the USA is a **secular** state and that there is no support for any religious group or denomination from federal or state governments. For example, public schools are strictly non-religious. Despite this, Americans are traditionally very religious. For example, during the 1950s, 95 per cent of Americans believed in God and church attendance was about 40 per cent. It is no surprise, therefore, that religion has always played a very important role in US culture. In the nineteenth century, anti-Catholic feeling was very strong, especially when millions of Catholic Irish and German immigrants arrived in the USA. Culturally, Protestantism played a very important role in the Southern states, the so-called **Bible Belt**.

Traditionally US politics and society were dominated by wealthy Protestants who lived in the Northeastern states (New England), loosely referred to as White Anglo-Saxon Protestants (**WASPs**). What mattered most was being white and Protestant. Up to 1989, most US presidents, except John F. Kennedy, came from this background.

WHAT ARE THE MAIN RELIGIOUS GROUPS IN THE USA?

America is a predominantly Protestant country with a large number of other religious groups or denominations. Many commentators refer to a **three-faith model**:

- **Protestants** comprise well over half of the population, but no one Protestant group makes up a majority. The most numerous are the Baptist, Lutheran, Methodist, Presbyterian, Episcopalian (similar to the Church of Ireland) and the different Pentecostal churches. There has been a tradition in the USA of home-grown churches, of which the Mormons, Christian Scientists and the Assemblies of God are probably the most famous. Protestants in the north and the west of the country tend to be more liberal, socially and culturally. However, in the south and midwest they tend to be more conservative. Commentators often refer to strict Protestants who place great emphasis on the Bible as **fundamentalists**. A high percentage of US Protestants describe themselves as **evangelical** or **born-again Christians**.

- **Catholics** are the largest single religious group in the USA, making up a quarter of the population. Geographically they are most numerous in the north-east and the south-west. There are major divisions in the Catholic church on social issues, such as divorce, and many of the faithful have ignored Church teachings on these issues.

- ⊙ **Jews** make up the third largest religious group in the USA, which traditionally has the largest Jewish population in the world. Jews are divided into Reform, Conservative and Orthodox congregations and communities. New York, New Jersey, Florida and California have the largest Jewish populations.

- ⊙ The numbers of Muslims and Orthodox Christians have grown considerably since World War II.

WHY WAS RELIGION IMPORTANT IN THE 1950s?

During the 1950s the United States was a very religious country. The Cold War against 'godless communism' helped to promote religion. American families living in the new suburbs sought to pass on values to their children by joining churches and nearly 70 per cent of the population belonged to a church. This established the church and family as the **twin pillars** of respectability for most Americans. In 1954, 'one nation under God' was added to the Pledge of Allegiance, while in 1956 'In God We Trust' was adopted as the national motto and put on coins and notes. President Eisenhower began cabinet meetings with a prayer – a tradition that was followed by later presidents.

In the USA there are a number of African-American Protestant churches. Most developed in the nineteenth century. Some resulted from divisions over slavery in mainstream churches. Among the largest are the National Baptist Convention, the African Methodist Church and the Church of God in Christ.

The fight against 'godless communism' was supported by most religious leaders and the majority of their congregations. Organisations such as Billy James Hargis's **Christian Crusade** and Fred Schwarz's **Christian Anti-Communist Crusade** vigorously attacked communism as godless and immoral. These groups helped sustain the anti-communist hysteria of the McCarthy period. Religion had now become a badge of patriotism.

During the 1950s, evangelical Protestant preachers attracted a large following. Preaching a simple message based on the Bible, they denounced affluence and consumerism, and called on people to turn away from 'sins' like drinking, smoking, gambling, swearing and dancing. One of the most popular of these preachers was the southern Baptist **Billy Graham** (see page 194). He had a weekly television show in which he urged viewers to make 'a decision for Christ'. Huge crowds attended his religious meetings. He was also a frequent guest of presidents.

WHAT ROLE DID RELIGION PLAY IN RACE RELATIONS?

Religion played a key role in the black civil rights movement. Most of the leaders were Protestant ministers such as **Dr Martin Luther King**. They used Christian ideals to fight racial injustice. However, a large measure of resistance to civil rights came from the socially conservative white Protestant churches of the southern states, where there was still a lot of religious segregation. For example, white and black Baptists went to their own churches. Even after the success of the civil rights movement this division remained. A poll in 1980 found that nearly 50 per cent of Americans, black or white, went to a service where there was no member of the other race present.

During the 1960s, the **Muslim** faith attracted growing numbers of black people in northern ghettos. They rejected both Christianity – the religion given to them by their 'slave masters' – and racial integration (see Chapter 4). They changed their 'slave' Christian names to Islamic ones. The most famous example was **Muhammad Ali** (see page 192). Though the majority of blacks continued to follow the Christian ideas of Martin Luther King, the growing popularity of militant Muslim views caused many whites to turn away from the civil rights movement.

WHY DID ORGANISED RELIGION DECLINE IN THE 1960s?

The 1960 presidential election saw a revival of anti-Catholic suspicion directed at the Democratic candidate, John F. Kennedy (the first Catholic US president). Many Protestants worried that he would take orders from the Pope. The **Southern Baptist Convention** passed a resolution voicing doubts that Kennedy or any Catholic could be president of the United States. Kennedy tackled these criticisms and his election was seen as a victory by US Catholics. However, he had to add the Protestant **Lyndon B. Johnson** to his election ticket as vice-president to win over those who harboured suspicions.

The 1960s were to prove a difficult time for religion in the USA. Rising affluence led to a decline in church attendance. This decline continued through the 1970s and 1980s. Religion played a smaller role in people's lives, especially among the baby-boomers (those born in the 1950s). It is estimated that up to 40 per cent of the population abandoned religion entirely. The introduction of the contraceptive **pill** led to a sexual revolution that scandalised conservative Americans.

Rock'n'roll music encouraged many US teenagers to espouse a different set of values from their parents (see Chapter 9). Organised religion was now challenged by a growing counter-culture that rejected religion as part of the 'establishment'.

The Supreme Court supported an agenda of civil liberties that gave more power to individuals to make choices about their private behaviour. This agenda was also supported and promoted by the powerful feminist movement.

Many people felt that their churches should take account of these changes in society. They were known as **liberals**. Many Catholics agreed with this view. However, on the other hand the social upheavals of the decade resulted in a growing demand for a return to traditional values. Americans were worried about the decline of morals in US society, pointing to increasing crime rates, the growth of feminism and soaring divorce rates. For many older people, going to church, building a career and being patriotic became political statements. This conservative reaction helps to explain Richard Nixon's victory in the 1968 presidential election. Since the 1960s those who are religious are more likely to vote Republican than Democrat.

Religion and the American People

Opinion polls suggest that religion was a very significant part of the lives of most Americans. Study the following results of opinion polls and answer the questions below.

1 Importance of Religion

Responses to the question: How important would you say religion is in your life?

	1952 %	1978 %	1990 %
Very important	75	52	54
Fairly important	20	32	36
Not very important	5	16	10

2 Church Attendance

Responses to the question: How often do you attend church?

	1955 %	1972 %	1989 %
Regularly (weekly)	50	41	35
Occasionally	27	30	28
Seldom	16	20	20
Never	7	9	16

Source: Roper Center for Public Opinion Research, University of Connecticut, www.ropercenter.uconn.edu/

QUESTIONS

1 From the evidence presented in the responses to question 1 above, how important is religion in the life of Americans?

2 What pattern has emerged in regular church attendance since the 1950s?

3 How do you explain the changes in some of the figures since the 1950s?

4 Are opinion polls reliable sources of information? Explain your answer.

WHAT ROLE DID THE MORAL MAJORITY MOVEMENT PLAY IN US POLITICS?

In the 1970s, the **conservative backlash** led to the creation of a powerful political movement that was called the **religious right** or the **Christian right**. This movement was dominated by evangelical Protestants. They had traditionally avoided politics but now they felt they had to act to 'save America'. They believed that the Supreme Court had interpreted separation of Church and State in a way that was hostile to religion – for example, prayer and Bible reading was now banned in public schools. Attempts to get schools to teach the biblical view on the origins of the world (**creationism**) were rejected by the Supreme Court. Evangelicals further worried about the refusal of courts to grant tax exemption to private Christian schools and universities.

The issue of tax exemption was very important as charitable organisations did not have to pay tax. The Supreme Court said that any institution that practised discrimination was not a charitable organisation and, therefore, could not be tax exempt. Many evangelical schools and universities were segregated or practised discrimination. For example, Bob Jones University did not admit African Americans until 1971, and did not allow inter-racial dating. When it was proposed to remove Bob Jones University's tax-exempt status there was outrage among evangelicals. They argued that as they did not receive federal funding, the government had no right to interfere in how they ran their schools or universities.

Legislation to allow **abortion** was, however, the most controversial issue for the Christian right. Allowing abortion drew very strong opposition from both evangelical Protestants and conservative Catholics. Both groups were further alarmed at feminism and the gay rights lobby.

One interesting aspect of American religious culture has been the growth of televangelism. Polls identify that a quarter of Americans watch religious programmes once a week. The use of TV to spread the Christian message started in the 1950s. In the 1980s, preachers like Oral Roberts, Pat Robertson, Jimmy Swaggart and Jim Bakker had a huge following that responded enthusiastically to appeals for funds. They were known as televangelists. Jimmy Swaggart's TV ministry generated over $150 million a year. Bakker and his wife also ran a theme park called Heritage USA – a Disneyland for Christians – that was the third largest in the USA. Many televangelists promoted the agenda of the religious right.

The most important force representing the religious right was the political lobby group called

Pope John Paul II makes his way to an open-air mass in Chicago during his visit to the USA in 1979. Many Catholics in the USA were opposed to the Church's position on divorce, contraception and abortion

President Reagan (right) chats with Jerry Falwell during a meeting with School Prayer Leaders in the Cabinet Room in the White House, July 1983

the **Moral Majority**. It was founded in 1979 by **Jerry Falwell**, a Baptist minister from Virginia. He believed that 'the idea that religion and politics don't mix was invented by the Devil to keep Christians from running their own country.'

Moral Majority received support from some Catholics and Jews because of its message of family values, prayers in schools, law and order, lower taxes and increased defence spending. It opposed abortion, feminism and gay rights. In the 1980 presidential election, there were three declared **born-again** Christian candidates – Carter, Reagan and John Anderson – but it was Reagan who received the support of Falwell and his organisation. Moral Majority played an influential role during his presidency and in his re-election in 1984.

Factors in the Growth of the Religious Right
- Decline in traditional values and morality
- Ban on religious activity in public schools
- Legalisation of abortion
- Growth of feminism and gay rights movement

The name Moral Majority was chosen as it suggested that it represented the views of the majority of Americans. However, opinion polls suggested that this was not the case.

Most Protestants and Catholics, while agreeing with some of the social views of the Moral Majority, disliked its political message. Some evangelical religious leaders were uncomfortable with the religious right and felt that the role of religion was to look after people's souls, not get involved in politics; for example, **Billy Graham** commented, 'I don't think Jesus Christ or the Apostles took sides in the political arena of the day.' Although an evangelical himself, Jimmy Carter was a strong critic of the political agenda of the religious right, especially its opposition to women's rights.

The movement was also weakened by a number of scandals involving some of the televangelists. One concerned **Jim Bakker** and his wife **Tammy Faye Bakker**. In 1987, Bakker was forced to resign following a sexual scandal involving a former secretary. He was later imprisoned after it emerged that he had been stealing from his own organisation to fund his lavish lifestyle. Another televangelist, **Jimmy Swaggart**, was discredited in 1988 after confessing on air to having been with a prostitute. He was expelled from his church and most of his audience deserted him. These and other scandals hurt the evangelical movement as contributions fell off and membership declined. They also played into the hands of the critics of the religious right, who accused the movement of hypocrisy.

In 1987, after a number of quarrels, Falwell left the Moral Majority movement and it was dissolved in 1989. Its place was taken by the **Christian Coalition of America**, set up by Pat Robertson, who had unsuccessfully stood against George Bush Sr in the Republican primaries in 1988. He

Opinion Poll on Abortion

Americans continued to be very divided on the issue of abortion, as the responses to the following question show.

Do you think abortions should be legal in all circumstances, legal under certain circumstances or illegal in all circumstances?

	1975 %	1989 %
Legal in all circumstances	21	27
Legal under certain circumstances	54	50
Illegal in all circumstances	22	18
Don't know	2	6

now built this organisation into one of America's most powerful lobby groups. Like its predecessor, it had a very influential role in the Republican Party.

In 1989, the USA was still a very religious society. There had been some decline in church attendance, but a majority of people still went to church at least once a month – 40 per cent went every week. Three-quarters of people described themselves as religious and nearly 70 per cent were members of their local church (nearly the same as in the 1950s). For most families, Christmas and Easter involved a visit to the local church. While there was a lot of disagreement about issues such as abortion, the Religious Right and gay rights, religion still played a very central role in US culture and everyday life.

QUESTIONS

1 What is meant by the separation of Church and State?

2 Explain the origin of the term 'Bible Belt'.

3 What are the main Protestant groups in the USA?

4 What role was played by religion in the 1950s?

5 What impact did the Protestant churches have on the civil rights movement?

6 Why did organised religion decline in the 1960s?

7 Why were many Americans worried about the developments in US society in the late 1960s and early 1970s?

8 What were the aims of the Moral Majority movement? How influential was it in US politics?

9 What was the attitude of Jimmy Carter and Billy Graham to the religious right?

10 How was the religious right discredited in the eyes of many people?

11 What evidence is there to show that the United States was still a religious society in 1989?

DOCUMENT

This is an extract from a speech given by John F. Kennedy to the Greater Houston Ministerial Association on 12 September 1960 at the Rice Hotel in Houston, Texas. The Ministerial Association was a group of Protestant ministers.

But because I am a Catholic, and no Catholic has ever been elected President, the real issues in this campaign have been obscured – perhaps deliberately, in some quarters less responsible than this. So it is apparently necessary for me to state once again – not what kind of church I believe in, for that should be important only to me – but what kind of America I believe in.

I believe in an America where the separation of church and state is absolute; where no Catholic bishop would tell the President ... how to act, and no Protestant minister would tell his parishioners for whom to vote; where no church or church school is granted any public funds or political preference, and where no man is denied public office merely because his religion differs from the President who might appoint him, or the people who might elect him.

But let me stress again that these are my views – for contrary to common newspaper usage, I am not the Catholic candidate for President. I am the Democratic Party's candidate for President who happens also to be a Catholic. I do not speak for my church on public matters – and the church does not speak for me.

Source: John F. Kennedy Presidential Library and Museum, www.jfklibrary.org/

1 DOCUMENT QUESTIONS

a) Why does John F. Kennedy feel that 'the real issues in this campaign have been obscured'?

b) What examples does he give to show he supports separation of Church and State?

c) What role does he say his religion plays in public matters?

d) Would you agree that John F. Kennedy was a liberal? Support your views with reference to the text.

2 ORDINARY LEVEL QUESTIONS

a) How and why did Billy Graham become such a popular religious leader in the United States? (Leaving Cert 2006)

b) What effects did events of the 1960s have on religion in the USA?

3 HIGHER LEVEL ESSAYS

a) How important was the role played by religion in US society between 1945 and 1989?

b) What was the contribution of religion to modern American culture? (Amended Leaving Cert 2013)

c) What impact did the social changes of the 1960s and 1970s have on religion in the USA?

11 Advances in Military and Information Technology 1945–1991

KEY QUESTIONS

This chapter examines the major advances in military and information technology in the United States between 1945 and 1989. The advances in space technology are discussed in Chapter 12.

WHAT WERE THE MAIN ADVANCES IN MILITARY TECHNOLOGY?

From 1945 onwards the United States established itself as the leader in military technology. The primary reason for this was Cold War rivalry with the USSR. In the second half of the twentieth century the US military spent vast sums of money in developing technology that would give it an edge over the USSR.

The USA's rise to superpower status came about as a result of its bombing of Japan (Hiroshima and Nagasaki, 1945), which ended World War II. While Germany made most of the technological advances in the war, the USA had made a number of significant contributions, especially in the air, with the **Mustang fighter** and the **B-29 bomber**. The USA also made the defining technological discovery of

the war, the **atomic bomb**. The largest scientific programme in history, **Operation Manhattan**, developed and tested an atomic device in July 1945. This new weapon was used with devastating effect on the cities of Hiroshima and Nagasaki in August 1945. The **nuclear age** had begun.

During the Cold War the military in both the USA and the USSR had two main types of weapon:

- **Conventional weapons** – non-nuclear weapons, such as tanks, missiles, etc. The Warsaw Pact had an enormous advantage over NATO in terms of conventional weapons.
- **Nuclear weapons** – weapons with enormous explosive power. As a rule US missiles were more accurate, while Soviet missiles were more powerful.
- There were three main ways to launch nuclear missiles and bombs:
  - ➜ Air – bombs and planes
  - ➜ Sea – submarine launch
  - ➜ Land – silos and mobile missiles.

There were also stockpiles of biological (e.g. anthrax) and chemical (poison gas) weapons.

The devastation caused by the atomic bomb dropped on Hiroshima. This bomb had the same yield as 13,000 tons of TNT. Bombs were later developed that were far more powerful than this

As the Cold War progressed, nuclear weapons were developed and 'improved' upon, leading to an **arms race** between the USA and the USSR. The Americans wanted to develop weapons in order to respond to a potential Soviet attack.

Nuclear weapons can be delivered in two ways: bombs and missile rockets.

Bombs

The **US Air Force** saw bombs delivered by planes, rather than missiles, as the best way to launch a nuclear attack. The first atomic bombs dropped on Japan were soon further developed so that the **yield** (power) was increased, while their physical size was reduced.

In 1952, the USA detonated the first **hydrogen** (H-bomb) or **fusion** bomb. The H-bomb was up to a thousand times more powerful than the atom bomb. In 1954, a bomb small enough to be dropped from a bomber was built. The yield of bombs was now measured in megatons (millions of tons) rather than kilotons (thousands of tons) of **TNT**. In the early 1960s the controversial **neutron bomb** was tested. It was designed to kill people but leave buildings undamaged. However, by the late 1950s, **rockets** had overtaken bombs as the main method of delivery.

Rockets

The Germans had used the first modern ballistic rocket, or missile, the **V2**, during World War II.

The mushroom cloud from the 'Mike' test of 1952, the first test of a hydrogen bomb. The blast completely obliterated the small island of Elugelab in the Pacific. The USA has carried out over a thousand nuclear tests. After 1963, these types of test were banned by the Test Ban Treaty (see page 97). The USA then carried out tests underground in Nevada

Both the USA and the USSR realised the significance of this new weapon. As the war ended, both tried to get their hands on German missiles and the scientists who developed them. The USA succeeded in capturing the head of the programme, **Wernher von Braun**, and most of his team. With their help the USA started developing rockets.

Progress was slow, however, as the US military thought bombs were more important than rockets until events in 1957 changed attitudes dramatically.

That year the Soviets launched their first **intercontinental ballistic missile (ICBM)** and a few months later the satellite **Sputnik I** (see Chapter 12). This led the USA to accelerate its rocket programme as it now felt very vulnerable to rocket attacks from the USSR. The feeling was that if the Soviets could launch a satellite into space they could fire a nuclear missile to the USA. Many commentators claimed that a **missile gap** had opened between the USSR and the USA. In December 1957, the USA tested its first ICBM, the **Atlas** rocket.

As with Sputnik, advances in rocket technology were closely linked to space exploration. Rockets were used to fire satellites and craft into space. For example, the Atlas rocket was used on both the **Mariner** and **Mercury** space programmes. Wernher von Braun later worked on the **Apollo** programme.

Developments in the 1960s

The 'missile gap' was in fact an illusion; the USA actually had more missiles than the Soviets. The USA was to pull further ahead of the USSR in rocket development during the 1960s. In 1962, the **Minuteman** ICBM was introduced to the US nuclear arsenal. The type of fuel it used meant that it could be prepared for use very quickly, hence its name. It was housed in reinforced concrete underground chambers (known as **silos**) throughout the western USA. It used a **computer guidance system** that improved its accuracy. It could fly 3,000km at a speed of 24,000km per hour, delivering a warhead of up to one megaton. A modified version of this missile still remains in service today.

An important development of the late 1960s saw **multiple independently targetable re-entry vehicles (MIRVs)** fitted on missiles. Individual missiles now had a number of separate **warheads** (the actual explosive device). These warheads could be programmed to hit a number of different targets.

Test launch of a Minuteman missile

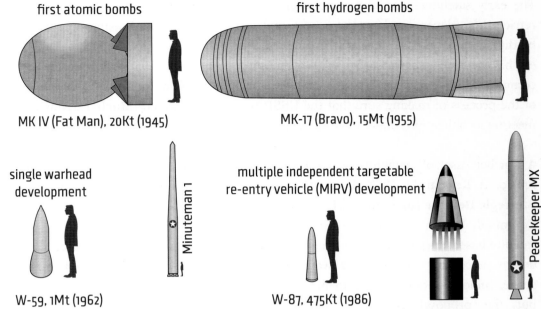

How US nuclear weapons have developed in both size and yield. (Kt = kiloton; Mt = megaton)

first atomic bombs

MK IV (Fat Man), 20Kt (1945)

first hydrogen bombs

MK-17 (Bravo), 15Mt (1955)

single warhead development

W-59, 1Mt (1962)

Minuteman 1

multiple independent targetable re-entry vehicle (MIRV) development

W-87, 475Kt (1986)

Peacekeeper MX

Early warning systems that used **radar** were developed to warn of a Soviet attack. Computers built by IBM were used to process signals and predict impact sites.

Submarines

In the 1960s, submarines started to be powered with **nuclear reactors** and could now fire nuclear missiles. The **Polaris missile** was the first submarine-launched system; in the 1980s it was replaced by the **Trident missile**. In the 1960s, the US government adopted the theory of **mutual assured destruction** (**MAD**) (see page 125). It believed that it could deter the USSR from ever using nuclear weapons by possessing weapons that were very difficult to locate and destroy. For the USA, it was important that the Soviets knew that even if they destroyed the USA, they themselves would also be annihilated. Submarines played a crucial role in deterrence as they were virtually undetectable.

> The US military refer to a lost nuclear weapon as a 'broken arrow'. During the Cold War the USA lost 11 missiles that were never recovered. There were also a number of accidents, most of which involved planes or submarines.

Further Developments in Nuclear Weapons

The number of rockets in the US nuclear arsenal peaked in 1970. By this time, US military scientists were concentrating on improving the **accuracy** of their missiles and reducing the size of their warheads. They wanted to land their missiles as close as possible to their target (referred to as **circular error probability**).

Tomahawk cruise missiles were introduced in the late 1970s. They flew at low altitude to avoid radar. They had an on-board computer guidance system and were very accurate. These missiles could be launched from the air, by land, from ships or submarines after being fitted with a conventional or nuclear warhead.

The **Peacekeeper missile**, introduced in the 1980s, had ten separate warheads. It could travel over 8,000 kilometres and deliver a warhead within 200 metres of the target. Each 300-kiloton warhead was 25 times more powerful than the bomb dropped on Hiroshima.

Nuclear weapons were not restricted to missiles and bombs. The USA developed nuclear artillery shells, landmines, depth charges and torpedoes.

Spy Satellites

One technological spin-off from the space race and rocket technology was the use of **spy satellites**. The USA launched its first satellite, called **Corona**, in 1960. It flew over the USSR and took pictures of military bases. This type of intelligence gathering was referred to as **national technical means**.

The early satellites used film cameras that were retrieved by planes, but later these were replaced by digital cameras that sent their images back to earth. The satellites were also used to monitor communications, nuclear tests, etc., and were part of the process of making sure that the USSR was meeting its obligations under the SALT agreement.

A further use of satellites was proposed by President Reagan in 1983. He announced the **Strategic Defense Initiative** (SDI) (see page 131). Commonly known as **Star Wars**, SDI would be a satellite-based nuclear defence system that would destroy incoming missiles and warheads from space. Billions of dollars were spent on research, but the proposal proved to be technically impossible.

Satellites allowed the development of **global positioning systems** – which enable soldiers to know where they are on the battlefield. These systems subsequently became very popular commercially.

Aviation

In aviation, the crucial technological change was the development of **jet engines.** First used by the Germans in World War II, these made planes fly faster. The **F86 Sabre**, one of the most successful early US models, was used in combat during the **Korean War**. The use of air power in warfare became a central part of US strategy. It could inflict massive damage to enemy equipment,

supply routes, buildings and fighting strength while minimising US dead and wounded.

In the 1950s, **supersonic jets** were developed that could fly at over 1,000kph, or faster than the speed of sound (**Mach 1**). New fighters, such as the **F-4** and **F-8**, were introduced that were very fast, manoeuvrable and armed with cannon and missiles. In the Vietnam War these planes helped give the USA **air superiority** over the Soviet-built **MiG** fighters used by the North Vietnamese.

Later models introduced in the 1970s, such as the F-14, 15 and 16, used computers in their cockpits and maintained US superiority over their Soviet counterparts.

The **B-52 Stratofortress bomber** was first flown in 1954. Powered by eight jet engines, it was designed as a nuclear bomber but could also drop conventional bombs. It played a major role in the Vietnam War, dropping millions of tons of conventional bombs. It has been so successful that the US Air Force say they plan to keep it in service until 2050.

Spy planes that could fly at great speed were also introduced. They flew far higher than normal planes, thus making them more difficult to shoot down. Introduced in the 1950s, the **U-2** plane could fly at an altitude of 70,000 feet. The **Lockheed Blackbird** remained the world's fastest and highest-flying plane during its operational career.

F-15 jets armed with missiles

Helicopters

Helicopters came into widespread use after World War II. One of the most important models was the Bell UH-1 Iroquois, known as the **Huey**, used extensively during the Vietnam War. It transported troops quickly to an area, evacuated the wounded and gave fire support to the men on the ground. It could also be used for reconnaissance. The Huey was replaced by the **Black Hawk** in the 1970s. This helicopter could carry more men and equipment than a Huey. **Apache** helicopters, introduced in the late 1980s, were designed to attack targets, including tanks.

Stealth Technology and Other Developments

The 1980s saw the development of a new category of plane that used **stealth** technology. These planes were designed to be invisible to **enemy radar** and therefore very difficult to detect. The **F-117** was the first fighter introduced using this technology, while the **B-2** was the first bomber. Stealth technology did not come cheap – it was estimated that each B-2 bomber cost up to $2 billion.

Introduced in 1980, the main US battle tank, the **M1–Abrams**, has a computer-guided firing system and can fight at night. Its powerful gun can destroy targets at a range of four kilometres. It was vastly superior to its Soviet rival, the **T72**.

Aircraft carriers were also nuclear-powered in the 1980s; they were heavily armoured and could stay at sea longer. They became central to US military strategy. A third of a kilometre in length, armed with missiles and carrying over 80 aircraft and helicopters, they could bring US military power to anywhere in the world.

The Military–Industrial Complex

The construction of nuclear missiles and other military equipment resulted in massive contracts for civilian companies. For example:

- **General Electric** worked on developing early missiles.
- **Boeing** built the Minuteman missile.
- **Lockheed Martin** constructed the Atlas and Trident missiles.
- **McDonnell Douglas** had part of the contract for the Tomahawk cruise missile.
- **IBM** built many of the computer systems that the US military used.

It was very unusual for so much money to be spent on weapons in peacetime. Many Americans became worried by the influence that these military contractors and the Department of Defense (the Pentagon) had on members of Congress. In 1961, President Eisenhower coined the phrase the **military–industrial complex** to describe this influence (see page 92).

The F-117 Stealth fighter

The weapons outlined above are not cheap. It is very difficult to find out exactly how much they cost (that is kept secret), but here are some approximate current costs:

- F-16 fighter: $25 million
- B-52 bomber: $119 million (with 20 Cruise missiles)
- Minuteman missile: $50 million
- Ohio class Trident submarine: $4 billion (with Trident missiles)

It is estimated that between 1942 and 1996 the USA spent $5.8 trillion on nuclear weapons alone.

The Modern US Army in Action

The modern US army displayed its technological ability during the **Gulf War** in 1991. Iraqi forces were overwhelmed by a US-dominated coalition. Here are some examples of the military technology that the USA used against the Iraqis:

- **Tomahawk** Cruise missiles launched from ships over 1,600 kilometres away hit targets in Iraq and Kuwait.

- **Laser-guided Smart bombs** targeted specific buildings.

- Often fighting at night, **M1-Abrams** tanks easily destroyed Soviet-built Iraqi tanks.

- **F-117** stealth fighters attacked Baghdad at night.

- **Global positioning systems** allowed troops to know where they were, move at night in the desert and keep their bearings during frequent sandstorms.

As a result the USA suffered minimal casualties in comparison to the Iraqis.

WHAT WERE THE MAIN ADVANCES IN INFORMATION TECHNOLOGY?

Information technology (IT) involves the use of computer **hardware** and **software** to convert, store, process and transmit information. Computers have revolutionised many aspects of American society, especially in the area of work.

This section focuses on the technological developments that brought the computer into most offices and homes, and examines its impact on American life. Computers shrank in size; where once they took up a whole office they could now fit on a desk. Most of the development in computer technology began in research laboratories working for the US military.

When talking about the history of computer development, historians refer to different **generations** of computers. Each generation of computer was faster and smaller than the previous one. As the table on the next page shows, the key development for each generation was with the '**brain**' of the computer that processed the information.

QUESTIONS

1. Why did the Cold War play such an important role in US military technological developments?

2. What was the importance of the hydrogen bomb?

3. Why did the USA not devote many resources to rocket development in the years immediately after the war?

4. In the late 1950s, why did many Americans feel that there was a 'missile gap' between the USA and the USSR?

5. Explain the following terms: ICBM; silo; early warning system; MIRV; MAD; circular error probability.

6. What was the major development in the use of submarines?

7. Explain why air power plays an important role in US military strategy.

8. What is a supersonic jet? Give an example of two models.

9. How were Huey helicopters used in Vietnam?

10. What major development occurred in military planes in the 1980s?

GENERATIONS OF COMPUTERS

Generation	First	Second	Third	Fourth
Time	1940s and 1950s	Late 1950s	1960s	1970s to today
Processor	Vacuum tubes	Transistors	Integrated circuits	Microprocessors

The Early History of Computers

Most Americans' first glimpse of a computer came on presidential election night in 1952. A TV network correctly predicted Eisenhower's landslide victory on 'an **electronic brain**'. Prior to that, computers were only seen in universities or government buildings.

The modern computer was developed during World War II. They were not computers as we know them today, but calculators designed to solve complex mathematical problems, such as code breaking. In Britain, **Alan Turing**'s decoding centre at Bletchley Park constructed **Colossus** to break the German **Enigma** code. This electronic computer was operated using 1,500 vacuum tubes, which were commonly used in radios at the time.

In 1946, scientists working for the US military at the **University of Pennsylvania** built the first general purpose computer, **ENIAC** (**electronic numerical integrator and computer**). This was a high-speed 18,000 tube digital computer weighing 30 tons. It was designed to calculate the flight paths of cannon shells and was later used on nuclear weapons research. It took up 550 metres of floor space and needed six people to operate it. It was controlled with wires plugging into outlets and it required the same power as a small town.

The first US computer, the ENIAC

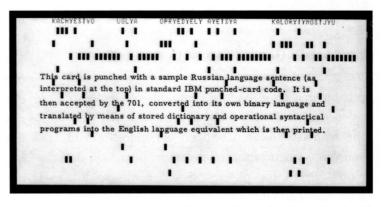

A punch card used in an early computer. It was used to translate Russian into English

The First Commercial Computer

The first commercial computer, **UNIVAC** (**universal automatic computer**), was introduced in 1951. It could solve complex addition problems in less than a second, multiplication in six seconds, and division in 12 seconds. However, it only had a storage memory for 1,000 words. At over $1 million, it was not cheap. **UNIVAC 1**, built

for the **Census Bureau**, was the '**electronic brain**' that predicted Eisenhower's victory. In all, 46 models were sold. Historians refer to these as the **first generation** of computers.

Other companies soon began building their own models. **International Business Machines** (IBM) came to dominate the market. They used **punch cards** to put information or data into their computers.

The Second Generation of Computers

Vacuum tubes were quite large, expensive, un-reliable and required large amounts of electricity to operate (and this generated great heat). In 1947, the **transistor** was developed, an innovation of enormous importance. Its inventors later won the **Nobel Prize** for physics. Some commentators have compared its significance to the invention of the printing press or the motor car.

Transistors were far smaller and cheaper to produce than vacuum tubes, which they soon replaced in radios and TVs, but at first they were not considered suitable for computers. This changed in 1959 when IBM produced the first affordable computer to be operated with transistors. The use of transistors led to the **second generation of computers**. By the early 1960s, huge vacuum tube machines were replaced by smaller, more compact, cheaper and faster digital computers using transistors.

The Impact of Early Computers

Computers in the 1950s and early 1960s were massive in size compared with later models. Data-processing departments – separate rooms in themselves – became commonplace. **General Electric** was one of the first companies to buy a computer, followed by **Du Pont**. Most major banks, the military, universities and insurance companies soon followed. They were also heavily used in the nuclear power industry.

These early computers did not have monitors (screens). Information was entered using **punch cards** and the results were printed. Crews of mostly female keypunch operators inserted information in a form that could be read by the machines. The machines were mainly used in businesses for payroll and storing data. Many people were concerned about their huge capacity to store data on individuals and to displace human workers, and about the potential impact that they might have on civil rights.

The 1964 **IBM 360** became the standard computer in business. Its success meant that by the mid-1980s, the 360 and its descendants had earned IBM over $100 billion. IBM's dominance of the market was such that the eight companies making computers were known as '**IBM and the seven dwarfs**'.

Third-Generation Computers: the Integrated Circuit

As computers were becoming more complex, connecting transistors together became more difficult. An important advance (again linked to the military) was the **integrated circuit** or the **silicon chip** – also known as the **microchip**. This combined a number of transistors on a single piece of silicon (a crystalline non-metal with semi-conducting properties). The research behind the development of this system was funded by the US Department of Defense. The Air Force decided to use the new chips to improve the guidance system on its new **Minuteman** missiles (see page 158). These Minuteman production contracts helped to bring the chip from the laboratory into the marketplace.

Their use saw the development of faster, smaller and more efficient computers, or **mini-computers** as they became known. The older, larger computers were now called **mainframes**. By the end of the 1960s, the modern computer was taking shape. Operators now typed in their data directly using keyboards (no longer using punch cards), and the results were displayed on monitors. The computers transferred the information into **bytes** (kilobytes = 1,000 bytes; and megabytes = one million bytes), and read that. **Operating systems** allowed the computer to run different applications at the same time. Computer science also led to interest in **artificial intelligence**. In the 1968 film *2001: A Space Odyssey*, a supercomputer, HAL, tries to take over a manned mission to Jupiter.

The Microprocessor

Fourth-generation computers were introduced in the 1970s, when the **microprocessor** was developed. A large number of integrated circuits were implanted on tiny silicon chips and these controlled the computer's operations. The company **Intel** introduced the first microprocessor in 1971. This development saw a dramatic reduction in the **size** of computers, which also made them more **affordable**. This first tiny microprocessor had as much power as the giant ENIAC computer. The most dramatic impact of this technological development was the growth of the **personal computer**.

The **floppy disk** was developed in the same year and it greatly improved the means of **data storage** and **transfer** between computers – a floppy could hold around one megabyte of information.

An IBM 360 computer at the Seaboard Coast Line Railroad office

NASA officials at Mission Control monitor data in 1971. Computers were widely used by NASA. For example, the Apollo missions carried specially designed on-board computers for guidance and navigation. On-the-ground computers were used to launch and control flights. They were also used for training and research

Advances in computer technology have been dramatic. The first microprocessor, introduced in 1971, contained 2,300 transistors and was capable of 60,000 operations per second. The one Intel introduced in 1974 was three times as fast. By 1989, the Intel processor was 50 times faster again, with over a million transistors. An advanced microprocessor today can have as many as 151,000,000 transistors.

The Personal Computer

The technology now existed for **personal computers** (PCs), but most companies chose not to develop one as they could see no need for them. It was left to two young men working in a garage to develop the first personal computer (**micro-computer**).

In 1976, **Steve Jobs** and **Steve Wozniak** created a computer and set up a company called **Apple Computers**. The following year they made the first personal computer, the **Apple II**. Affordable and easy to use, with colour graphics, it soon proved very successful and over two million models were sold.

Meanwhile Harvard University dropout **Bill Gates** launched the **Microsoft Corporation**. His company developed the **DOS (disk operating system)** structure. This made computers easier to use for everyone.

In 1981, in response to Apple's success, a computer revolution occurred when IBM brought out its **personal computer**. It used an Intel processor and the Microsoft DOS operating system. This model soon became the standard design for personal computers. Soon the market was flooded with other companies making IBM-compatible machines or **clones**. In 1982, *Time* magazine made the personal computer its 'Person of the Year'.

Developments in the 1980s saw computer speeds increase dramatically, while they also became more affordable for the public. The 1984 **Apple Macintosh** introduced the use of **dropdown menus** and a **mouse**, which made computers far easier to use. **Software** to accompany computers became more user-friendly and graphics improved.

An early model of an IBM personal computer with printer

The Spread of the Personal Computer

In 1985, the **Microsoft Windows** operating system was introduced and this soon became the standard operating system on nearly all computers. In 1989, Microsoft topped sales of $1 billion for the first time. In 1982, the **CD-ROM** (compact disk – read only memory) was introduced. It could store millions more bytes of information (megabytes) than a floppy disk. By the end of the 1980s, portable computers (**laptops**) were becoming commonplace. Computer ownership rocketed from ten million in 1983 to 30 million by 1986.

A spin-off of computer developments was the growth of **computer games**. In 1962, the game **Spacewar** was developed for computer use. Gaming took off in the 1970s, and home video games could be played on TVs or computer monitors. In the 1980s, **Nintendo** games become popular in the USA and 1989 saw the release of the **Game Boy**, the first **hand-held console** (small machine).

Many of the leading computer companies in the USA are located in Silicon Valley. This is an area near San Francisco in California. The term was first coined in 1971 and comes from the use of silicon in microprocessors.

The Internet

By the late 1980s, the Internet started to become available to businesses and the public. Originally called **ARPANET** (Advanced Research Projects Agency Network), it had been developed for the US military by American universities in the late 1960s. The Department of Defense wanted a communications system that would survive a nuclear attack.

ARPANET grew slowly until developments in **fibre optic** technology allowed more information to be transferred down a telephone line, using a modem attached to a computer. The Internet took off, linking universities first in the USA, and then in Europe. By 1989, there were over 100,000 **hosts** online and by 1992 this figure had passed a million. In 1990, the first **search engine** (device to search the hosts that exist on the Internet) was developed and **websites** started to come into use.

The Internet revolutionised communications more radically than the telegraph and the telephone in the nineteenth and twentieth centuries.

The Changing Nature of the Office

By the end of the 1980s, computers had revolutionised the American office. Routine tasks once performed by hand – such as data storage, sending letters, preparing and designing research reports – were now computer-driven. Typewriters, filing cabinets and calculators are largely things of the past. Computers in a company are now networked and staff can transfer files to each other or contact each other by email. Companies can order goods automatically by computer.

Another practical effect of the use of computers was the introduction of **automated teller machines** (ATMs) in the early 1970s – a system where an account holder can withdraw money from the bank without dealing with bank staff.

> The computer revolution saw the creation of many new companies that are today household names, such as Microsoft, Apple, Compaq, Dell, Google and Intel.

QUESTIONS

1 Describe what the ENIAC computer looked like.

2 How did the UNIVAC computer come to the attention of the general public?

3 Why was the development of the transistor such an important step?

4 How do we know IBM was such a successful company in the 1960s?

5 What was the microprocessor and why was it an important advance?

6 What role was played by Apple in the development of the PC?

7 Why were IBM PCs and Apple Macs so important in greatly increasing computer ownership?

8 How important were Intel and Microsoft in computing?

9 Outline the early history of the Internet.

10 How have computers changed the way businesses operate in the USA?

END-OF-CHAPTER REVIEW

DOCUMENT

This an edited account of the Bravo Test conducted on one of the Marshall Islands in 1954. It is from the American PBS site called Race for the Superbomb.

On 1 March 1954, the USA tested an H-bomb design on Bikini Atoll that unexpectedly turned out to be the largest US nuclear test ever exploded. Scientists had grossly underestimated the size of the explosion. They thought it would yield the equivalent of five million tons of TNT, but, in fact, 'Bravo' yielded 15 megatons – a thousand times bigger than the bomb dropped on Hiroshima.

The blast gouged a crater about a mile wide in the reef. Within seconds the fireball was nearly three miles in diameter. Physicist Marshall Rosenbluth, about 30 miles away, remembers that the fireball, 'just kept rising and rising, and spreading

... And the air started getting filled with this grey stuff, which I guess was somewhat radioactive coral.'

A similar gritty, snow-like substance began raining down on the Japanese fishing vessel, the Lucky Dragon, that was about 80 miles east of Bikini. The 23 men aboard had no idea the ash was fallout ... When they returned to port two weeks later they were all suffering severe radiation sickness. One Tokyo newspaper headline demanded that the US authorities 'Tell us the truth about the ashes of death.'

Marshall Islanders were also exposed to the fallout. One islander on Rongelap, about 100 miles east of Bikini, remembers hearing 'a loud explosion and within minutes the ground began to shake. The children played in the colourful ash-like powder. They did not know what it was.' ... The Marshall Islanders weren't rescued for another day, by which time many of them had severe burns and were beginning to lose their hair.

Note: Fallout is radioactive dust created by a nuclear explosion.

Source: *The American Experience: Race for the Superbomb*, PBS, www.pbs.org/wgbh/amex/bomb/peopleevents/pandeAMEX51.html

1 DOCUMENT QUESTIONS

a) What mistake did the scientists who planned the Bravo Test make?

b) What was the effect of the explosion on the Atoll?

c) How did Marshall Rosenbluth describe the blast?

d) What happened to the *Lucky Dragon* and what was the reaction in Japan?

e) What effects did the fallout have on the Marshall Islanders?

f) Are atmospheric tests carried out by the USA today? Explain your answer.

2 ORDINARY LEVEL QUESTIONS

a) What have been the most significant developments in military technology?

b) How has the computer improved since 1945?

3 HIGHER LEVEL ESSAYS

a) How did the Cold War contribute to advances in military technology?

b) What was the impact of the main developments in information technology?

⑫ The Moon Landing (Case Study)

KEY QUESTIONS

'We choose to go to the moon in this decade and do the other things, not because they are easy but because they are hard.' (President Kennedy, 1962)

During the Cold War, rivalry between the superpowers was evident, and not just in the political arena. For a long time the obsession of a few dreamers, **space exploration** turned into a desperate race between the two superpowers. This struggle became known as the **space race**. It was a contest for prestige between the USA and the USSR. Each sought to prove, through space exploration, the superiority of its own political and economic system. The propaganda potential of such successes was enormous, while rocket development had military implications for the **arms race** between the two countries.

At first, all of the major advances came from the Soviets. However, it was the USA that achieved the greatest goal of all, landing a **man on the moon**.

WHAT WERE THE ORIGINS OF THE SPACE RACE?

After World War II, both the USA and USSR worked to build missiles that could travel thousands of kilometres and deliver nuclear warheads. These missiles were called **intercontinental ballistic missiles** (ICBMs) (see Chapter 11). It soon became clear that they could be used to send satellites and people into orbit.

The Americans thought that they had the technological edge over the USSR in missile development.

For example, many German scientists, such as **Wernher von Braun** (see page 158), worked for the US military. During World War II they had developed the first modern missile: the **V2** rocket.

Therefore, in 1957, the USA was shocked when the USSR launched the first man-made satellite into space. The satellite, **Sputnik I**, had a spectacular propaganda impact. The USSR quickly followed this success with the launch of **Sputnik II**. The second probe contained a dog, causing the US press to nickname it 'Muttnik'.

A Glossary of Space Terms

astronaut From the Greek words *astron* (star) and *nautes* (sailor). US term for its spacecraft pilots

booster Rocket engine used to set the space vehicle in motion

capsule Container on a rocket for people, animals and/or instruments. Usually recovered after the flight

cosmonaut 'Sailor of the universe'. The name the USSR gave its space people

countdown Process of checking all the equipment and systems before launching the rocket

docking Manoeuvre in space flight in which two vehicles approach one another and join together

heat shield Covering on a spacecraft that absorbs heat and protects the people inside during re-entry to the earth's atmosphere

launch pad Platform from which rocket is launched

launch vehicle Rocket or combination of rockets used to launch a spacecraft

module Self-contained unit of a spacecraft

orbit Path of a satellite around its parent body, e.g. moon around the earth

re-entry Spacecraft's descent into the earth's atmosphere

stage One of the propulsion units of a rocket

weightlessness Condition of zero gravity in a spacecraft

The Foundation of NASA

It seemed to many in the USA that it was losing the technological battle in both space exploration and rocket development. The military implications were significant as it meant that the Soviets had now developed missiles that could reach and destroy the USA.

The first US satellite, **Explorer I**, was only launched in early 1958. The same year, responding to the Soviet advances in space, **President Eisenhower** authorised the creation of the **National Aeronautics and Space Administration** (**NASA**). Its objective was to develop the US space programme. A space race between the superpowers had now begun in earnest.

Слушай, страна,
Мечта людей зовет!
Сегодня твой народ
Ликует и поет.

ВСЯ ВЛАСТЬ СОВЕТАМЪ!

Soviet poster commemorating the launch of Sputnik I and Sputnik II. The text at the top left translates as, 'Listen, country, the dream of the people is calling! Today your people rejoice and sing.' The lower flag reads, 'All power to the Soviets!'

HOW DID THE SPACE RACE ESCALATE?

To the dismay of the USA, the Soviets seemed to be making all the major advances in the Space Race.

- In 1960, the **Luna II** probe became the first man-made object to land on the moon.

- The following year the Soviets scored a crucial victory when **Yuri Gagarin** became the first man in space, in his craft **Vostok 1**, and the first to orbit the earth. His safe return proved that space flight was possible for humans. This was another massive propaganda victory for the Soviets. His achievement was headline news around the world and he became a hero in the USSR. The Soviets were keen to show him off and he visited the West, where he described his experiences. He was quickly followed by an American, **Alan Shepard**, whose flight lasted 15 minutes. However, the Russians had got their man in space first.

Yuri Gagarin (1934–1968), the first man in space, in 1961. He was seen by both sides as a pioneer in space exploration, and a crater on the moon was named after him. He was killed when his MiG-15 jet crashed

John F. Kennedy's Promise

One of the defining moments of the space race occurred in the same month as Shepard's flight. The new US President, **John F. Kennedy**, was conscious of the propaganda value of the space race and the need to challenge the dominance of the Soviets. In his first **State of the Union Address** to both Houses of Congress, he announced the goal of landing a man on the moon and returning him safely to earth by the end of the decade. As well as the obvious Cold War rivalry, this commitment appealed to Americans' sense of wonder and adventure.

The Problems

Given that an American had only spent 15 minutes in space prior to President Kennedy's announcement, a number of major problems had to be overcome. These included:

- Developing a rocket that could take a craft out of the earth's atmosphere.

- Navigating this craft to the moon.

- Developing life support to ensure that astronauts could survive in space for a number of days.

- Getting craft to dock with and separate from each other in space.

- Landing a craft on the moon.

> NASA chose astronauts from among active-duty military pilots. There were no female astronauts at this time. This contrasted with the Soviets, who sent the first woman, Valentina Tereshkova, into space in 1963.

In order to tackle these problems and fulfil Kennedy's commitment, the **Mercury**, **Gemini** and **Apollo** space programmes were developed. Vast amounts of money and resources were now put into developing the technology needed to get a man to the moon. This gave the US economy a major boost. The programme also had knock-on effects in other areas and it contributed substantially to progress in computers, medicine and communications.

By the mid-1960s, NASA's budget had risen to over $5 billion a year and there were 500,000 people employed directly or indirectly on the space programme. In total, over $27 billion was spent on getting a man to the moon.

The Moon – Some Facts

The observations of astronomers and probes sent by both the USA and USSR had gathered a lot of information about the moon, including:

- It is a quarter the size of the earth.
- At its greatest distance it is 406,494 kilometres away from the earth, at its closest 363,104km.
- The temperature on the moon rises to 121°C during daylight and falls to –162°C during the lunar night.
- Contrary to popular myth there is gravity on the moon, although it is about one-sixth that of the earth's (an astronaut weighing 82kg on earth weighs only 13.6kg on the moon)
- The moon's pull on the earth causes the tides.
- There is no atmosphere or water on the moon.
- There is no life on the moon. NASA was not sure about this at first and placed the crews who landed on the moon in quarantine on their return.

The Mercury Programme (1959–1963)

The one-man **Mercury** missions' major aim was to see if a person could survive in space. They helped to develop hardware for safe space flight, including the return to earth. A lot of information was gathered on how human beings would fare in space. From 1959 to 1963, the United States flew many test flights and six manned Mercury missions. In 1962, **John Glenn** became the first American to orbit the earth. This event caught the popular imagination in the USA. Glenn became a national hero and was given a ticker-tape parade in New York.

Project Gemini (1963–1966)

Once the Mercury programme had proved that manned spaceflight was possible, the two-man project **Gemini** was launched to conduct experiments and work out other issues relating to a moon mission. Ten manned Gemini missions were flown from 1964 to 1966. These missions helped to improve techniques of spacecraft control, docking and space walking.

For example, in 1965, the **Gemini 4** mission performed the first American **extra-vehicular activity** – or space walk. The Soviets had carried out the first space walk earlier the same year.

WHY DID THE USA TAKE THE LEAD IN THE RACE TO THE MOON?

The USA feared that the Soviets would get men to the moon first. However, unknown to the Americans, the Soviets had lost their lead in the space race. There were a number of reasons for this:

John Glenn entering his craft, Friendship 7, before his flight, 1962

- Their programme had long ceased to compare with that of the USA in both scale and resources.

- While the USA was committed to one politically determined goal (that of putting a man on the moon), the Soviet programme increasingly lacked direction.

- The Soviet government did not authorise a manned moon programme until 1964. This meant that they started later than the USA and soon fell even further behind.

- The new Soviet leadership that replaced Khrushchev in 1964 was not as enthusiastic about the programme. However, Kennedy's successor, Lyndon Johnson, was as committed to the space programme as his predecessor.

- The Soviets were sending unmanned craft to the moon, but they were encountering difficulties. There were problems with their new N1 rocket and the results of the unmanned flights to the moon were not promising. They were unwilling to take the risk of manned flight to the moon.

As the Soviets hesitated, the USA jumped in. Developments during the **Apollo** programme were to give the USA victory over the Soviets in the race to put a man on the moon.

HOW DID THE USA PLAN TO LAND ON THE MOON?

Originally conceived in the late 1950s, the aim of the **Apollo** space programme was changed after President Kennedy's dramatic announcement in 1961: its aim was now to land a man on the moon and to bring him back.

In 1967, the programme started badly with the **Apollo 1 tragedy**. Three astronauts – Gus Grissom, Ed White and Roger Chaffee – were killed by a fire in their command module during routine testing. A shocked NASA put a halt to manned missions until the craft was examined.

However, 1967 was to end on a positive note with the successful first test of the **Saturn V** rocket. This rocket, designed by Wernher von Braun, was the most powerful rocket ever built. It consisted of three parts and its first launch astounded everyone who saw it. This was to be the rocket that would power the Apollo spacecraft.

The same year **Colonel Vladimir Komarov** became the first person to die in a space accident. His **Soyuz** craft crashed into the earth after its parachute failed to open correctly.

(Left to right) Gus Grissom, Ed White and Roger Chaffee, who were killed in the Apollo 1 accident. Ed White had been the first American to perform a spacewalk

In October 1968, after over a thousand modifications to the craft, **Apollo 7** was launched successfully into orbit around the earth. In December 1968, **Apollo 8** completed the first manned orbit of the moon. It proved conclusively that it was possible to navigate to the moon and back.

The **Apollo 10** mission was a dress rehearsal for the moon landing. The astronauts separated the lunar module from the main craft. Manned by two astronauts, it descended to within fifteen kilometres of the surface of the moon. The way was now open for the first moon landing.

QUESTIONS

1 Why did the USA feel it had an advantage over the USSR in rocket technology?

2 In what ways did the USSR beat the USA during the early years of the space race?

3 Why was John F. Kennedy's speech in 1961 so important in the space race?

4 Outline some of the practical difficulties faced in getting a man on the moon.

5 Examine briefly the advances made in both the Mercury and Gemini space programmes.

6 Explain why the Soviets fell behind the USA in the race to the moon.

7 What was the Apollo 1 tragedy?

8 Outline the importance of the Saturn V rocket.

9 What were the main developments during the Apollo programme that made a moon landing possible?

APOLLO 11 MISSION – THE FIRST MANNED MISSION TO LAND ON THE MOON LENGTH OF MISSION: 8 DAYS			
Commander	Neil Armstrong	16 July	Launch from Kennedy Space Center
Lunar Module pilot	Edwin 'Buzz' Aldrin	19 July	Reached orbit around the moon
Columbia pilot	Michael Collins	20 July	Landing on the moon 2½-hour moon walk
Take off	Kennedy Space Center, Florida	22 July	Return to earth
Mission Control	Johnson Space Center, Houston	24 July	Landed in the Pacific Ocean

The Journey to the Moon

At 9.32 a.m. on Wednesday, 16 July 1969, experienced astronauts **Neil Armstrong**, **Buzz Aldrin** and **Michael Collins** lifted off the launch pad at the **Kennedy Space Center**. (Cape Kennedy, Florida, is now known as Cape Canaveral. Between 1963 and 1973 it was called Cape Kennedy in honour of J.F. Kennedy.) This was the beginning of their eight-day mission. A million people lined the Florida shoreline to witness the launch. Although Apollo 11 was the heaviest spacecraft ever fired into space, the lift-off went without a hitch.

The rocket contained three stages that fired the spacecraft into orbit around the earth. After orbiting the earth one and a half times, the Saturn thrusters fired and the craft reached a speed of 25,000mph (over 40,200kph). The journey to the

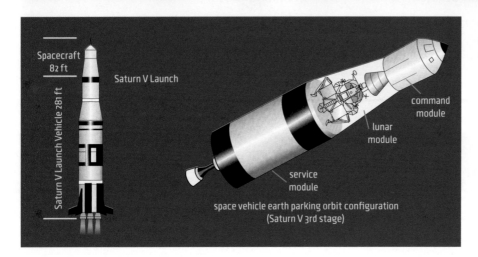

A diagram based on a NASA press release showing the launch and space vehicle

Spacecraft 82 ft

Saturn V Launch

Saturn V Launch Vehicle 281 ft

command module

lunar module

service module

space vehicle earth parking orbit configuration (Saturn V 3rd stage)

moon had begun. Throughout the mission the men reported back to **Mission Control** at the **Johnson Space Center** in Houston.

Getting the Astronauts to the Moon

The spacecraft that took the astronauts to the moon was 110 metres high. It contained the Apollo 11 craft and the Saturn V rocket. The craft itself was made up of three parts: the command module, the service module and the lunar module.

The **command module**, Columbia, was about the size of a large car and carried the astronauts. It was made up of two million parts. Its exterior contained a heat-shield layer that could withstand

temperatures of 2,760°C. It was the only part of the spacecraft to return to earth. Below the command module was the **service module**. Its rocket engine powered the craft. The module also contained the electrical power system and fuel for the rocket engine.

The **lunar module** weighed 15 tons and was 6.7 metres high and 9.4 metres wide. It was nicknamed 'the bug' because of its four legs which supported it on the moon's surface.

The module was made up of two parts or stages. The **descent** (lower) stage was equipped with a rocket motor to slow the rate of descent to the surface of the moon. It contained exploration

The launch of Apollo 11. The rocket used up 151,000 litres of rocket fuel per minute

Photo of the earth taken by the Apollo 11 crew from a distance of 120,700 kilometres

equipment and remained on the moon. The **ascent** (upper) stage contained the crew compartment and a rocket motor that returned the astronauts to the orbiting command module.

WHAT WERE THE MAIN EVENTS DURING THE MOON LANDING?

On 19 July, the spacecraft reached the moon. It went into orbit 111km from the surface of the moon. In all, the spacecraft was to stay orbiting the moon for nearly 60 hours. This was as close as **Michael Collins** would get to the surface of moon.

The following day, Aldrin and Armstrong were transferred to the **lunar module**. This separated from the Columbia to begin its descent to the moon's surface.

Guidance computers at mission control took the lunar module (the Eagle) out of orbit and controlled its descent, until it was about 50 metres from the moon's surface. Suddenly it became clear that the chosen landing site was covered with boulders.

Short of fuel and seconds from disaster, Armstrong took control of the Eagle from mission control. He brought the craft down safely in the smooth terrain of the **Sea of Tranquillity**. It was 4.17 p.m. back at the launch site in the USA. Armstrong coolly reported: 'Tranquility Base here. The Eagle has landed.'

There was wild cheering and loud applause from the scientists, engineers and reporters back at mission control.

'One Giant Leap'

After a number of hours were spent checking that the Eagle was undamaged, Armstrong and Aldrin put on their lunar spacesuits. They opened the hatch and Armstrong climbed down the ladder. As he descended, he pulled a rope that released a TV camera that recorded his first step on to the moon. He stepped on to the surface at 10.56 p.m. with the historic words, 'That's one small step for man – one giant leap for mankind.' The moment was watched on TV by an estimated 600 million people.

Men on the Moon

After a further 20 minutes, Aldrin came down the ladder and joined Armstrong on the moon.

The two men stayed on the moon's surface for about another two hours. Armstrong activated a second television camera to record all the astronauts' activities and set up the American flag. This was left on the moon, along with a number of mementos from the earth, including a plaque.

Finally, they were ordered by Mission Control to 'head on up the ladder'. The first moonwalk was over.

The Journey Home

Nearly 22 hours after the astronauts had landed on the moon, the top half of the lunar module blasted off on its journey back to the Columbia.

The men now returned home, reaching the earth on 24 July. As the ship entered the atmosphere the heat shield protected the spacecraft as the exterior reached a temperature of 2,760°C.

It safely splashed down in the Pacific, about 1,600km from Hawaii. The men were transferred

This plaque was left on the moon by Armstrong and Aldrin. What does it say about the motives behind the mission to the moon? They also left medals as memorials to dead Soviet and American astronauts such as Yuri Gagarin. It is believed that footprints left on the moon by the Apollo 11 astronauts will still be visible one million years from now!

by helicopter to the aircraft carrier the USS *Hornet*. Here, they were greeted by **President Nixon**. They were placed in quarantine for three weeks with the samples they had collected from the moon.

One of the most famous images ever. Buzz Aldrin with Neil Armstrong reflected in his visor

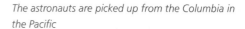
The astronauts are picked up from the Columbia in the Pacific

President Nixon laughs with the astronauts in quarantine; ticker-tape parade for the Apollo 11 crew in New York; Apollo astronauts at an audience with Pope Paul VI

WHAT WAS THE IMPACT OF THE MOON LANDING?

John F. Kennedy's commitment of 1961 to send a man to the moon and return him safely had been accomplished.

Armstrong, Aldrin and Collins returned home to a tumultuous welcome in the USA. There were speeches, parades, interviews and tours. Thousands lined Broadway in New York, when the astronauts were treated to one of the city's famous ticker-tape parades. At the White House, President Nixon awarded them the nation's highest civilian honour, the **Presidential Medal of Freedom**.

Conscious of the international propaganda value of their achievement, a Presidential Goodwill Tour was organised, in which the astronauts visited 24 countries in 45 days, each receiving a hero's welcome and meeting dignitaries such as the Pope.

The Media and the Moon Landing

The successful moon landing was carried live by radio and TV throughout the world. It had the largest television audience in history. Despite the war, American soldiers in Vietnam stopped to listen. Streets were deserted as people stayed indoors to watch their TVs.

Not all countries gave the event such prominent coverage. The moon landing was not just an achievement for humankind, but it was a victory for the USA in the Cold War and media coverage reflected this. The Russians tried to jam **Voice of America** radio broadcasts and buried reports on the moon landings in routine news broadcasts. China, North Vietnam and North Korea ignored the story.

Newspaper treatment of the event also reflected Cold War politics.

In the West: The event was front-page news every-where. Many newspapers printed special editions and saw their circulation increase dramatically. For example, the London *Evening Standard*'s circulation doubled when it printed a colour supplement about the landing. Neil Armstrong's famous quote was displayed prominently and many papers renamed the following day, a Monday, 'Moonday'.

In communist countries: The event was treated differently. Chinese papers did not carry the story on their front pages. *Pravda*, the official Communist Party newspaper in the USSR, placed the news on the bottom of the front page. The French communist daily *L'Humanité*, while praising the achievement, managed to keep the words 'United States' off its front page!

QUESTIONS

1 Describe briefly the main parts of the Apollo spacecraft.

2 What was life like in space for the astronauts?

3 What was the role of Michael Collins during the mission?

4 Describe the events when the men landed on the moon.

5 How do we know that the astronauts were regarded as heroes?

6 How did the Cold War influence the reporting of the moon landing?

WHY DID THE SPACE RACE END?

In total, there were five more manned moon landings, starting with **Apollo 12** in November 1969, and ending with **Apollo 17** in December 1972. These later missions carried out vital scientific work and explored and collected more material from the moon.

One of the missions, **Apollo 13**, came very close to disaster when an oxygen tank in the service module exploded. The drama that followed gripped the world as the crew clung to life during their four-day return journey on the damaged ship. During the crisis the USSR offered to help.

Later missions were usually less eventful. **Apollo 14** was commanded by **Alan Shepard**, who had been the first American in space. During the mission, he played golf on the moon!

After the first moon landing, there was a sense of anti-climax. Public interest, briefly revived by the Apollo 13 crisis, declined. A number of factors led to the end of Apollo missions:

- The USA had won the space race and there seemed to be little to be gained politically by repeating the effort.

- Economic prospects were not so good and resources were scarce. Space exploration did not have such a high priority. The budget to NASA was reduced. This forced NASA to cut back on the Apollo programme.

- The Apollo mission had achieved most of its scientific goals and there was a shift in emphasis away from the moon to space stations and unmanned missions to the planets.

The space race was essentially over, and politically times were changing. The 1970s was an era of improving relations between the superpowers that became known as détente (see Chapter 8). As a result competition between the superpowers declined.

Furthermore, due to recession and the worsening US economy, funding to NASA was cut. The

Celebrations in Mission Control at the safe return of the Apollo 13 crew, 1970

The Skylab space station orbiting the earth. Long-term weightlessness caused the Skylab crew members to grow by one inch!

emphasis was now on near-earth, cost-effective missions. There were two main developments in this period:

1   The **Skylab** space station.

2   The reusable space vehicle: the **Space Shuttle**.

HOW DID MANNED SPACE EXPLORATION DEVELOP?

NASA hoped to create a permanent human presence in space. In May 1973, the USA used one of the last Apollo vehicles to launch an experimental space station, **Skylab**. The station remained in use until February 1974. Three separate crews worked on the station, which was about the size of a small house, with sleeping areas, a kitchen, a bathroom and a shower. The astronauts carried out experiments and studied the medical effects of weightlessness.

Only one other US crew went into space during the 1970s. In a highly symbolic gesture of international co-operation, an Apollo and a Soviet Soyuz spacecraft met 225km above the earth in July 1975. The event was watched by millions on TV. The crews spent two days working together before they came back to earth. To many this event signalled the end of the space race.

The Space Shuttle

It had long been an aim of NASA to develop a reusable craft. The project was given the go-ahead in 1972, but with tight financial restrictions. The function of this craft was to deliver and retrieve satellites and perform scientific research. It was designed to be launched like a rocket and return like an aircraft gliding on to a runway. It was planned that the Shuttle would have an operational life of about 100 missions. The first Shuttle, named **Enterprise**, made its experimental flight in 1977. It was named after the craft used in the TV series *Star Trek*.

In 1981 the Space Shuttle **Columbia** blasted off from Cape Canaveral. The first flight was successful and within a year the Shuttle was fully operational. A total of five craft were built.

However, the Shuttles were neither cheap nor easy to operate. While NASA had hoped for 24 flights a year, it proved difficult to launch more than six.

The Space Shuttle also proved very dangerous. In 1986 the Space Shuttle **Challenger** exploded soon after take-off. All seven astronauts were killed. A further accident occurred in 2003 when the **Columbia** broke up on re-entry, killing its crew of seven.

The launch of the Space Shuttle Columbia, April 1981

The ill-fated Challenger crew. Back row (left to right): Ellison S. Onizuka, Christa McAuliffe, Greg Jarvis and Judy Resnik. Front row (left to right): Mike Smith, Dick Scobee and Ron McNair. In just over a hundred flights there have been two crashes, making the Shuttle a very dangerous form of transport

Height of the Cold War between the superpowers

⬇

Launch of Sputnik 1 started the Space Race

⬇

Soviets were winning when Yuri Gagarin became the first man in space

⬇

President Kennedy pledged to land a man on the moon by the end of the decade

⬇

Caught popular imagination in the USA

⬇

Massive resources directed to the space programme

⬇

Mercury, Gemini and Apollo programmes set up to achieve Kennedy's aim

⬇

Soviets, with fewer resources, fell behind the USA

⬇

Apollo 11 landed the first man on the moon. The USA won the space race

SPACE RACE TIMELINE 1957–1975

1957	Sputnik I, the first man-made satellite, launched
1958	NASA set up
1959	The Soviets land the first probe on the moon, Luna II
1961	Yuri Gagarin becomes the first man in space and the first to orbit the earth
	Alan Shepard is the first American astronaut in space
1962	John Glenn becomes the first American astronaut to orbit the earth
1963	Valentina Tereshkova is the first woman in space
1967	Apollo 1 fire kills three astronauts
1968	Apollo 8 successfully orbits the moon
1969	Apollo 11 lands on the moon
1970	Apollo 13 mission nearly ends in disaster
1972	Apollo 17 is the last mission to the moon. Apollo programme ends
1973	Launch of Skylab space station, which remains in space until 1979
1975	US Apollo and Soviet Soyuz spacecraft dock in space

QUESTIONS

1 Outline the main events that occurred on Apollo flights after the moon landing.

2 Mention two reasons why the Apollo programme was eventually ended in 1972.

3 What were the two main aims of NASA after the ending of the Apollo programme?

4 What were the two manned space flights launched by NASA in 1973 and 1975? What was their importance?

5 Outline the main events during the development and successful launch of the Shuttle.

6 Why did the Shuttle fail to live up to expectations?

DOCUMENT

This is an extract from the *New York Times* Report of 21 July 1969.

Houston, Monday, July 21 – Men have landed and walked on the moon.

Two Americans, astronauts of Apollo 11, steered their fragile four-legged lunar module safely and smoothly to the historic landing yesterday at 4:17:40 pm., eastern daylight time.

Neil A. Armstrong radioed to earth and the Mission Control room here: 'Houston, Tranquility Base here. The Eagle has landed.'

The first men to reach the moon – Mr Armstrong and his co-pilot, Col. Edwin E. Aldrin, Jr of the Air Force – brought their ship to rest on a level, rock-strewn plain near the southwestern shore of the arid Sea of Tranquility.

Mr Armstrong opened the landing craft's hatch, stepped slowly down the ladder and declared: 'That's one small step for man, one giant leap for mankind.'

A television camera outside the craft transmitted his every move to an awed and excited audience of hundreds of millions of people on earth.

Source: www.nytimes.com

1 DOCUMENT QUESTIONS

a) What significant event was reported on Monday, 21 July 1969?

b) What message did Neil Armstrong radio to Houston?

c) Where had the craft landed?

d) Are newspapers an objective source for a historian?

e) Outline the usefulness for a historian of newspaper accounts such as this document.

2 ORDINARY LEVEL QUESTIONS

a) How was it possible for the United States to achieve the moon landing in 1969? (Leaving Cert 2007)

b) What was the importance of the moon landing in 1969?

3 HIGHER LEVEL ESSAYS

a) To what extent can the moon landing (1969) be seen as both a major advance in technology and a statement of American foreign policy? (SEC Sample Paper 2006)

b) How did the Americans achieve a successful moon landing in 1969 and what was its importance for the USA? (Leaving Cert 2014)

Key Concepts and Personalities

KEY CONCEPTS
Glossary of Terms

consumerism

Growth of prosperity that saw increased spending power for the general public, leading to a booming market in goods for consumers. The growth of consumerism saw a dramatic increase in advertising, especially with the advent of TV.

corporate capitalism

Capitalism is an economic system where goods and services are provided by private enterprise for profit. In corporate capitalism this system is dominated by large companies. These companies operate in many countries and are called multinationals.

discrimination

Treating a person unfairly because of their religion, race or gender. For example, a whole series of laws in southern states led to wholesale discrimination against African Americans.

feminism

A campaign for equal rights for women that grew in popularity in the 1960s. Feminists wanted greater equality and more opportunities for women in American society. They rejected the traditional role of a woman as wife and mother who stayed at home to rear her children while the husband worked.

fundamentalism

A Christian movement that wanted a return to traditional values. It hoped to see a greater role for religion in everyday life and it was opposed to liberalism. Very influential in the Republican Party.

globalisation

Increased economic co-operation between countries all round the world. Globalisation has developed through free trade, technological advances, multinational investment and movement of people. It has led to a decline in cultural differences between countries.

imperialism

Movement to acquire colonies and an empire. While the USA had traditionally opposed European colonialism, many critics of US foreign policy used this term to describe US actions in Asia and South America after World War II. In this sense it is a pejorative term and one rejected by most American politicians.

internationalism

After World War I the USA rejected participation in the League of Nations. During the 1920s and 1930s it did not get involved in international affairs and showed little interest in events beyond the USA. This policy was known as 'isolationism'. The USA stayed neutral when World War II broke out in 1939, only joining the war after Japan attacked the US naval base at Pearl Harbor in December 1941. After World War II, the USA decided that it needed to play a role in world affairs in order to protect American interests. Isolationism was dropped. The USA became a founding member of the United Nations (UN), with a permanent seat on its Security Council. As post-war tensions grew between the USA and the USSR, the Americans formed a defensive

	military alliance with other western countries (NATO). This new policy became known as 'internationalism'. Those who supported internationalism believed that it was the duty of the USA to promote freedom and democracy around the world and to prevent the spread of communism.
liberalism	A view that government should not interfere in how citizens live their private lives and that people should be free to make choices about their own behaviour. Liberals believe in complete separation of Church and State. Politically, many liberals supported civil rights, abortion and government intervention to help the poor.
mass media	A term that refers to the increasing influence after World War II of the media, particularly TV and newspapers, on everyday life and on political decision-making.
military–industrial complex	A term coined by President Eisenhower in his farewell address. He used it to describe the growing political power of the army and the armaments industry to influence the decisions of politicians. Used widely by critics of the Vietnam War.
Moral Majority	A 1980s coalition of religious groups that supported traditional Christian values and opposed abortion and gay rights. They claimed to speak for the majority of Americans.
presidential bureaucracy	The vast number of federal agencies and the millions of people (public servants) who work for the federal government. The increase in the role of the government was as a result of the New Deal Programme of the 1930s and World War II. Many Americans criticise the waste and sheer size of the federal government.
public opinion	The attitude of ordinary people to the government's actions. With the growth of TV and opinion polling, public opinion is a major factor influencing the decisions of presidents and politicians.
technological development	Inventions and improvements that saw changes in military hardware, space travel, industrial production and the widespread use of computers. Many technological developments have had a profound impact on people's everyday lives.

KEY PERSONALITIES

Note: the two US presidents who are Key Personalities (Truman and Johnson) are covered in Chapter 1.

Harry S. Truman (1884–1972)

For information on Truman, see pages 9–10.

Lyndon B. Johnson (1908–1969)

For information on Johnson, see pages 12–13.

The Organization Man by William H. Whyte (1917–1999)

William H. Whyte wrote *The Organization Man* in 1956. The book was influential at the time, selling over two million copies. In it, Whyte described changing attitudes to work and career in contemporary America.

Whyte, a former editor of *Fortune* magazine, studied people who worked for large American corporations (companies). He was concerned about the power and influence these corporations had over the individuals who worked in them. Not only did employees work for them, but it appeared they belonged to them as well. 'The organization man', Whyte claimed, was 'so completely involved in his work that he cannot distinguish between work and the rest of his life.'

This new trend saw Americans abandoning the old values of hard work, entrepreneurial risk-taking and individual self-reliance. Instead a new ethic was emerging. It was based on co-operation, security and teamwork. Whyte called this the 'Social Ethic', in which the individual became subsumed into the needs of the organisation. It also led to the development of a corporate culture. What mattered was conformity, behaving the way the corporation expected its employees to behave. The rewards for the organisation man were promotion and job security.

Whyte's organisation men were 'middle managers', a new managerial class largely made up of young war veterans. Having gone to college on GI Bill grants, they then went on to work for large corporations, such as IBM, or federal government organisations, such as NASA or the FBI. The organisation man had strong loyalty to the corporation, believing that his own prosperity was connected to the corporation. If the corporation did well, so would he. He was prepared to work long hours. Always eager to please the corporation bosses, he knew his place and learned never to challenge the accepted norms by acting independently or showing any creativity at work. The important thing was to be well liked and to conform to the organisation's expectations.

Whyte's book went beyond the world of work: *The Organization Man* also exposed the conformity of life in the new suburbs. In the middle-class suburb of Park Forest, Illinois, Whyte found that there was no room for privacy, individualism or non-conformity. The organisation man lived in a new ranch-type house with his wife and family. His wife stayed at home to take care of the children and the house. He was the breadwinner, working hard in the corporation to provide a range of consumer gadgets for the home, and giving his children a good education.

Betty Friedan (1921–2006)

Betty Friedan was born Betty Naomi Goldstein in Peoria, Illinois. Her father, a Russian Jewish immigrant, had a jewellery business. Her mother had worked as a newspaper writer, but left her job to marry and become a mother.

Friedan graduated with an honours degree in psychology in 1942, and in 1943 moved to California, where she was offered a scholarship to do a PhD. Few woman at this time studied for doctorates. Owing to cultural and personal pressures, she turned down the scholarship.

In 1944, she moved to New York City, where she got a job with a left-wing news agency. She reported on strikes and industrial disputes and came into contact with discrimination cases in the workplace. She was concerned about the fact that women were not paid the same wages as men for doing the same job.

In 1946 she married Carl Friedan, an actor, and in 1949, she was dismissed from her job when she asked for maternity leave. As a result, the family moved to the suburbs, where Friedan became a full-time wife and mother.

She records that she found life in the suburbs frustrating, and began writing articles for magazines. However, many editors of women's magazines were not interested in publishing stories about women who did not follow their traditional role. In 1957, Friedan sent a questionnaire to her former classmates. The responses revealed that her ex-classmates were largely feeling frustrated and disappointed with marriage and motherhood. The survey showed that these educated and talented housewives in their mid-30s were leading lonely lives in the suburbs.

Over the next five years she interviewed thousands of American women. The results of her research were published in her book *The Feminine Mystique* (1963). By 1966, it had sold more than three million copies.

The Feminine Mystique challenged the myth of the happy American housewife. Friedan discovered a gap between what society expected of women and their own private expectations. She called this 'the problem that has no name'.

Unwittingly, Freidan had started the modern **women's liberation movement**. In 1966, inspired by the civil rights movement, she helped set up the **National Organization for Women (NOW)** and became its first president, a post she held until she retired in 1970.

Until the 1990s, Friedan went on lecture tours, organised protests and demonstrations, and promoted equal rights for women. However, she had little time for the younger, more militant generation of feminists. She did not support an all-out war on men, and criticised the more radical feminists for being **female chauvinists**. She advocated a society in which men and women were equal.

In 1981, she wrote *The Second Stage*, a book that was widely criticised by younger feminists as a move away from the ideas of women's liberation.

Viewed as a moderate feminist, Friedan is remembered as the founder of the modern feminist movement in the USA. She was uncompromising in her demands for equality for women, and remained a dominant influence in feminist politics during the latter half of the twentieth century. She died, aged 85, in February 2006.

Martin Luther King (1929–1968)

Martin Luther King, born in Atlanta, Georgia, was the son and grandson of Baptist ministers. Both his father and his maternal grandfather were active in the National Association for the Advancement of Colored People (NAACP).

King studied at a theological seminary in Pennsylvania. In 1951 he won a scholarship to study for a PhD at Boston University, which he received in 1955. While at Boston, King met **Coretta Scott**, a music student from Alabama, and they married in 1953.

In 1954, King moved back to the south, working as a pastor in a Baptist church in Montgomery, Alabama. He also served on the executive committee of the Montgomery branch of the NAACP.

When the Montgomery Bus Boycott began in 1955, King emerged as leader. Influenced by Christian theologians and Mahatma Gandhi, King advocated non-violent direct action. He believed that if African Americans united in peaceful, dignified protest they could bring about an end to the system of racial discrimination in the south. He insisted that persuasion and civil disobedience would triumph over the forces of hatred and violence.

The boycott and King's leadership attracted the attention of national and international media. The success of the boycott led to king's emergence as the leader of the civil rights movement.

In 1957, King helped to set up the **Southern Christian Leadership Conference (SCLC)**. Its aim was to continue working for change, using non-violent tactics.

In 1958, the SCLC began its crusade to double the number of African-American voters in the south by 1960.

In 1960, some African-American students began 'sit-ins' at segregated lunch counters. King supported them and was arrested in October 1960. In April 1963, he led a non-violent demonstration in Birmingham, Alabama, and was again arrested. In August that year, King led a march on Washington, DC. Over 200,000 protestors joined the march, and he made his famous 'I have a dream' speech. *Time* magazine named him 'Man of the Year' for 1963. The following year King received the Nobel Peace Prize, the youngest man ever to receive that honour.

As a result of King's campaigns, legislation was introduced in 1964 and 1965, outlawing discrimination and the restrictions on African Americans voting in the southern states.

However, younger and more militant African-American groups became impatient with the slow rate of reform. When King tried to extend non-violent protest to northern cities there was a backlash against him, led by militant African Americans demanding 'black power'. He was physically assaulted at a demonstration in Chicago.

During 1967, when urban riots broke out in the black ghettos of some northern states, King spoke out against social and economic inequality. He also became critical of US involvement in the Vietnam War, pointing out that the war drew attention, and funding, away from domestic problems.

In 1968, King went to Memphis, Tennessee to support striking black sanitation workers. While there, on 4 April 1968, he was assassinated by a white southerner, James Earl Ray. News of his death resulted in riots in black neighbourhoods. Violence erupted in 125 cities and 70,000 troops were brought in to suppress the upheaval.

Joseph McCarthy (1908–1957)

Joseph McCarthy was born in 1908 in Appleton, Wisconsin. His mother, Bridget Tierney, was from Co. Tipperary, and his father, Tim McCarthy, was born in America but had an Irish father.

In 1935 he graduated with a law degree. In World War II McCarthy enlisted in the Marines. He became an intelligence officer in the Pacific but would later exaggerate his war record. In 1946 McCarthy stood as a Republican candidate, and was elected to the Senate. There he made a name for himself as an opportunist who exchanged votes for favours from business groups. He also got a reputation for drinking and gambling.

As his Senate record was unimpressive he was in danger of not getting re-elected. He needed an issue to save his political career and found one in the growing popular fears of communism. On 9 February 1950 he made a dramatic speech announcing that he had a list of 205 names of communists working in the government. In the following weeks he repeated and expanded his claims and by March he was making newspaper headlines across the country. Although he never produced the list he was featured on the cover of *Time* and *Newsweek*.

McCarthy was re-elected as a senator in 1952, and appointed Chairman of the Senate Permanent Subcommittee on Investigations. He used this position to further his investigations of alleged communist subversives (spies). He was helped by his friend J. Edgar Hoover, head of the FBI. For the next two years he carried out a witch hunt of various government departments. Few dared to criticise him for fear of being labelled a communist supporter. Many government employees lost their jobs when they admitted to having supported left-wing or communist organisations in the past.

McCarthy seemed to offer simple solutions to complex questions about the Cold War. In the 1950s many Americans could not understand why such a powerful nation as the USA failed to contain communist expansion in Europe and Asia. The USSR had developed atomic weapons, and controlled Eastern Europe. China 'fell' to the communists, and Korea looked to be heading the same way. McCarthy explained that these events happened because spies and traitors were working within the USA, employed by the government in high-ranking positions. His wild accusations made sense to many ordinary Americans. Opinion polls showed that over 50 per cent of Americans supported his claims.

In the 1952 presidential election he attacked Truman, his administration and the Democratic Party. His crusade helped win the election for the Republican candidate, Dwight Eisenhower.

In 1954 McCarthy began investigating communist activity in the US army. This led President Eisenhower, a former high-ranking army general, to finally condemn him. The Senate hearings lasted 36 days and were televised. The army rejected his allegations and McCarthy was exposed as a ruthless bully and liar. In December 1954 the Senate passed a resolution condemning him for bringing the Senate into disrepute. The media lost interest in him, and his political career soon ended. He died in May 1957.

The term *McCarthyism* came into use, standing for militant anti-communism, intolerance of dissent, and irresponsible accusations. McCarthy's activities had created a mood and attitude that affected many aspects of American life in the early 1950s, damaging social and political life at home and America's reputation abroad.

Norman Mailer (1923–2007)

A very well known and controversial American writer, Norman Mailer was the creator of the **non-fiction novel** in the 1960s. This is a form of journalism that combines actual events, autobiography and political commentary with the rich storylines of the novel. He was the author of over 40 books.

He was born in New Jersey and grew up in Brooklyn, New York in what he called a 'typical middle-class Jewish family'. A gifted student, he went to **Harvard University** at the age of 16 to study aeronautical engineering. He became interested in writing and completed his first novel when he was 18. During World War II he served in the US Army in the Pacific.

In 1948 he wrote his first book, *The Naked and the Dead*, regarded as one of the classic novels about World War II. The book was inspired by his wartime experiences fighting in the Philippines. It enjoyed enormous success, making Mailer a national celebrity at the age of 25.

He settled in Greenwich Village in New York and became involved in left-wing politics, He was one of the founders of the alternative newspaper the *Village Voice*.

In the 1960s Mailer reported on the social upheavals occurring in US society, such as the civil rights and anti-war movements, and covered the Democratic and Republican conventions.

A strong critic of US involvement in Vietnam, Mailer was arrested during an anti-war demonstration at the Pentagon in 1967. This experience was recounted in his book *Armies of the Night* (1968), which received the **Pulitzer Prize** for non-fiction. His political involvement led to an unsuccessful campaign for Mayor of New York City in 1969.

Of a Fire on the Moon (1971) explored the Apollo 11 moon landing and *The Prisoner of Sex* (1971) brought Mailer into conflict with the growing feminist movement. *The Fight* (1976) was a book-length description of the Muhammad Ali–George Foreman boxing match in Zaire in 1974. In 1980 Mailer won a second Pulitzer Prize for *The Executioner's Song*, which related the life and death by firing squad of convicted murderer **Gary Gilmore**. He also wrote a number of biographies of figures such as **Marilyn Monroe, Pablo Picasso** and **Lee Harvey Oswald**.

In the 1960s, Mailer directed a number of independent films and also worked on screenplays, contributing, for example, to the screenplay for Sergio Leone's *Once Upon a Time in America*.

He was a regular on radio and TV talk shows and he had a strong influence on public opinion in the USA during the 1960s and 1970s.

Muhammad Ali (1942–)

Regarded by many as the greatest boxer in history, Muhammad Ali's outgoing and colourful style both in and out of the ring heralded a new type of media-conscious sports celebrity. At the height of his fame, Muhammad Ali was described as 'the most recognisable human being on earth'.

Through his statements on black pride, his conversion to the Muslim faith, and his outspoken opposition to the Vietnam War, Muhammad Ali became a highly controversial figure during the turbulent 1960s in the USA.

Muhammad Ali was born **Cassius Clay** in 1942 in Louisville, Kentucky, and he took up boxing at the age of 12. In 1960 Clay won a gold medal at the **Olympic Games** in Rome. His treatment when he returned to his home town after the Games angered him. He wrote: 'When I came home to Louisville, I still got treated like a nigger. There were restaurants I couldn't get served in. Some people kept calling me "boy".'

He became a professional boxer in 1960 and won all 19 of his early fights. In 1964, to many people's surprise, he defeated Sonny Liston to become the World Heavyweight Champion. In the early 1960s boxing was in decline and dominated by the Mafia. Ali's victories dramatically raised the profile of professional boxing. The sport had a new hero. In all, he defended his title nine times between 1965 and 1967.

In 1964 Clay rejected his 'slave name' of **Cassius Clay**, changing his name to **Muhammad Ali**. Ali did not support the civil rights movement, because it wanted to break down barriers between black and white; but he supported the **Nation of Islam**, which wanted a separate nation for black people. **Martin Luther King** called him 'a champion of racial segregation, and that is what we are fighting against.'

Ali opposed US involvement in Vietnam and in 1967 he refused to serve in the army. He defended his decision by claiming that Vietnam was a white man's war. As a result he was stripped of his heavyweight title and banned from boxing. Found guilty of draft evasion, he was sentenced to prison but on appeal he avoided serving any of his sentence. This stance made Ali a hero to the anti-war movement.

After he returned to boxing he took part in some of the most famous fights in boxing history. In 1971 he lost to Joe Frazier in an epic fight. The 'Rumble in the Jungle' (1974) in Zaire saw Ali recapture the world crown when he defeated **George Foreman**; and in the 'Thrilla in Manila' (1975) he overcame **Joe Frazier**.

He was world champion from 1974 until 1978. In 1979 he announced his retirement, but made a brief return in 1980. He retired for good in 1981 with a career record of 56 wins and 5 losses.

He was diagnosed with **Parkinson's disease** in 1984. Despite his disability he remains a popular and active figure. In 1996 he had the honour of lighting the flame at the 1996 Summer Olympics in Atlanta.

Marilyn Monroe (1926–1962)

Born Norma Jeane Mortenson in 1926, Marilyn Monroe had a troubled upbringing. She lived with foster parents until she was 7, and then went to live with her mother. In 1935, when her mother was hospitalised following a nervous breakdown, she was sent to an orphanage. At 16 she married James Dougherty. During World War II Dougherty served in the US forces and Monroe went to work in an aeroplane factory. There an army photographer spotted her and encouraged her to join a modelling agency. As a result she became a successful model. This publicity brought her to the attention of Hollywood, and in 1946 she signed a contract with one of the major film studios, 20th Century Fox. Shortly after joining Fox she adopted her stage name, Marilyn Monroe.

Over the following years she had minor parts in movies and continued modelling. In 1953 she got her first major role in a big budget film when she starred in *Niagara*.

During the 1950s she had several successful film roles, many of them as 'dumb blonde' characters. She featured on the cover of *Life* (1952) and *Time* (1956). Her screen performances, as well as her high-profile photographs, earned her a name as a sex symbol, which Hollywood was quick to exploit. With the spread of American popular culture in post-war Europe she became a household name there.

In 1955 she starred in *The Seven Year Itch*, a box office hit, which featured the famous skirt blowing scene. Her role in *Some Like It Hot* (1959) is considered her best ever performance. Her last completed film was *The Misfits* (1961), written for her by Arthur Miller. She longed to be taken seriously as an actress, but was never nominated for an Oscar.

Monroe had many problems in her personal life. After divorcing Dougherty in 1952, she married the New York Yankee baseball star, Joe DiMaggio, in 1954. The huge publicity Monroe attracted put a strain on the marriage and the couple divorced after a few months. In 1956 she married playwright Arthur Miller. She stood by Miller during his ordeal with HUAC (House Un-American Activities Committee), risking her own career, but nonetheless they divorced in 1961. She was known to have had affairs with several famous Hollywood actors, and there were rumours of affairs with both President Kennedy and Robert Kennedy.

Her personal unhappiness drove her to psychotherapy and drugs. In 1961 she was admitted to a psychiatric clinic. Her career suffered as her dependence on drugs increased. She became difficult to work with and got a name for being late for shoots. She was found dead from an overdose of sleeping pills at her home in August 1962. The official verdict was probable suicide. However, the circumstances of her death led to many conspiracy theories. Her troubled life and tragic death inspired many writers, artists and musicians. She remained a Hollywood icon, and her fame continued long after her death.

Billy Graham (1918–)

Billy Graham was born in North Carolina in 1918. His parents, originally Presbyterians, joined the Southern Baptist Church in 1934. After graduating from Wheaton Bible College in 1943 he travelled around the country preaching at Youth for Christ rallies. In 1949 he organised a mission in Los Angeles, which was intended to run for three weeks, but was so successful it lasted eight. This was to be the first of what became known as Graham's evangelical crusades. Over the next fifty years these crusades would take him around America and the world.

In 1950 he set up the *Billy Graham Evangelistic Association*, to organise and promote his crusades. Wherever a crusade was planned this group would rent out a large venue, such as a stadium or a park, and make sure the event got maximum possible publicity. A choir, sometimes of thousands of singers, would sing hymns before Graham took to the stage to preach on the gospel.

Another important factor in Graham's success was his skill and ability as a public speaker. A gifted showman, he could captivate his audiences. Crowds flocked to hear him speak, and often followed him to other venues around the country. He made great use of the media, hosting radio and television shows and writing newspaper articles. His television shows brought in over 50,000 letters a week from admirers in the 1950s. They also brought over $2 million dollars in contributions, which was used for future crusades. Graham wrote 25 books.

Graham's popularity continued to grow during the following decades. In the 1980s a number of scandals involving other evangelical preachers hit the headlines. However, Graham's reputation as an honest and committed evangelist remained intact. In 1999 *Time* magazine called him the 'Pope of Protestant America'.

In the 1950s Graham was a strong supporter of Senator Joe McCarthy. He believed that communism was evil and that it was America's mission to stop it spreading around the world. By the 1980s, however, his views had mellowed and he called for world peace.

Graham was minister to several presidents, and was consulted by all the presidents between 1945 and 1989. He spoke at Johnson's funeral in 1973 and at Nixon's in 1994. In a poll Americans rated him the seventh most admired person in the twentieth century. Graham's influence can still be felt in the USA, where 40 per cent of Americans identify themselves as evangelical Christians.

INDEX